Welcome to the EVERYTHING® series!

These handy, accessible books give you all you need to tackle a difficult project, gain a new hobby, comprehend a fascinating topic, prepare for an exam, or even brush up on something you learned back in school but have since forgotten.

E FACTS
Important sound bytes
of information

You can read an *EVERYTHING®* book from cover-to-cover or just pick out the information you want from our four useful boxes: e-facts, e-ssentials, e-alerts, and e-questions. We literally give you everything you need to know on the subject, but throw in a lot of fun stuff along the way, too.

E SSENTIALS
Quick handy tips

We now have well over 100 *EVERYTHING®* books in print, spanning such wide-ranging topics as weddings, pregnancy, wine, learning guitar, one-pot cooking, managing people, and so much more. When you're done reading them all, you can finally say you know *EVERYTHING®*!

E ALERT
Urgent warnings

E QUESTIONS?
Solutions to
common problems

Dear Reader,

Why is managing people so complicated? Well, to start with, it's because humans are complicated, with unique motivations, frustrations, skills, deficiencies . . . all of which they bring to the workplace. Just like their managers.

Life as a manager in today's business environment means directing and balancing multiple, and often competing, missions. And at the moment when you think you know the lay of the land in your office or company, something changes. Departments merge, employees transfer or quit, companies change ownership. While company goals may seem like a moving target, it's your job to be sure they are being met. You must do more—faster, and with fewer resources.

You might not have the power to change the workplace, but you can improve your abilities to function within it. Whether you have just received your first promotion or are firmly entrenched in middle management, whether you work for a megacorporation or a family business, your success as a manager depends on your people skills. It's not enough to know processes inside and out; you also must know what motivates and supports the people who make those processes happen.

This book is a guide to understanding how people function within the workplace, and how you as a manager can help them grow to be more productive and successful . . . so you are, too.

Sincerely,

Gary R. McClain

Deborah S. Romaine

THE
EVERYTHING®
MANAGING
PEOPLE BOOK

Quick and easy ways
to build, motivate, and
nurture a first-rate team

Gary McClain, Ph.D., and Deborah S. Romaine

Adams Media Corporation
Avon, Massachusetts

EDITORIAL
Publishing Director: Gary M. Krebs
Managing Editor: Kate McBride
Copy Chief: Laura MacLaughlin
Development Editor: Michael Paydos

PRODUCTION
Production Director: Susan Beale
Production Manager: Michelle Roy Kelly
Series Designer: Daria Perreault
Layout and Graphics: Arlene Apone,
Paul Beatrice, Brooke Camfield,
Colleen Cunningham, Daria Perreault, Frank Rivera

An Everything® Series Book.
Everything® and everything.com® are registered trademarks of F+W Publications, Inc.

Published by Adams Media, an F+W Publications Company
57 Littlefield Street, Avon, MA 02322. U.S.A.
www.adamsmedia.com

Produced by Amaranth.

ISBN: 1-58062-577-0
Printed in the United States of America.

J I H G F E D

Library of Congress Cataloging-in-Publication Data
McClain, Gary, Ph. D.
The everything managing people book /
by Gary McClain and Deborah S. Romaine.
p.   cm.
Includes index.
ISBN 1-58062-577-0
1. Supervision of employees. 2. Personnel management.
I. Romaine, Deborah S., 1956- II. Title.
HF5549.12 .M375   2001
658.3–dc21   2001046319

Illustrations by Barry Littmann.

This book is available at quantity discounts for bulk purchases.
For information, call 1-800-872-5627.

Visit the entire Everything® series at everything.com

Contents

Introduction

In the early days of the Industrial Revolution, managing meant getting product out. Nameless workers stood side by side on assembly lines, going through the same movement, one after another. The process was refined by men with stopwatches, who decided how to best break down the tasks for maximum speed and repetition. Not only did workers have to do the same thing over and over, they also had to do it within specific time parameters. If employees took breaks when they weren't supposed to, or if they suddenly couldn't do the work, they were gone. Managing back then was simple.

Then along came unions. The workers were not so easy to push around. If managers wanted them there beyond eight hours, they actually had to compensate them for their work. And there were more changes. More women entered the workplace, as did minority groups. They demanded equal opportunity and equal pay. Time marched on, bringing new workplace complications: Affirmative action. Sexual harassment. Equal opportunity. These have become guiding principles as well as government mandates. In fact, government—federal, state, and local—now rules the workplace to nearly the same extent it rules other dimensions of American life. And ignorance of the law (which is increasingly complicated) risks lawsuits not only from employees but also from communities within which companies operate. Managing has become very complicated.

To survive as a manager in today's world requires more than setting goals and backing them up with ultimatums. People have different work styles that they bring to the job, and managers are expected to understand and accommodate them. Emotions, which used to have no place in the workplace, have to be acknowledged and even discussed not just among friends but in meetings as well. Company goals still require that employees work at their highest level of productivity, but companies also realize that attaining this productivity requires vacations, creature comforts, and opportunities for growth and advancement. While there are very few managers and companies who long for the "good old days" of half a century ago, the world of management has become a much more challenging (but also interesting) place.

The Everything® Managing People Book provides a window into this world. It is your guide to being a manager, covering key information that a manager needs to know, from performance evaluations to government regulations to team building. And we know you want practical advice, so we've included lots of examples* from the real world of work. Managers have to mediate between the needs of the company and the needs of their employees, and we have kept this balance in mind throughout the book. Managers also have to grow and develop professionally, so we've included a few ideas in that direction.

Managing is an exciting opportunity to make an impact on people, on your organization, and on your own career and personal development. We hope that *The Everything® Managing People Book* helps you along the way.

*The examples and stories in this book are composites created from the shared experiences of numerous people; all names, circumstances, and details have been altered. Any resemblance to real people or situations is purely coincidental.

CHAPTER 1
Ideals and Realities

So, you're a manager. If you're new to your position, you probably have lots of ideas about how to do things differently—and better. Though you've had plenty of training in the skills your jobs have required, no one's really teaching you how to be a manager. You've had your share of bad managers, and you don't want to become one of them. That's why you're reading this book.

If you've been a manager for a while, you know it's far more work and worry than glory. You've probably been able to implement some of the great ideas you had when you first became a manager, and have had less success with others. Perhaps you know you could do better if you knew what to do and how to do it. Maybe you're worried that you're becoming the manager you always hated having. That's why you're reading this book.

Everyone who's ever worked has a "bad boss" story. Does that mean every manager is destined to become one of those stories? The risk is there, certainly, in an employment climate that emphasizes the bottom line above all else. But wide opportunity is there, too, for you to break the mold and be the manager who stars in a story that begins, "Yeah, I've had a lot of bad bosses in my time. But once, I had this really great manager . . ."

This is really why you're reading this book.

The Changing Landscape of Today's Business World

If there is one constant in today's business world, it's change. "Today" is really the operative definition. While yesterday offers many lessons and some foundations, the future holds both promise and uncertainty. Today, in great respect, is all that matters. Factors that drive the business world's stability and volatility include:

- The economy at large, both domestic and global
- Consumer demand and purchasing patterns
- Technology

Let's take a look at each of these as they affect you—a manager in today's business world.

The Economy

When Bill Clinton ran for president in 1992, the United States was coming out of one of the worst recessions in recent times. Clinton campaigners took up the slogan, "It's the economy, stupid!" Crass, perhaps, but it made the point that when the economy is good, life is good. If you want a good life, you'll need a good economy.

This holds true outside of politics as well. Economic realities are the guiding force of this—and any—country. When the economy is booming, especially with a new paradigm driving hopes and expectations to new levels, then there is a lot of concern for people.

FACTS

Companies want to make sure employees are happy, so they strive to establish fun, creative work environments. But when the economy slows, companies tighten up and attitudes shift. Instead of worrying about employee happiness, companies panic about profits and losses. There might as well be a sign on the wall saying, "If you don't like it here, don't let the door hit you on your way out."

The 1980s was the decade of technology. Personal computers were beginning to dominate the business landscape. It wasn't just the accounting people who powered up every morning; everyone from the receptionist to the marketing representative to the executive vice president was learning how powerful this business tool could be. Companies that developed software to give computers new capabilities were riding high on the bubble of success.

It wasn't unusual for such companies to splurge on their employees. After all, it was only fair to share the wealth. At one such company, for example, profits were so obscenely high that everyone had the best of everything: private offices, management training sessions, champagne brunches, lavish parties to celebrate every little success, generous bonuses, stock options, and gifts. Programmers could requisition stereos and mid-level managers were free to order leather couches for their offices. Sales reps earned fabulous trips to exotic locations as rewards for meeting mediocre goals. Companies constructed glorious buildings with their names in lighted letters on the outside and full health club facilities for employees inside.

Then there was a bad quarter, and another. Wall Street lowered its expectations, and an analyst's report suggested the market niche was saturated. Companies changed their tone almost overnight. Gone were the brunches, and training sessions became morning meetings. There were no more gifts or bonuses, and stock options dropped significantly in value. The company bought a smaller company that gave new meaning to the concept of running a tight ship. That company's president took over, and work was no longer fun for anyone. Consolidated operations meant people shared offices with two or three other people. There was much grumbling in the hallways and the break rooms.

The new management regime had a new definition for communication, too. Rather than involving employees in the decisions that were being made and finding ways to encourage them to participate in restoring the company to profitability, the company's leadership merely passed down word of new cuts and new restrictions. People complained about working too many hours, and many resigned. Those who stayed resented their managers for these heavy-handed tactics, while managers resented their own managers for the same reasons. The corporate culture became one of negativism.

While certainly this company's leaders had the opportunity—and some would say the obligation—to handle circumstances differently, it's only fair to recognize that those circumstances were not entirely their doing. The entire economy was in a downswing.

If you were a manager in the 1980s, you probably felt as helpless as your employees did. Many aspects of daily operations spiraled beyond your control, and there was little you could do about it. Yet your employees probably held you accountable; it's human nature to place blame. And to some degree, you probably held yourself accountable as well, because you're a concerned and compassionate human being. (If you were a manager in the 1990s, think dot-coms. And if you're a new manager, take notes—your time of challenge will come, just as surely as the business seasons cycle.)

Economy downturns are not always the fault of corporate extravagance, although when times are tough it's easy to look back at better days and wish you'd been more cautious. Many factors drive the economic cycle, including those beyond domestic boundaries. From the break-up of the Soviet Union to the conflicts in the Middle East, global events have far-reaching effects. Some have positive consequences, such as new marketing opportunities. Others create uncertainty and confusion that results in caution and prudence.

Natural disasters such as floods and earthquakes have consequences we can measure in terms of human tragedy as well as dollars and cents. The devastating 1996 earthquake that struck Kobe, Japan, for example, devastated the Japanese economy, causing the Nekei Stock Index to drop 40 percent in 24 hours. The repercussions rippled around the world, leaving no economy untouched. The economic ramifications extended over months and even years in some industries that had become dependent on manufacturers and suppliers in the Kobe region.

Technology, which we discuss a few pages ahead, has greatly reshaped the global economy as well. It once required a significant infrastructure to conduct business with companies in other countries. Today, only a Web site is required. Many businesses work with vendors located in countries where labor and supply costs are lower than in the United States. A book publisher, for example, can have books printed in Southeast Asia or Hong Kong for as little as 20 to 30 percent of what it would cost to have the same work done in the United States.

ESSENTIALS   As a manager, it's no longer enough for you to know what competitors across town are doing. To stay on top of your game, you must know what competitors are doing around the world.

Consumer Demand

Remember pet rocks? Talk about a product with no purpose! Yet the painted novelties became favorites among a fickle market that happened to take a fancy to them, creating a multi-million dollar boom. Then pet rocks fell out of favor, and the bottom dropped out of the market.

Consumer demand drives the market, in products as well as service. It was consumer demand that resulted in the "service excellence" movement of the late 1980s and early 1990s, for example. Cost-cutting measures had all but put an end to the practice, as well as the concept, of customer service during the recession years of the early 1980s. But people got fed up with being treated poorly, and started complaining. Smart companies realized that they needed to listen. As a result, it became important not only to sell thirty-five widgets an hour, but also to be nice when you did so.

Because it's hard to be nice to your customers when you're not nice to your coworkers or when your manager isn't nice to you, the emphasis on restoring customer service became a movement to alter corporate culture. Managers received training in quality systems, and learned how to measure and improve service in tangible ways. It became their responsibility to uphold corporate service standards.

Technology

Few factors have influenced the business landscape to the extent that technology has. While some "old timers" who were in the workforce before the 1980s can remember when the IBM Selectric typewriter was the standard by which all other office technology was measured, a growing percentage of today's employees have never known life without computers. In just two years—from 1998 to 2000—PCs in the workplace surged from 67 percent to 80 percent. Today, few companies (indeed, perhaps no companies) can survive without e-mail and the Internet. Electronic technology has become an essential tool in many industries and most companies—and for nearly all managers.

This has given rise to a new way of working: telework, also called telecommuting. Telework, say many analysts, is the greatest revolution in the American workplace since the assembly line. (Chapter 4, "This Is Not Your Daddy's Workplace," discusses telework in detail.)

QUESTIONS?

What does telework mean?
Employees who telework (or telecommute) work from home or other locations, connecting with coworkers via computer and telecommunication. According to a 2000 report from the U.S. Department of Labor, workers telecommute in 70 percent of American companies with more than 5,000 employees and in 43 percent of those with fewer than 1,000 employees.

Nearly 70 percent of employees use computers to conduct at least a portion of their daily job tasks. Among managers, the percentage is even higher, approaching 90 percent. Today's managers must not only keep their own technology skills sharp, but also must ensure that their employees have both the technology and technical training to use computers and other electronic gadgetry productively and efficiently. It's not just a computer on every desk, but also a handheld organizer in every hand, a pager on every waistband, and a cell phone in every briefcase. Moving at the speed of light seems sluggish in comparison to keeping pace with technology.

Paradigms Lost, Paradigms Gained

They came of age surfing the Web, and rode the wave of the Internet to positions not only as employees but also as managers and even owners of multimillion dollar companies. They were the "wunderkind" of the new economy, young people fresh from (or dropped out of) college. They upended the old paradigm of hard work, patience, and commitment, replacing it with a new paradigm rooted in WIIFM (What's In It For Me). They worked incredibly long hours, took great risks, and demanded huge stock options. People came and went as they pleased, working whatever hours their creative muses dictated. It was an exhilarating ride . . . until the wave broke and dropped them in the sand.

People with little business and no management experience suddenly found themselves in roles of responsibility and accountability. Even in a world they created, they could not escape the expectations the old paradigm had established. Customers insisted on products and service, and employees demanded opportunities and compensation. Yet delivery was erratic and unpredictable; products sometimes dropped entirely from the company's offerings without warning or notice to customers. The opportunities employees had come to believe were their right evaporated as the company's opportunities dried up. It was entirely possible for employees to show up to work, only to find that the company had moved to another floor or another building.

Employees jumped jobs on a whim, going with whatever lucrative offer came their way. The demand for people with technology backgrounds was intense, yet most Web wizards had little formal education or training. They knew one thing and they knew it very, very well—but in the end they still knew only one thing and it wasn't enough.

The dot-com boom went bust. The conventional paradigm returned with a vengeance, thrusting the dot-com paradigm into oblivion. Many dot-com "wunderkinds" found themselves in search of jobs, any jobs, shell-shocked by the events that jolted them from their alternate realities into the reality that pundits had warned was certain to catch up with them. These are the people who might now be working for you, or applying for jobs that are available in your company. And they present unique challenges for managers who must find ways to both cultivate and corral their talents and creativity.

Of the 300 Internet-based public companies offering products and services to consumers in June 2000, only five were earning a profit. In the 52 weeks between November 1999 and November 2000, dot-coms listed on the Bloomberg U.S. Internet Index lost 60 percent of their value overall.

Balance Sheets and Bottom Lines

The harsh reality in the business world is that companies have to make a profit. (Even not-for-profit organizations must still meet goals and keep constituents happy.) Businesses must balance profitability, customer or client satisfaction, and quality products or services. Nowhere has this lesson been so graphically illustrated as in the dot-com industry.

Until the mid-1990s, few people had even heard the term "dot-com." The buzz word was familiar primarily to those on the inside of the technology industry, those brimming with ideas to turn the information superhighway of the Internet's World Wide Web into the greatest economic boom of all time. And for a while, it looked as if they might succeed. Amazon.com burst onto the stage in 1997, launching itself into cyberhistory and etching technospeak into the vernacular. Investors swarmed to fund anything and everything, quite literally, that could put a ".com" at the end of its name. In 1997, 34 dot-coms went public and raised $1 billion; in 1999, nearly 300 dot-coms generated more than $24 billion through their IPOs (initial public offerings).

"Never give a sucker an even break," W. C. Fields always said. At the turn of the century, it was clear that the Internet was on the same page. By the end of 2000, dot-coms had lost 60 percent of their stock value. Many simply disappeared from the cyberscene altogether. Even dot-com giant Amazon.com consolidated operations and cut its workforce. A few—those that got in at the beginning of the cycle and functioned more like conventional business models—survived and became successful.

FACTS

The dot-com industry is not the only one to come from nowhere to enjoy phenomenal success and then fade into the background. In fact, it is only the most recent to have followed the cycle. Similar cycles in the steel, auto, telephone, airline, railroad, and computer industries have been continually restructuring the American economy throughout the twentieth century.

Yet despite the collapse of the dot-com kingdom, the influences of cyberspace remain strong. As we said earlier in this chapter, technology rules. The Internet and its World Wide Web have become essential commerce and information channels for businesses of all sizes and kinds. If anything, the dot-com cycle drove home the reality that unless they can ride the technology curve, companies will not survive. They need to hire people with technology skills and to invest in equipment and training. And they will expect their managers to make it all happen.

Of Upstarts and Mega-glomerates

Upstarts and mergers have dominated the business landscape for the past two decades. From fusion in the oil industry to consolidations in the entertainment industry, the large fish are gobbling up the smaller ones at a phenomenal pace. No sooner does a bright young company show signs of success than another company wants to acquire its potential. The ever-changing scenery poses challenges for managers who might go to work one day for a small operation and return the next to find themselves assimilated into a mega-glomerate.

If you work for a small company, odds are you wear many hats and have a broad base of functions and responsibilities. A small operations manager often worries about the details of day-to-day activities, from filling the copy machine's paper trays in the morning to brainstorming new products in the afternoon. If you're a manager in a large corporation, you likely wear a single hat and have a comparably singular focus in your work. A corporate manager might know little about what goes on beyond the boundaries of his or her department.

Whether your company is large or small, its human needs remain the same. What motivates people remains the same. And in the end, the role of managers remains the same. You are the face of your organization, both to employees and to customers.

FACTS

Early research in industrial psychology demonstrated that employees were more productive when they perceived that management was interested in them. In a study conducted from 1924 to 1927, researchers manipulated the lighting in a work group, telling employees that management was trying to make improvements in their working conditions. Even when researchers created adverse conditions, productivity continued to rise within the work group. The researchers concluded that this was because employees viewed the situation as the company taking an interest in them.

What Companies Care About

The cynics say that companies care only about profits. And of course, companies must care about whether they are earning or losing money, as we discussed earlier. Unless companies can stay on the plus side of the balance sheet, nothing else will matter. But good companies—those with staying power—are the ones whose corporate visions reach beyond earnings statements. Good companies try to involve employees at all levels of the corporate chain in decision making. They emphasize and practice open, two-way communication. And they provide opportunities for learning and advancement. They understand that employee productivity relies on factors such as:

- Personal satisfaction
- Opportunities for self-expression
- A feeling of having some control over personal destiny
- Having a voice in what happens within the company

The challenge for managers is to balance the needs of the organization, the demands of the marketplace, and the desires of the employees.

What the Dynamic Business Environment Means for Today's Managers

Jack be nimble, Jack be quick . . . a children's nursery rhyme could well be the new maxim for today's managers (adapted to be gender-neutral, of course). A manager must accommodate rapid changes not only in technology but also in shifting corporate directions as business responds to the environment in which it exists.

Even with all of the trends, people are still people and they are most productive when well managed. It remains a central role of every manager to understand what makes people tick, and to know how to use that understanding to motivate and manage them. This is your job, in addition to the myriad other responsibilities your job description specifies.

CHAPTER 2
Life As a Manager

Being a manager is an achievement many people strive toward as they further their careers. However, few people are adequately prepared for the rigors that face them. As an employee, you had a clear-cut definition of your role and responsibilities. It was fine for you to show initiative by doing more than what was expected of you, but everyone knew your efforts were above and beyond the call of duty.

As a manager, little is clear-cut. Your job description no doubt includes the phrase "and other duties as necessary," which often seems to be the core rather than the periphery of what your daily activities entail. You are expected to wear many hats and to know which one to wear for each circumstance. How did you get yourself into this position? Many managers enjoy the diversity of their roles, once they figure out how to play them.

Coach, Mentor, Teacher, Parent, Mediator, Cheerleader: Who Are You?

Expectations are high for managers today. Subordinates and superiors alike might expect you to:

- Know your own job inside and out
- Know the jobs of your employees inside and out
- Know what everyone needs, and provide it for them
- Maintain both motivation and discipline
- Enjoy coming to work in the morning more than you like leaving in the evening

As a manager, your roles are nearly endless. You might be friend, confidant(e), advocate, drill sergeant, counselor, sage, and even enforcer. But in the end, as a manager you are a leader. Leadership means many things to different people. But to you, there is only one meaning: knowing which hat to wear and when. Is that the theme song for *Mission Impossible* playing in the background?

Coach: Bringing Out the Best in Others

Odds are, you remember a coach from somewhere in your past. Perhaps it was a track coach who pushed you to run faster or jump farther than you thought was possible . . . or a swim coach who pushed you to the edge of your endurance. Good memories or bad, these are powerful reminders of the influence a single person can have in the lives of many others.

While the other roles you adopt as a manager tend to focus on each individual's needs and capabilities, the role of coach additionally requires you to bring people of diverse skill levels and backgrounds together to work as a unified team, in such a way that the synergy among them generates a product or result that surpasses each individual's abilities. Sounds like a tall order? It is! But it's really nothing more than ongoing reinforcement of what employees are doing and learning.

An effective coach:

- Provides timely and specific feedback. "Good job!" feels good but says little; "You really nailed the point in your proposal!" lets an employee know what was good
- Establishes standards and goals that are high enough to make employees stretch, but not so high that they're impossible to reach
- Tells the truth with kindness and caring—but still tells the truth
- Shares ideas and offers suggestions, but resists telling employees how to do things
- Teaches people how to cook rather than taking them out to dinner, metaphorically speaking

FACTS

It hasn't taken long for the business world to adapt the concepts of coaching for use in the employment environment. Thousands of consultants offer business coaching services that target motivation of work groups and individuals to improve efficiency and increase productivity. Business coaches charge anywhere from several hundred to several thousand dollars a day for their services. How do you know if they're worth it? Ask around, and check references.

Good coaches inspire loyalty and respect, characteristics that are increasingly rare in the workplace. How do you become a good coach? The most effective way is to watch a good coach in action. If you feel that your workplace is deplorably lacking in such role models, attend some high school or college athletic events. You'll see good coaches, bad coaches, and mediocre coaches, and you'll see how their teams respond to their methods.

Mentor: Trusted Guide

Although we view mentoring as a modern concept, the original Mentor debuted in Homer's classic of Greek mythology, *The Odyssey*. When Odysseus, the mythical king of Ithaca (known to Westerners as Ulysses), goes off to war, he appoints his close friend Mentor to look after his family and household, including his son Telemachus and wife Penelope. When the sea nymph Calypso imprisons Odysseus on her island, Athena, the Greek goddess of war, takes over Mentor's body to guide Telemachus in safeguarding his mother from the actions of greedy suitors chasing his father's riches. When Odysseus finally returns home after ten years, Mentor helps him devise the "test" by which he proves to Penelope that he is, indeed, her long-missing husband. Mentor also makes appearances in other Greek myths, often as the disguise for a helpful god or goddess.

Today's mentors are ordinary people who have achieved extraordinary success helping others reach their goals. Most mentoring is unofficial, though some corporations have structured mentoring programs to groom potential upper-level managers and executives. More typically, a person with expertise takes interest in a subordinate's career and takes that subordinate under his or her wing. A mentor helps an employee:

- Set long-term goals and short-term objectives
- Explore new directions to achieve goals
- Identify personal strengths and weaknesses
- Find ways to develop and grow

One of the most effective methods of mentoring is shadowing. You put your employee in situations where he or she can observe your actions without participating in them. Your employee might sit in on a conference call or a sales meeting, for example, or read and discuss with you a report you've written, or accompany you to an event for which you are giving a presentation. These "lessons" are far more effective than any explanations you can offer. Not only do they let your employee see the master in action, but they also show that the master is still human. If you're exceptionally good at what you do, it's because you learn from your mistakes as well as your successes. The better you are, the smaller the increments of measurement. These are subtleties that are difficult to convey in any other way.

Mentoring extends beyond teaching in that it relies on establishing a relatively long-term relationship that revolves around sharing and mutual respect. A mentor shares knowledge as well as wisdom—a fine line, perhaps, but a crucial distinction. While knowledge can be learned, wisdom must be acquired. Knowledge is having the right words; wisdom is knowing when and how to say them—and when to keep them to yourself.

Most mentors have in mind the goal that the employee will become as good at something as they are—perhaps even better. This benefits your employee, of course, by providing opportunities for growth and advancement. But it benefits you, the mentor, as well. If you can create and shape your own replacement, you are freed to pursue new opportunities yourself.

ESSENTIALS

Consider this valuable bit of advice offered by General George S. Patton of the U.S. Army: "Never tell people how to do things. Tell them what to do and they will surprise you with their ingenuity."

Teacher: Imparting New Skills

A teacher is someone with expert skills and knowledge who has the ability to share this expertise with others. A good teacher—one whose students learn—improves both the individual and the company. But it isn't always easy to find a balance between "let me show you" and "get out of the way, I'll do it myself!"

Ron was hired to do PR for a software company. The company was small, and it hired Ron because he was a good writer with a technical background. But Ron had never combined these skills to write press releases, and his debut in his new job was less than spectacular. In fact, it was a bit of a spectacle. After bleeding all over Ron's first few attempts with her red pen, Ron's manager called him into her office. For the rest of the afternoon, she became his journalism teacher. She explained and demonstrated the basic principles of journalism. She showed him how to establish those principles—who, what, where, when, and why—in the first paragraph of virtually anything he might write. She showed him how to make up quotes that would pass muster with corporate executives, how to put words in their mouths that they would wish they had actually said (and would say, after reading the stories generated by the press release).

Now, Ron's manager could have reamed him out. After all, Ron had been hired to write press releases—and he wasn't doing a very good job of it. Ron's manager could have counseled him for his unacceptable job performance, and placed a memo in his personnel file. But she didn't. She put on her teacher hat and turned her office into a classroom. She not only showed Ron just what she wanted him to do, but also taught him the skills he needed to apply the same lesson to other situations. For a few weeks after, Ron's manager met with him to strategize the approach for each new press release. Ron went to his desk to do the writing, then sat down with his manager to review the results. Within a few months, Ron was getting compliments from senior executives. Not only did Ron's skill level improve tremendously, but his self-confidence grew as well. He even enrolled in an evening continuing education class at a local community college to further hone his writing skills.

Not all situations end in such success, of course. Some people resist the suggestion that they need to clean up rusty skills or learn new ones. Some managers lose patience when improvements fail to be immediate and dramatic. Some managers know what they want from their employees but don't know how to express their needs in ways their employees understand. If the teaching hat doesn't fit you very well, consider alternatives (as your budget allows):

- Hire consultants to conduct workshops or seminars for your work group or department
- Send employees to training courses (all expenses paid, of course)
- Reimburse or otherwise compensate employees for taking classes that directly improve their job skills

Parent: Setting Limits

If one of your non-work roles is parent, you might look forward to work as a relief from parental responsibilities—in the same way you might gaze upon the peaceful faces of your children as they sleep, and marvel at the miracle that brought them into your life. Fantasy is quite pleasant when it's removed from reality! Many people view the workplace as an alternate home, and the people there as surrogate family members. After all, you spend more waking hours at work than at home or anywhere else. Coworkers are pseudo-siblings or pseudo-spouses. And managers become—you guessed it—pseudo-parents.

> Just as parents need to set limits and structure at home, managers need to establish boundaries and organization for their employees at work. As a manager, it is your job to tell employees what they can and cannot do.

As much as you might like to toss this particular hat out the window, it's one that comes with the territory. Just as you might have to tell your ten-year-old son to stop spitting out the car window, you might need to tell a thirty-two-year-old administrative assistant that she can't swear on the telephone or a fifty-year-old sales representative that he can't shave during the morning staff meeting. It seems petty and counterproductive . . . and sometimes it is. But people push limits just to be sure those limits are still in place. Everyone needs to feel there's a certain level of stability in their lives, and limits allow them to do so. Limits also establish equity and accountability (more on these topics in later chapters).

In the role of parent, you are often training your employees in basic behaviors. This differs from teaching them skills. Training, in this context, addresses such rudimentary ideas as explicitly identifying circumstances in which it is okay to laugh and those in which it is not okay. You might find yourself repeatedly reminding employees to ask clients if there is anything else they can do for them before rushing to the next call, just as at home you might find yourself repeatedly reminding your kids to unball their socks before putting them in the laundry basket. And your parent role might frequently compel you to reinforce core values and the behaviors that support them, such as prioritizing client requests even when that requires interrupting other work.

Sometimes being parental also means providing a listening ear. It might mean listening to complaints and even whining, and being able to listen between the lines to understand the real issues. You often must sense when your employees feel overworked, and help them to prioritize their tasks and responsibilities so that they can still eat and sleep. And sometimes wearing your parent hat means being firm and saying, "Yes, I understand this is a lot, but you have to perform at this level if you want to be considered senior."

FACTS

A study reported in the February 2000 issue of *Entrepreneur* magazine found that having managers they could respect ranked at the top of the list of what employees want in their jobs. The survey concluded that the relationship employees have with their managers is a key factor in whether employees stay or leave.

Parents sometimes need to intercede with a child's school, stepping in to say that a particular teacher's homework load is unreasonable or another child's bullying is out of control. There are times, too, when you need to become an advocate for your employees, going to your manager and saying, "We have to pull back a bit because we are starting to overwork certain people." This is about getting support to help meet personal and company goals, not to manipulate "mommy" or "daddy" to get out of responsibilities.

When you are functioning effectively in your manager-as-parent role, your employees:

- Know and follow established guidelines and procedures
- Understand that there are clear and consistent consequences for stepping outside the boundaries
- Accept accountability for meeting project timelines rather than pointing the finger of blame at others if things go wrong
- Are comfortable in coming to you with problems or concerns
- Respect you, but don't fear you

Remember, though, that you are not, of course, really a parent to your employees, and the work group is not really a family. There are important differences, many of which are performance-based. Your employees are adults, and have adult rights and responsibilities. It does not serve them well, in the long run, for you to make decisions for them as you might for your children. They have been hired to perform specific tasks and accomplish particular goals. You can restrict your daughter's television when she forgets to do her chores, but it's a more serious matter when an employee fails (by forgetting or by intent) to complete an assignment. The lines are not always clear, but it's essential for you to know where they are.

You might re-examine the amount of time you spend wearing your parent hat if:

- You look at the employees sitting in your office airing yet another dispute, and realize that if they were younger and shorter, they'd be tattling.
- "Nobody told me I had to do that" is a familiar chorus in staff meetings.
- Employees ask permission to go to the restroom or take a break.
- No assignment gets completed without repeated visits to your office to be sure it's being done right.
- You make excuses to your superiors when your employees fail to complete projects either on time or correctly.

Mediator: Finding Balance

Acting as a mediator is familiar territory for many managers who feel that all they do is mediate. You might help employees resolve disagreements among themselves, investigate disputes between clients and employees, or negotiate differences between the priorities of upper management and the needs of employees. Mediation is more effective (and successful) when it is a process of collaboration rather than compromise. This is more than just word play. Collaboration comes from the Latin *collaborare*, meaning "to labor together." Compromise, despite its core word "promise," implies giving up something of value, or conceding, to reach agreement. The implications are important because they set the tone for the discussion. Few people are happy when compromise means they get less than they hoped for or expected, yet most are pleasantly surprised to get more.

QUESTIONS?

What does mediation mean?
To mediate is to be in the middle or intervene to settle a dispute between two parties. Mediation is the process of finding common ground, of seeking win-win solutions to differences and disagreements that will be acceptable to both parties.

Mediation is most effective when you:

- Focus on common goals and look for common ground to help you reach those goals
- Treat all parties, and their viewpoints, with respect
- Propose win-win solutions
- Remain interested but impartial
- Establish a process for assessing the success of the agreed-upon solutions

Cheerleader: Rallying the Troops

When you reached the manager step on the corporate ladder, did you think you'd need to pull out the pom-poms and the bullhorn? It's a significant aspect of your job to motivate and excite your employees. Leading the cheering section demonstrates that you believe in your team and its ability to succeed. This is important on a day-to-day basis, and becomes critical in times of change.

Change frightens and confuses many people. There is an inherent insecurity when the not-yet-familiar replaces the tried-and-true. People worry about their jobs and their abilities to complete new tasks and assignments. They need someone (you) to rally them back to believing in themselves.

But you have to have those pom-poms always at the ready. It's not acceptable to sit in your office all week, then pop out when a productivity report tells you your department is in jeopardy of missing its deadlines. Cheering on the troops is only effective when the troops know that you truly care—not just about their projects and assignments and meeting your department's goals, but also about them as people and individuals. And they won't know you truly care unless you're involved in what's going on every day.

FACTS

When Total Quality Management (TQM) and its many variants entered the American business vernacular in the 1980s, many employees resisted efforts to make them "better" workers when they perceived that nothing changed within their work environments to support the "new employee" that upper management wanted to see. When companies began involving employees in identifying problems and designing solutions, there was a dramatic leap in buy-in. Once employees felt they were owners in the process of improvement, they became enthusiastic supporters of improvement efforts.

Do you watch sporting events? Do you watch the cheerleaders? (It's okay, you can admit it.) They're always interacting with the crowd, no matter what's happening on the field or the court. They're chanting and dancing and smiling, working to stay engaged with the spectators. Their mission is to create a roar of support beyond what they themselves can generate, that motivates the players to give the proverbial 110 percent.

But the players know that the cheerleaders are there, and are always there. And they know that even when the crowd boos, the cheerleaders are still there, cheering.

This is your role, too. Even when your superiors—or your clients or customers—are unhappy with your team's work and productivity, you need to stay right there on the sidelines, cheering your team on even when things aren't going so well. If you've been there all along, they will respond.

- "Great job getting out that report, Joan. I know you came in early every day this week to make it happen, and I appreciate your effort."
- "You all worked really hard on the Johnson proposal, and we made it to the final round. I know no one likes to work Saturdays, but if we can all give one last effort on these final questions, we can get the phase two proposal done for delivery on Monday."
- "We're short-staffed right now, and I know that's not your issue. But we still have customers to serve, so let's give it our best. I'll lead the first team; who wants to lead the second and third teams?"

Sometimes you will find yourself switching back and forth between your cheerleader hat and your coach hat. That's where the business world differs from the sports field. While you'll never see one of the Dallas Cowgirls calling the play on third and short, you will find yourself doing the corporate equivalent. You can't very well expect your employees to buck up when you have no idea (and they know you have no idea) what goes on in their daily lives.

Stay Connected

Chapter 7, "Communication and Feedback," goes into comprehensive detail about the need and ways to stay in touch with both employees and superiors. This is such a critical message, however, that it's worth mentioning here. There is no replacement or substitute for effective communication. The 1980s were pivotal in changing the ways employers and employees treated each other. It was the decade of "management by walking around" (MBWA to its advocates), as well as a focus on collaborating (there's that word again!) to meet customer needs and exceed expectations. While many aspects of this transformational decade have evolved into more sophisticated forms, the need for continual communication remains unchanged.

Today, it's a rare (although not yet extinct) manager who believes it's possible to manage effectively from a distance. If you don't know how life is for your employees, you can't know how they're doing. You must roll up your sleeves and get your hands dirty, metaphorically speaking, to stay connected to the daily grind.

ALERT

Some managers (and we know you're not among them) believe that their promotions mean they've earned the right to climb out of the trenches. Nothing is further from the truth. If anything, you've acquired the responsibility to know the trenches every which way—and the people who toil in them every day.

It's not as thankless as you might think. In fact, the rewards are pretty impressive. For starters, your employees respect you. They work more efficiently and effectively, not just because they know you're watching but also because they want to earn your respect (because they know you're watching). While they might never name their firstborn after you, they will go the extra mile for you because they know you'll do the same for them. When your employees do well, you do well. And when they look good, you look good. It doesn't get any better than that.

Living with Your Limitations

Are you feeling a little bit like part of your job description reads, "walk on water"? Don't worry—it's fine if your sidestroke can get you to shore. It's okay to have limitations. Everyone does. What matters more is knowing what yours are, and being able to compensate for them. If you're not a good teacher, have someone else do the teaching—just be able to recognize when it's necessary. Your superiors, as well as other managers in your company, might be good resources. And if you need to improve in an area, there's guaranteed to be a book that can help. Which, of course, you already know since you're reading this one. See? It's not that hard to find the support you need to be the kind of manager you would like to have as your manager!

Stepping Up to the Challenge

It's not possible for a new manager to step in and maintain the same atmosphere that existed under the previous manager. Managers are people, and people (of course) are uniquely individual. A new manager has different abilities, interests, and priorities. The work group will eventually reflect this, and everyone knows it (even you). Even when a change in management is desirable, employees might meet it with resistance. It's frightening and threatening to lose a manager. Even if the new manager is someone promoted from within the company, he or she is still an unknown. People may outwardly agree that the new manager offers new opportunities, but inwardly feel worried. They want to know:

- What will happen under the new "regime"?
- Will things be better or worse than they were before the changing of the guard?
- If the previous manager was fired, what happens to former allies that still work in the department or work group?
- What and how will job descriptions and responsibilities change?

ESSENTIALS

When you step into a new position, be sure you communicate consistently and diligently with all of your employees. You must both talk and listen. You need to hear about what concerns your employees. Even if there's little you can do about their worries, listening to them acknowledges that they are valid.

Talking with the employees who now report to you will help you to establish an environment of mutual respect, even if there is disagreement.

Explain your perspectives and expectations, and discuss the expectations of your superiors. You can't talk away disappointment, disagreement, disapproval, or fear, but bringing these emotions out into the open gives everyone permission to begin dealing with them.

Replacing a "Bad" Manager

"Bad" and "good" are simplistic, judgmental designators we like to apply to difficult situations. Reducing concerns to such a basic level makes us feel better about them, somehow. This has much to do with a sense that we've lost control—even though control might not have been present in the first place. More often than not, however, circumstances change and the people within them don't, or else they change in different ways.

What is a "bad" manager? Often, this is a judgment that exists in the eye of the beholder. After all, no one is perfect. But what employees perceive as good or bad in a manager is not necessarily the same as how executive management sees the situation. Consider the following sections; although the names have been altered to protect those who wish to remain unidentified, the circumstances are real.

The High Cost of Management Mistakes

Albatross All-Tech started as a small company run by a trio of entrepreneurs who were great visionaries. No matter how dark the horizon, they always found the silver lining—and found ways to display it to employees. They were great cheerleaders who excelled in motivating employees to give more than should have been possible. As a result, the company grew into a huge success. Revenues skyrocketed, and things began to change. The single office where it all started spread to a suite, then a floor, then a building. The three founding entrepreneurs became executives, and rewarded dedicated employees by making them managers.

Layers of management grew as the company did, and soon local level managers lost contact with the executives. Managers like Cheryl were outstanding cheerleaders and coaches, but now the company had other needs. Many managers were able to adapt, but Cheryl could not. She didn't see why she had to, either; after all, she was the reason the company had gotten where it was. While this was true enough, it was shortsighted. One Monday morning when employees came to work, there was someone new in Cheryl's office.

"Good morning," he said from his doorway when it was clear that everyone was in. "I'm Carl, and I'm your new boss."

Carl was no stranger to the employees, and by noon the grapevine had divulged his story: He was on his way to the executive suite, but his superiors wanted him to have some hands-on management experience. His mission: to improve the department's productivity. Over the next few days, Carl held numerous meetings in his office during which he outlined the changes that would take place. Cheryl had been fired, he explained, because she had been unable to take the department's performance to the next level. Each meeting ended with the admonishment that Carl expected everyone's full support.

Well, he got what he asked for—just not in the way he had in mind. The employees bonded together to undermine Carl at every opportunity, even to the extent of placing department and company goals at risk. They supported the unspoken effort to oust him. They succeeded. Why? Because Carl was a bad manager? In their eyes, yes. But Cheryl also had been a bad manager, at least in the eyes of upper management. And in truth, the department knew that even though everyone liked Cheryl, she was ineffective as a manager.

Though Carl was ultimately responsible for his own demise, the way in which Cheryl departed resulted in angry and hurt feelings that employees immediately transferred to Carl. People went home for the weekend fully expecting to see each other come Monday, but it turned out that Friday was the last time they would see Cheryl. In a way, it was as though she'd been killed in a car accident—she simply disappeared without so much as a "see ya." Because her bond with employees was primarily personal, everyone was hurt by this abrupt departure. If she had truly cared about them as they all believed she did, why would she leave without saying good-bye, or at least asking a representative of senior management to say good-bye on her behalf? People were worried:

Would she be all right? Where would she go? What would she do? Did she need anything from them?

When Carl stepped into the picture as though he had painted it, the resentment spilled over onto him. There was no transition; he was just there Monday morning to assert that he was now in charge. Senior management erred by not paving the way for his entrance; his abrasive and arrogant manner simply made more potholes. With no other outlet, employees vented their feelings at Carl. And by failing to recognize the attributes and talents of the employees—which were abundant despite Cheryl's poor management skills—he alienated the people he needed most. Though in the end employees felt that they won when Carl was fired, in reality theirs was a hollow victory. They felt betrayed by the company to which they'd given their loyalty and commitment. The rapport that had existed with Cheryl at the department's helm was gone, and work was just work.

FACTS

Some managers feel such a need to be liked by their employees that they gossip with them, badmouthing company policies and the executives who create them. While employees might laugh too, they soon lose trust in such managers. They begin to wonder what the managers say about them. In the end, these actions cost managers from both sides. Employees no longer want to associate with them, fearing they'll be painted with the same brush, and executives no longer trust them to represent the company's interests.

When the Last Manager Truly Was Bad

Sometimes, of course, the former manager truly was bad, no matter whose standards form the measurement. Managers can be dictatorial, disorganized, selfish, unfair, lazy, and abusive. Neither employees nor executives appreciate these characteristics (although nearly everyone has had a boss somewhere along the line who has personified them). When you are replacing a manager who was bad by all accounts and standards, you have both a responsibility and an opportunity.

Jonathan joined WonderWidgets with rave reviews from the upper level executives who had hired him. Within weeks, however, his employees were singing a very different song. Jonathan seemed to call in sick every time he had accumulated enough leave time to cover a day out of the office. At least once a week he called to say he would be working from home, although no one answered the phone when employees called with questions. When he was in the office, Jonathan was disorganized, volatile, and unpredictable. He flew off the handle for no apparent reason, cancelled or missed appointments, redefined assigned projects and tasks without consulting those doing the work, and often refused to make decisions about even the most mundane matters (like ordering toner for the copy machine).

Jonathan played favorites, promoting one person and squelching others. It was never safe to be in Jonathan's good graces because his fancy turned faster than a child's whimsy. Without warning, yesterday's favorite became today's scapegoat. Most people that Jonathan promoted he soon fired. This was supposed to keep the person from showing him up, but it didn't work because everyone in the office was on to Jonathan's game. Fortunately, upper management was on to it as well, and Jonathan was fired (upon hearing the news, the employees had a party).

The new manager, Joanne, started her first day on the job by meeting with everyone. She asked the group to talk about what worked and what didn't, from a process perspective. She explicitly said she did not want to hear names and stories. This freed the employees to focus on workflow, assignments, goals, priorities, and other issues related to productivity rather than personality. Over the next two days, Joanne went around to talk privately with each employee, allowing people to express their personal feelings. On Friday of her first week, Joanne called another department meeting. She shared her improvement plan with the group, talking about what seemed to work well and what didn't. She gave everyone a few days to think about and respond to the plan, and then created a revised improvement plan that incorporated many employee suggestions.

Joanne continued talking with employees, both individually and at group meetings. Employees learned they could trust her, and grew to like as well as respect her. Within six months, the department was so far ahead of its goals that it was necessary to revise the plan again.

When It's Your Turn to Clean Up After a Bad Manager

Cleaning up after a bad manager is among the most difficult challenges you can face as a manager. Unless you handle the situation just right, you, too, will look incompetent. All managers, good and bad, have loyal followers. Always assume this to be true. It isn't necessary to treat these employees any differently (and in fact is probably better for you not to), but it is vital for you to know who they are, because your first mission is to get everybody on board, and the loyalists will be the most resistant. (Get out your pom-poms!)

- Express clear and concise goals and objectives. Explain why these are important to each employee, to the department, and to the company.
- Ask each employee for comments and thoughts. Respond to negative expressions without judgment or attempting to refute them. "Yes, that's a good point. We'll come back to that."
- Respond directly but nonconfrontationally to efforts to undermine your authority and the process. If an employee persists, quietly and calmly request that he or she meet with you in your office after the meeting to discuss those concerns.
- Continue to gather input and information from every employee. Meet with individuals and small work groups as well as the entire department.
- Listen to what people are saying, and also to what they're not saying. Question, nonconfrontationally, what doesn't make sense to you or seems out of context.
- Integrate employee suggestions into improvement plans. If you can't use a suggestion directly, use it indirectly and credit the employee or employees with providing the impetus for the necessary change.
- Be consistent. If you change direction, have a good reason and present it to your employees.

It's easy to turn the last manager into a bad guy, whether or not that was actually the case. Human nature causes us to want to look as good as we can; sometimes this tendency (rooted in insecurity) leads us astray. You might be tempted to think that by making someone else look bad, you can at least look better—if not downright good. Resist! Although extremes in perception are common during times of transition, eventually the fog clears and balance returns to judgment. When this happens, you're in a much stronger position if your attributes stand on their own merits. On the flip side, turning the last manager into a bad guy can backfire by instead turning him or her into a martyr. It's also human nature to put a halo on the last manager's head. People forget how bad things really were, and begin to reminisce about the good old times (however few of them there actually were). Before you know it, you become the bad guy. Just a little something to think about. . . .

Replacing a "Good" Manager

What happens when the manager before you was almost superhuman? Those are tough shoes to fill. This can be just as significant a challenge. As always, good communication is essential.

- Listen to employees so you know what concerns them, and talk with them so they know what concerns you.
- Confront the ghosts head-on. Ask what employees liked about the previous manager's approach, and what they would change if they were in your shoes.
- Focus on processes, procedures, and policies. Whether or not employees like you, this is the foundation of the workplace.
- Refrain from presenting your views to change the world at the first meeting. Save your perspective for subsequent meetings, when you can temper your comments with understanding that you acquire by listening to employees' concerns and views.
- Do not comment about the previous manager's ways of doing things. Remain neutral and supportive of the company's goals. Whatever role you're playing, you are above all the face of the company.

Just like bad, good is in the eye of the beholder. Change doesn't inherently mean the end of good; it can mean a different kind of good. Any good manager can (and should) have an open-door policy in which employees feel comfortable seeking him or her out, an open exchange of ideas, and procedures that support the work group's productivity and happiness.

Rebuilding a Work Group: Picking Up the Pieces

We all want to feel that we have some control over our lives. We want to know that others listen to us, value us, and care about us. Everyone needs this. When circumstances and people change, particularly at work, it causes concern and stress. It's natural to wonder whether things will improve or deteriorate, whether work will be a place we enjoy going to or can't wait to escape from. These are issues that threaten our comfort levels. We worry about what will happen to our work situations, to our opportunities for advancement, and to our careers and livelihoods. Yet we often find ourselves in situations where many aspects are out of our control. If you want to stay in the job, you must accept the changes. Can you hear the stress-o-meter starting to whir?

Sometimes a manager steps into an existing work group or department that remains intact aside from its change of leadership. The employees are seasoned and knowledgeable, and passing the baton is a smooth transition. When the previous manager has been fired, however, there are very likely productivity issues. Other employees might have been fired or transferred as well, leaving some positions vacant. If you are a manager in this type of situation, your mission is to rebuild.

Rebuilding can arise from several circumstances. Perhaps there is a new market, making it necessary for a company to revamp its product and service lines to meet changing customer demands. In such a setting, your job as manager is to identify the key strengths and abilities existing employees offer, and look for ways to fit them into the new structure.

You will need to motivate employees to feel that they are valued contributors in the new order.

ALERT

It's important to make sure each person understands his or her role and responsibilities, as well as those of the others in the work group or department. And it's essential to clearly articulate and support new goals and procedures. Ambiguity breeds mistrust, and that's not what you need to succeed.

Maybe your company has reorganized because of new ownership or to consolidate operations (save money). The employees who remain are likely to be suspicious and reluctant to support (or even appear to support) new corporate mandates. It is fertile ground for resentment, distrust, anger, and fear to thrive. But you're not going to let these negatives grow, because you see the situation as a great opportunity. Pull out your parent, coach, and cheerleader hats—you need to mobilize these people. But first, allow for some mourning. While the public view tends to spotlight the people who lose their jobs in corporate shake-ups, these have been traumatic events for the employees who remain. It can be more distressing to be among the survivors than to get a pink slip. These people need time to assimilate and adjust. A good manager acknowledges feelings, and then helps employees focus on the future and encourages a positive outlook.

After all is said and done, however, your key role is still to craft a cohesive and productive work group. This entails communicating both with the group as a whole and with individual employees to:

- Clarify goals
- Identify roles and responsibilities
- Establish procedures for how people work together
- Get acceptance and support from employees

The sooner you articulate a clear path, the sooner employees can get on with their work lives. People recover more quickly when there is a plan in place that helps them move forward, toward new responsibilities and broadened abilities. You, their manager, are the one who can—and must—lead them.

It's Lonely in the Middle

As a manager, it is also your role to be an advocate for employees. Sometimes they might not want you to take on this role, or might not recognize that you have. At the same time, you represent the company. You can't really belong to either side if you are to function effectively. That's why it's called "middle" management!

You're not always a welcome presence, which is probably not news to you. Employees might resent you, often for reasons that have nothing to do with you personally. Even your superiors might be impatient with what they perceive to be your lack of progress if improvements take longer than expected. You alone cannot make things all better; miracle worker is not among your many roles, although both subordinates and superiors might act as though it is.

Your accountability requires you to maintain a distance from both employees and upper management. Think of this as a "clear vision" boundary that helps you to see both sides without becoming immersed in either. In fact, you might begin to see your job as one defined by boundaries. Without boundaries and limits, you and your employees might easily lose sight of the real reason you're together: to help the company meet its goals. You can be colleagues, after a fashion, but you can't really be friends. Keeping a safe distance from upper management keeps your vision from becoming rose-tinted. You are the one who needs to be able to tell the executives which policies and procedures are working and which ones are counterproductive or even dismal failures.

Maintaining a balanced distance gives you the ability to support company policies and procedures in front of your employees; even if you disagree with them, you don't share this with your employees. Instead, you take your disagreements privately to your superiors and express your concerns. This preserves trust and respect from both sides.

Riding the Waves of Change

The turbulent 1980s gave rise to the use of a phrase from Shakespeare's *The Tempest* to describe the magnitude of the upheaval in the business world: "sea change." The new environment was dramatically different from the old one, as were the new ways. Such upheavals are like volcanic eruptions; they blow existing structures to oblivion and construct new ones, often simultaneously. One minute there's a mountain and the next there's a smoking crater. But downslopes are new hills and valleys and rivers and lakes, a ready-made environment to replace the old one. In the business world, such eruptions take the form of mergers and acquisitions. One day there's a giant conglomerate that dominates the corporate landscape, and the next there's a smattering of small companies scattered all around.

It's as much a reality of your career as it is of nature: Things change. Companies change, people change, needs change. The typical American worker may have as many as seven careers during his or her working life, and three or four times that many jobs—a significant change in the course of a generation. In commerce, as in nature, change results in new and often unexpected growth. Those who thrive are those who can adapt to new needs and new demands, and respond to difficult situations with positive attitudes. The reality is that people are going to leave your work group and people are going to join it. You yourself will move into different positions, perhaps for the same company, but more likely for other companies (or your current company under different ownership). Job security is more a matter of skills security, of making sure that your abilities and knowledge keep you a desired commodity.

CHAPTER 3

It's Not about You, It's about Them

It's exciting to be promoted to manager. You're proud of yourself—and rightly so, you've earned this—and you can't wait to share your excitement with your coworkers. But wait—they're not your coworkers any more. They report to you. And they can't wait to put you to the test.

If your euphoria survives this jolt, it's certain to lose luster when you realize that there are still people—your superiors—holding you accountable for your productivity and efficiency. In fact, there might be more of them paying attention to your actions and efforts than ever before, and that accountability includes the productivity and efficiency of all the people who report to you, too. But don't take the interest personally. Oh, your superiors probably like you well enough and are pleased to have you in the management ranks. The interest they have in you is vested in your ability to advance the company's goals and objectives.

What Employees Want from Managers

At one level, what employees want from their managers is fairly simple. They want direct and truthful information about your expectations of them, honest feedback, and fairness in how you treat them compared to other employees. Of course, managers are human just like their employees (although employees don't always grant them this generosity). But as a manager you must moderate your humanness. Who hasn't had a manager whose . . .

- Mood, alternately wretched or exhilarated, determined whether an employee's performance was good or bad?
- Favored child this week became next week's orphaned outcast, without rhyme or reason for either choice?
- Interpretations of policies and procedures change faster than the weather, and with about as much predictability?

These managers might seem fine at first, when their inconsistencies benefit you. But sooner or later they turn on you, and suddenly the unfairness of it all becomes painfully clear. Because you can't predict when or which way such a manager will turn, you (and all the employees in your work group) become distrustful. The higher into the ranks of management this person rises, the greater the discontent below. Eventually employees will transfer to other departments or leave for jobs with other companies to get away from this destructive and counterproductive behavior. Of course employees behave in similar ways. But when you, a manager, act with such inconsistency, it reflects a negative image not only on you but also on the entire organization.

SSENTIALS   Being a manager isn't about you, except to you. To everyone else, it's about them. Subordinates want to know what you can do to help them, and superiors want to know what you can do to help the company. That's why we call it middle management.

Consistency, Consistency, Consistency

It's not very glamorous. But in the end, consistency scores big points with employees because it shapes as well as supports their expectations. Larisse was a manager for a company that gave bonuses for completed projects. When the company first implemented the policy, the procedure was simple: Each employee had one project at a time, and each project had a timeline. Each time the timeline was met, the employee received a bonus. The company grew and its market became more sophisticated. Projects became increasingly complex, and employees often handled several projects at the same time. To meet timelines, employees started working together.

A manager's dream come true, right? Only until bonuses were due, and then it turned into a nightmare. At first, the company tried splitting bonuses among the various employees who worked on the project. This worked only until employees began complaining that two of them did most of the work, while the others made only token contributions. Because there was no formal company policy about shared bonuses, Larisse was a frazzled wreck. There was no way she could be consistent because there was no structure to support her judgments and decisions. Employees began to feel that she was fickle and arbitrary, even though she often spent hours pouring over project time logs to determine which employees had made what contributions.

Though the last thing Larisse wanted was yet another set of rules, she finally felt compelled to ask her superiors for a more comprehensive policy. Within a month she—and every employee—received a copy of the new, detailed guidelines for bonus payments. There was the usual grumbling as everyone dissected the new policy. Even Larisse found guidelines that she thought were unfair. But she enforced the policy anyway, because as a manager that was her job. In the end, that consistency restored peace and productivity. And Larisse found great peace of mind, because she no longer had to remember how she had handled a bonus on a previous project and try to figure out if this project had a similar set of circumstances.

Consistency is crucial not just because it establishes standardized procedures, but also because it affirms fairness. Even if employees (or managers) disagree with human resources (HR) policies or department procedures, they will accept them when they know everyone else must, too. Your company and your department should have written policies and guidelines that are available for employees to review at any time. A word of warning: If yours doesn't, don't just leap to your keyboard to begin writing your own policies. Talk with your superiors first. A written policy, even something you send out as an e-mail or a memo, represents your company. Its content can have legal ramifications. Many companies have policies that outline the process for writing new or revising existing policies and procedures. (Chapter 4, "This Is Not Your Daddy's Workplace," goes into much more detail about legal issues.)

What Organizations Want from Managers

We'd say consistency, consistency, consistency again, but that would be repetitive (even though it's true). As a manager, you are the face of your company (also repetitive but true). You represent upper management to your employees. Your superiors expect you to:

- Reflect and support company goals and objectives, even if you don't agree with them
- Reflect and support company policies and procedures, even if you don't like them

- Communicate the company's needs to employees
- Give upper management feedback about how employees perceive and respond to company goals and polices
- Give upper management feedback about what works and what doesn't about how the company does business

If your enthusiasm for these last two points exceeds your reluctance for the first three points, take five here to pull yourself back to reality. This is not a license to blast your company's executives for all the shortcomings, perceived or real, that employees complain about. Remember that mediator hat we discussed in Chapter 2, "Life as a Manager"? Put it on before reading any further.

To be consistent and effective in supporting a company's principles, managers must also be committed to them. This doesn't mean you live or die by them, but you must feel enough commitment that you can and do use them as the guiding force in your interactions with employees. If you deeply resent certain corporate policies or goals, this commitment will be difficult for you. Ask yourself:

- What is it, precisely, that I don't like?
- Why do I feel so strongly about it?
- Do other managers share my feelings?
- What have I done to attempt to change the policy or goal?
- Could I live with this policy or goal if I understood the reason it was in place?

Often, simply exploring the reasons for your feelings brings your concerns to the surface where you can examine them to decide if they truly have merit. Sometimes how we feel about certain policies or goals has little to do with the principle, but instead relates back to some personal experience for which we're still carrying around baggage. If you think about it, companies don't have anything to gain by implementing policies and procedures that are unreasonable. Sometimes the original purpose for the guideline gets lost in the process of moving it through the process of approval. Once someone points this out, it's possible to correct the flaws.

Successful companies create working environments in which employees and managers feel welcome to share their views and concerns. This kind of dialogue helps companies to avert potential problems. After all, the company doesn't exist solely for the purpose of creating rules. Rules are in place to support the company's mission and goals, whatever those are. Like nearly all other dimensions of doing business, rules must be dynamic to remain effective. This means that a company must continually review and reassess its policies, to be sure the policies are keeping up with changes in the business environment.

As a manager, it is your role to facilitate this process.

ALERT

As a manager you need to let your superiors know when there are problems. Who knows better how to make improvements than the people who do the work—your employees? Listening to them is more than just good business. It's the employees who feel there is no audience for their concerns who may leave in anger.

Are You Bridging the Gap or Stuck in the Middle?

Organizations, whether for-profit or not-for-profit, must be in a constant state of development. The market requires this in response to new technology, changing trends, and shifting opportunities. Managers must be ready to adjust to these demands as well. Sometimes your role is to interpret the change for employees and help them adjust to it, especially when it results in corporate policy that directly affects them. Sometimes your role is to listen to employees, collect their suggestions and reactions, and interpret them for upper management.

A savvy manager sees change as opportunity and is able to actively bridge the gap. To do this effectively, you must be a good listener and a good diplomat, as well as able to get things done through prioritizing and implementing action. Unfortunately, managers often shy away from bridging the gap. This reflects their insecurity with change. They don't want to expend the extra energy required to be an active rather than a passive manager.

Jolene was a manager whose hands-off yet supportive style engendered tremendous loyalty among the employees who reported to her. The work group was open, fun, and hard-working. But Jolene's style wasn't as popular with the superiors to whom she reported, who felt uninformed about her work group's activities. As the company grew, upper management wanted all managers to establish better procedures to account for staff time and resources, and to shift assignments among employees for improved efficiency. Jolene resisted these efforts, believing they were unnecessary intrusions into her work group's operations. As a result, the company put a new manager in place between Jolene and upper management, in effect curtailing Jolene's authority.

The new manager, Marilyn, was more formal and procedure-oriented, and Jolene didn't like her. Though Marilyn's approach was much more consistent with the direction the company was headed, Jolene continued to resist. She bad-mouthed Marilyn to her employees, and encouraged them to resist Marilyn's changes. The tactic backfired. Jolene and her most loyal employees lost their jobs when Marilyn, implementing upper management directives, reorganized the department. Instead of stepping up as a leader and bridging the gap between employees and the company, the old ways and the new ways, Jolene allowed herself to become trapped in the middle and ultimately squeezed out.

FACTS

The U.S. Bureau of the Census reports that the number of twenty- to thirty-four-year-olds declined by 6 million in the 1990s, while the number of people over age fifty increased by 12 million. By the year 2020, 20 percent of the American population—62 million people— will be age sixty-five or older. By the year 2010, there will be more people age fifty or older holding jobs than people under age fifty.

It can be difficult to be the bridge, especially if you disagree with the company's new direction or methods. But resistance is generally futile and ends up tainting your reputation. Jolene was, overall, a good manager.

She just couldn't respond to the demands of change, and it cost not only her but also her employees. If your disagreements about upper management directives are strong, you have an obligation to discuss them with your superiors. But as a manager, you have an equal obligation to support those directives in dealing with your employees. By doing so, you help them change and adapt if that's what they choose to do, and you keep yourself well positioned to move on to other opportunities.

From Whiz Kids to Novice Seniors: The Age Gap

The workplace has always had its mix of young and old. What's different about today's workplace is that roles and responsibilities are seldom linked to age. In former generations, "kids" were hired on and "old-timers" took them under their wing, teaching them both job skills and social roles. Younger workers respected the wisdom of older workers, knowing that someday it would be their turn to be the older workers on the receiving end of such deference.

Now it is someday, but the workplace has changed. The American population is aging, and so is its workforce. Technology, typically the glory field for the young, has upended the status quo. There is still a mix of young and old in the workforce, but older workers are just as likely to be learning the ropes from younger employees.

As new technologies such as personal computers and the Internet began booming, companies hired whiz kids—young people with brilliant skills in narrowly focused technology areas—like crazy. Competition was hot, growth was fast, and the stakes were high. Web-based upstarts and established companies alike vied to lead the pack into a technology-driven future. In such an environment, the young hotshots flashed to the top. Once there, they hired people like themselves—smart risk-takers who supported, but didn't challenge, each other's ideas. People who didn't fit the new mold suddenly didn't fit in at all.

Older employees and even managers who had been in the workforce long enough to understand its dynamics grew frustrated. Corporate structure forced them to take advice and direction from superiors who knew little beyond the scope of their technology world. They didn't know about business models, they didn't know the market. What could have been a "dynamic duo" level of collaboration instead became a standoff. As older employees tried to get comfortable with the new technology, the whiz kids resented their "interference" and continued to dictate solutions. Meanwhile, the older people continuously tried to take a new technology and mold it to their own outdated ways of doing business. The result was often a disaster. Each age group resisted the other's knowledge. In many companies, the rocky start ended in disaster, with the company falling apart or returning to its previous business models. Ultimately, both sides lost.

The clash of cultures presents unique challenges for managers. Younger and older employees tend to have different attitudes and approaches toward work. Younger people often want to be left alone to complete assigned projects without interference. They expect managers to trust them to do this. If they fail to come through, there's always an external reason. This is not, in the young employee's mind, an effort to escape accountability, but simply the way things turned out. Game over, push restart. Move on. Older employees are generally accustomed to, and comfortable with, more structure. Their experiences have taught them that progress is a series of steps, and moving through them is a matter of taking them one at a time, not all in a single leap. They expect their managers to show interest in these steps and to appreciate their steady progress toward completion. Today's manager must be able to work with both extremes, taking the time to understand the issues each generation's culture brings to the workplace.

The Employee Wants to Know: What's in It for Me?

People work for myriad reasons that funnel into three core factors: They want to be entertained, feel appreciated, and earn money. The job description that covers these needs might read, "Our company offers challenging work, opportunities for career growth, and a comprehensive compensation and benefits package." The excited employee who applies for the position might think, "Finally—a job that will let me use my skills and knowledge in ways that make me happy, a company that will see how good I am and promote me, and a paycheck that will cover payments on a new car!"

On the surface, an employee's expectations are often brief and clear. He or she wants a reasonable paycheck, reasonable work assignments, reasonable hours, and a reasonable level of respect. The aspect of these expectations that continues (and often intensifies) centers around a single word: reasonable. What reasonable means, however, is different for each employee as well as at different times in an employee's career. A young, single person at the start of his or her working life might be eager for opportunities to travel and willing to work long hours to complete complex projects. For a married person with a family, however, travel and overtime might be resented intrusions.

What Employees Expect from Their Jobs

Expectations vary among individuals, of course. But common to most people are three basic needs:

1. To engage in work that is interesting and provides a sense of accomplishment
2. To feel that the job offers economic stability
3. To grow toward personal potential

An employee's expectations begin with the job position posting or advertisement. Someone—hopefully a person who intimately knows the job's technical skill requirements and work environment—attempts to summarize the position's needs in one hundred words or less. This can be a considerable challenge, even for the entry-level jobs employees might apply for to gain experience. Most job descriptions include a certain amount of "planned ambiguity" to accommodate the rapidly shifting needs of the business world.

Usually, this benefits both the company and the employee. Employers need to be able to change a job to fit new needs. Workers generally appreciate the opportunity to learn new skills. But managers and employees alike who establish rigid expectations based on the job description in place at the time of hiring are likely to resist changes that arise. This can lead to angry confrontations and dissatisfaction on both sides of the management line.

FACTS

Employees often expect their jobs to provide a certain level of social interaction. Going to work is a chance to reconnect with friends and acquaintances, to share stories about pets or children or misadventures at the shopping mall. Human beings need this interaction. In most situations, this need is not necessarily incompatible with productivity and efficiency. People work better when they're happy, and interacting with other people is a way to be happy. The challenge for managers is to keep such interactions appropriate for the workplace.

What Employees Expect from Their Managers

What do you think your employees expect from you as their manager? Put a checkmark in front of the statements that are true for you.

My employees expect me to . . .

_____ Know what they want, even if they don't say anything

_____ Understand that they have lives away from work that sometimes interfere with work

_____ Pick up the slack for them or intercede in some way when they aren't able to get their assigned job tasks completed on time

_____ Be available at any time of the day to answer questions and resolve problems

_____ Treat them fairly, which they define as considering any and all extenuating circumstances before passing judgment or taking action

_____ Help them acquire new skills, even if that means they will then become qualified for different jobs

_____ Advocate for them when they have needs that require upper management decisions

_____ Occasionally take them to lunch or bring in goodies as a show of appreciation for the good work they do

_____ Give them full credit for the department's successes and take full blame for the department's shortcomings

_____ Always remember that they are only human, but never reveal this about yourself

Most managers will check seven or eight of these expectations, chuckling over some and groaning over others. Some are not very reasonable or realistic, while others are essential. Some seem selfish— and they are. As we've said, when you become a manager, it's no longer about you. It's about your employees, what they need and want, and how you respond.

The Manager Wants to Know: What's Left for Me?

Managers succeed by putting other goals before their own agendas. They succeed by placing the company goals first, and they succeed by helping employees achieve their goals. When employees are functioning at their best, then the department is, too. And that is what makes the manager succeed. For this chain of events to occur, however, managers must understand what makes different employees tick.

To hear all the talk about meeting employee needs, you'd think companies don't consider managers to be employees. Of course you are just as much an employee as are the people who report to you. But an odd thing happens on your climb up the corporate ladder: your expectations are supposed to become more global. While upper management hopes that line-level employees care about the company in some way, it expects that you, as a manager, care about the company at least as much as you care about yourself. Fair or not, that's the way it is. As the company invests more in you—salary, training, responsibility, perks—it expects more from you.

When Doug got his first job in management, he could hardly wait to share the good news with his family. After everyone congratulated him, his older brother took him aside. "I know you got a raise with your promotion, but let me tell you something," he said. "Your hourly rate just went down."

Doug soon learned that his brother was right. Doug was a working manager, accountable for his primary position as a corporate trainer. And he was responsible for the four employees who now reported to him, watching over their work and providing the guidance they needed. Sometimes Doug's day-to-day responsibilities were so demanding that he couldn't break away from them, so he worked late, and even on weekends, reviewing the work of his subordinates. He felt like he had ended up with two jobs—and no appreciation.

Even before Doug received his first paycheck as a manager, reality shattered his expectation that he would cheerfully delegate work to a staff happy to take on new responsibilities, grateful to Doug for making such a positive difference in their lives. Instead, Doug found himself mediating often-petty disputes and telling people what to do. The people who had last month been his peers and who had joined with him to discuss solutions for work group problems now expected him to have all the answers.

Sometimes being in the middle leaves you feeling left out. The demands managers face today can be overwhelming, causing you to wonder if accepting this promotion or position was such a good idea after all. For some people, the answer will be no, it wasn't such a good idea. On the other hand, many people do enjoy or even thrive on the challenges that come with being a manager.

ALERT

Not everyone is cut out to be a manager. Many people who are among the best in their professions are among the worst when it comes to managing other people, because that's not where their strengths lie. Only by being truthful with yourself can you know if you are one of these people.

What Managers Expect from Their Jobs

Management is often a thankless job, which catches both new and experienced managers by surprise. It's human nature to expect others to appreciate your efforts on their behalf, but somehow in today's corporate culture it has become the norm to view what a manager does on behalf of his or her employees as just part of the job. So why, then, would anyone want to be a manager?

Because being a manager has its rewards, even if you have to dig a little deeper on some days to find them. There are the tangible, extrinsic rewards: higher salary, an office of your own (or at least a work area with a wider frame of space separating it from everyone else's space), and perhaps other perks such as stock options or parking privileges. For many managers, however, the rewards that matter are intangible and intrinsic. Being a manager is an opportunity for you to take your knowledge and the skills you have learned, and leverage them out over a group of people to achieve collective results that transcend the capabilities of each individual. The sense of accomplishment can be a real rush, as can the recognition that follows. And before you turn up your nose at the thought that you might actually enjoy such ego gratification, take a moment to relive your greatest achievement as a manager. Weren't you pleased (even thrilled) that others noticed? The ego is more willing to put up with wear, tear, and abuse when it knows that lurking somewhere in the shadows of the future is some serious stroking.

These are personal rewards, and without them your job would soon become drudgery. Perhaps you had already reached that point before your promotion, feeling that you knew pretty much all there was to know about your job. Becoming a manager gives you the opportunity to test your knowledge by putting it to work at a different level, where the higher stakes make the challenge more exciting. For most managers, the thrill exceeds personal gratification; there is also the satisfaction of taking your employees, your department, or even your company to the next level.

If you're thinking that this isn't the case for every manager, you're absolutely right. There are all too many people promoted to management positions because they excel in their jobs. In many industries, collective wisdom dictates that employees who are at the top of the skill or knowledge ladder in their fields must leap to the management ladder to have a continuing relationship with the best. Take the cream of the crop and put them in charge, this wisdom holds, and they will make everyone better. It would be great if this were true, but unfortunately it's usually not. It's also unfortunate that the American system has few ways other than promotion to reward people for work well done.

Being the best at what you do doesn't necessarily qualify you to manage. It takes a very narrow, intense focus to excel as an employee—a dedicated, almost single-minded concentration on the tasks at hand. It takes a much broader, though equally intense, focus to excel as a manager. As a manager, you must manage a process, not a product. It's no longer your job to write computer programs or assemble components. It's now your job to manage the people who perform these tasks. You can't step in to rescue them when they become overwhelmed; instead, it's your job to find ways to help people help themselves. In fact, a manager's rescue efforts are likely to alienate employees, who often interpret them as not-so-subtle suggestions that they can't do the work themselves.

Managers don't instinctively know what to do to manage. You probably went to school or studied in an apprenticeship program to learn what you know about your job. You relied on the expertise and knowledge of others to show you the way to proficiency. Managers, too, need training. In some respects, however, the situation is similar to the familiar lament about parenting—it's one of life's most vital responsibilities, yet there is no training program to teach new parents how to shape and nurture the young lives that are now their responsibility. Most people learn about parenting from their parents and grandparents, and from friends who became parents before them. They might learn methods that are ineffective, yet lack the framework to identify them as such. Similarly, most managers learn about managing from the managers they've had through their careers. They absorb the good, the bad, and the ugly. Without a framework for understanding the intricacies of human relationships, they might perpetuate methods that are ineffective or even damaging.

You, of course, could be among the fortunate ones who have had positive role models to guide your development as a manager. Or your company might have a training program for new managers. If neither of these is true for you (or even if they are), there are other ways for you to learn how to be a manager. You could:

- Enroll in continuing education courses. Many universities and community colleges offer noncredit programs that cover a wide range of management topics, from legal issues to communication techniques. (Your company might pay, or reimburse you, for this.)
- Ask a manager you respect and would like to emulate for suggestions and advice. You might be able to "shadow" this person for a day or so, to see him or her in action.
- Ask your company to pay for you to attend management workshops, or at least allow you the time off from work to go.
- Find out what professional magazines your company's executives and human resources staff subscribe to, and borrow them. This will expose you to the many dimensions of management from varying perspectives.
- If there are management certifications available in your industry or profession, find out what it takes to meet the requirements. Ask your company to sponsor, in full or in part, your certification efforts.
- Read books, like this one as well as those that present specific management methods or issues. Read about your industry or profession as well as beyond it.

You can't learn too much about management, about people, and about communication. The broader your base of understanding, the better equipped you are to handle the unexpected. As an employee, your outstanding job performance convinced your superiors that you were worthy of promotion. As a manager, you must demonstrate your ability to transcend daily details and visualize the bigger picture.

What Managers Expect from Employees

How would you describe the ideal employee? Go ahead . . . take a few minutes to think about this, and jot down some of your thoughts if you like. Most managers seldom have the liberty of considering what kinds of employees they'd like to manage. Instead, as a manager you typically inherit a work group whose members span the "why is this person still working here?" continuum. Some employees barely do enough to count as contributors, working as though they're using teaspoons to dig their way through mounds of work. Others bulldoze right through, clearing multiple projects with apparent ease and even taking on the responsibilities of other employees in the process.

Most managers would be satisfied to manage a work group in which each employee completed his or her assigned tasks correctly and on time. This would allow them to be what they are—managers—instead of what circumstances often force them into—hall monitors, babysitters, scoop patrol. "If only these people would act like the adults they should be!" is a common manager's lament. Are your expectations simply too high? No. In fact, they might not be high enough. As a manager, you have the ability to shape the attitudes and behaviors of the people you manage. Don't misunderstand—you can't change them. True change comes from within. But you can set and model the standards of acceptability. (Are you reaching for your parent hat? Good!)

FACTS

The tendency to use promotions as rewards has given rise to the "Peter Principle." This concept, put forth in the book of the same title by Laurence J. Peter (first published in 1969), asserts that people rise through organizations to the highest level of their competencies. The final promotion a person receives is to a level beyond his or her competency, and it is at this level that the person remains. Though Peter's observation of this phenomenon was somewhat tongue-in-cheek, the Peter Principle has become part of the modern business vocabulary.

People establish patterns of behavior based on conformity. No one likes to be the odd one out. The department with one truly bad apple (or one outstanding performer) is rare; far more common is the work group bound together by mediocrity. The peer pressure that was so molding in high school simply metamorphoses into new forms in adulthood. If there are no incentives to complete work on time and correctly, nor any consequences for failing to do so, why bother? People need reinforcement to do the right things. Your job as a manager is to provide that reinforcement.

Articulate your expectations to your work group as a whole, and to new employees who join it. Be specific but not restrictive:

- "I expect you to be at your work station and ready to work when your shift starts." (Not: "Everybody is to be sitting at their desks, pencils in hand, when the clock strikes eight.")
- "I expect you to complete projects by their deadlines. If this is not going to happen, I expect you to tell me about it as soon as it becomes clear to you." (Not: "For your monthly report, do an outline, then your research, then your draft, then your final.")

If you want people to act responsibly, you have to give them responsibility—and hold them accountable for meeting it. Most people work best when they understand what you expect from them and when you expect it, as long as they have the necessary knowledge, tools, and resources to complete their assignments. If they don't, then the issue is not one of personal but rather organizational responsibility.

ESSENTIALS

If there is a problem or things have gone badly, discuss the situation with employees without pointing fingers or placing blame. Focus on processes, not people. You can accept accountability without taking the fall; seeing you do this helps your employees see that they can do so as well.

Be generous and consistent with feedback and recognition. Some managers hold meetings at the end of the week to recognize completed work and discuss problems and challenges. This method holds employees accountable before their peers as well as before you, and also gives them the opportunity to shine in front of their coworkers. Give credit to everyone who participates in bringing a project to completion, and compliment teamwork.

What if your employees consistently fail to meet your expectations? Ask another manager whom you trust to casually observe your work group and your interactions with employees at different times over a week or so, then give you feedback. Objective observation can reveal attitudes and behaviors that give messages counter to the ones you articulate. This is somewhat like watching yourself in the mirror or having someone play audience as you practice a presentation or speech. It's a method performers, athletes, and others who are in the public eye use as one of the many tools to help them improve their abilities. Once you can see yourself as others see you, you can shape your behaviors to reflect the attitudes you want to convey.

Money Matters

It used to be that there was a set salary range for a position, and it established the boundaries for negotiation. It was a range that didn't vary much from company to company. Most people started at the lower end of the scale, ostensibly so there would be incentive for them to improve (which really meant there would be money to give them raises for staying in the job). Those with exceptional abilities or unique skills might start at the middle of the range. Few started at the top; those who had the qualifications to do so were probably overqualified for the job in the first place, so the reasoning was, and would soon move on when it became clear that there was no room for advancement within the position. Money and ability were like twins, seldom separated. Like bell-bottoms and tie-dye shirts, this is a vestige of a bygone era.

Salaries today are often open territory. To a great extent, this reflects the influence of the dot-com explosion of the 1990s, which blew salary conventions into oblivion. With skills that were in high demand, the sky was literally the limit. People moved from mundane salaries to five-, six-, and even seven-digit paychecks. As enticing as all this sounds, however, money is not very high on the list of reasons people take and stay in jobs. People expect to receive reasonable salaries for their work, of course, but numerous surveys reveal that other factors are more important. Key among them are:

- Interesting job tasks and responsibilities
- The tools and support necessary to do good work
- Recognition and appreciation for work well done
- Opportunities to improve and advance

Yes, employees expect to be well compensated. Sometimes money talks and employees walk—to competitors who offer deals too good to refuse. But for the most part, money moves up and down on an employee's list of dissatisfiers (things he or she does not like about the job) rather than on the list of satisfiers (things he or she likes about the job). People who leave one job for another solely for money are either woefully underpaid in the jobs they leave (which really is an issue bigger than the size of the paycheck) or they aren't going to find the satisfaction they seek in the new job, either.

Of course you care about your salary. To a degree, salary is the universal language that identifies how much a company values your abilities and contributions. If you earn significantly less than other managers in your company, all other factors being equal, read the writing on the paycheck. It should be telling you, "You're not meeting our expectations." If you are this manager, it's time to meet with your superiors, with an open mind and nonconfrontational approach, to find out where they feel you're coming up short. And there are situations in which companies use salary to drive someone out of the organization, or take advantage of a manager who won't challenge salary decisions. For the most part, however, the current competitive job market forces companies to pay competitive wages. Doing so is just good business.

Recognition and Reward

Who's not familiar with the carrot-on-a-stick image of fable fame? There's the hapless donkey, trudging around and around to grind grain on a millstone or pull water from a well. A stick fastened to his harness hangs over his head, a carrot dangling from it. He's worn a deep tread into his circular path as he plods on, eternally chasing the carrot just out of reach. He never gets it, but he sure keeps trying. Why? Because every night when he's put to pasture, his owner pats him on the back and tells him what a good job he's done. Of course, people are not donkeys (most of them, anyway). But in many respects they come to work each day to do the work that grinds your company's grain, motivated by both tangible and intangible prospects.

ESSENTIALS   Recognition is important to everyone. In a 1999 Gallup poll, 62 percent of those who reported dissatisfaction with their jobs also said they felt that their managers failed to recognize and appreciate their efforts and accomplishments. The most effective managers have a word of praise for each employee, every day.

Loyalty and Job Security

There is a risk associated with being a manager that differs from the risk of taking a job as a nonmanager. If your management job doesn't work out, what do you do? You might be able to go back to your old job, and even be the high performer you were before that caught the attention of your superiors. But chances are, both you and the company would find this regression too embarrassing to be effective. Coworkers might resent you, if you had been in a position of authority over them for any length of time. And human nature being what it is, it would be hard for you to become a subordinate again. When you become a manager, the only place you can go is up. If you can't meet your goals and responsibilities as a manager, your opportunities are seriously limited. It's fair to say that managers have less job security than their employees do.

Lee started working for the Great Gizmo Company as a customer service representative. A few months after he was hired, there was a major reorganization in his department and Lee was promoted to manager. Over the next six months Lee seized on a few well-timed political opportunities and became the department's vice president.

He angered a lot of people during his rapid climb to the top, and once he got there it quickly became apparent that he was in over his head. By now the company had invested a lot of time and money in Lee, and it didn't want to just let him go. So Lee was offered a job as a sales representative, where he at least had the opportunity to make good money. But he failed at that, too, and a few months later he was out the door.

Most companies are loyal to employees and managers, but that loyalty has limits. Once you stop being productive and are no longer contributing to the organization's goals, that loyalty ends. Yet, ironically, managers are expected to demonstrate extraordinary loyalty to the company. It is up to managers to promote loyalty among their employees, even when they don't feel the company is being loyal to them. Though it seems they have it made, managers are on the line more than anyone else.

Work Should Be Fun!

Each day is an adventure for Carolyn. When she steps through the doors of the software game company where she works as a team manager in the fantasy game division, she never knows what she will encounter. Employees often dress up as the characters they are creating. There are toys everywhere, from collectible movie figures to toy swords and lasers. Sometimes all the light bulbs are red or green or yellow; sometimes blacklights give off an eerie glow. It isn't unusual for Carolyn to walk into the middle of a "battle" or other scene enactment. Often, a hail of soft foam arrows greets her arrival, flying at her from behind doors and under desks. Boisterous laughter follows.

This work group has fun. So much fun, in fact, that some employees work around the clock when creativity is hot. And their fun pays off. The computer and video games they develop rank at the top of the market. Of course, this environment is a bit extreme for other kinds of work groups. But it supports the needs of its members, and that's what matters most.

Enjoying what they do at work ranks near the top of the list of job satisfiers for most people. Employees should want to come to work each day. Many companies have implemented casual dress policies (such as "casual Fridays") and minimized formality, especially if there is no direct interaction with customers. Numerous studies conclude that employees who are relaxed and comfortable are better able to concentrate on job tasks.

People spend more of their waking hours at work than anywhere else. If you aren't having any fun when you're at work, those are long hours indeed. As a manager, it's your responsibility to cultivate a work environment that employees find supportive and pleasant.

It's important to find out what your employees define as a comfortable workplace. Not everyone wants to—or should—spend the day shooting foam arrows and staging battles. The work environment needs to support the work being done within it. Do employees spend a lot of time on the telephone, or need quiet to help them concentrate? Then they might need office space with walls that go to the ceiling and doors that close. Do projects require employees to discuss possibilities and brainstorm ideas? Then a more open floor plan is probably better. Of course, these elements are not always within your ability to control. But if you do reshape what you can control to meet employee needs and requests, we're willing to bet that your work group's productivity and efficiency will improve.

Helping Employees Build Their Careers

Once (perhaps when you first entered the workforce), it was enough to land a job. People were happy to have paychecks, and employers were glad to have productive employees. Then it becomes apparent that there's a difference between a job and a career. People no longer stay in the same job or work for the same company for all of their working lives. On average, people have three to five different careers and work for a dozen or more companies from the time they enter the workforce until the time they leave it. More of either is not uncommon.

As a manager, it is one of your roles to help your employees develop their careers. Sometimes you want to help do this because they are good people who have really worked hard and you want to see them grow. They might quit if you don't. Sometimes you need them to grow so that they can take on more responsibilities—and free you up for the same reason. If employees don't feel like they are growing, they generally become stagnant. And over time, the department will grow stagnant and so will the organization. It often doesn't require that much for you to provide the opportunities your employees want and need. You might:

- Create a departmental training committee so employees can assess training needs and present ideas for meeting them
- Ask employees with particular proficiency in certain areas to conduct short workshops for other employees
- Sponsor brown bag lunch training sessions in which experts from other parts of the company or outside sources conduct short presentations during lunch breaks
- Establish a mentoring program in which employees pair up to learn from each other

When people are growing, their loyalty—to their managers and to the company—also increases. They perform better. And you have more time to focus on strategic issues, including your own career objectives. In a sense, it's an upward domino effect.

The Influence of Technology

New technology helps people work faster and more efficiently. This can be motivating because employees feel like they are both current and even in the fast lane. Technology can also be scary. If people work faster and more efficiently, then they can do more work. It doesn't take a rocket scientist to figure out that this means fewer jobs. But like it or not, technology has forever altered the business landscape. Nearly everyone is connected—we use online calendars to schedule meetings and appointments, Web-based purchasing to manage inventory, and handheld organizers to keep in touch with the office anywhere in the world.

As a manager, you need to actively embrace technology. It is not just the future, but also the present. But you must also carefully and effectively communicate the role of technology, so employees understand how technology benefits them. Make sure your employees receive the training they need, and have the resources available to use technology for the greatest effectiveness. If company resources are so tight that training budgets are nonexistent, ask employees with expertise in key areas to conduct informal training sessions for their coworkers.

And get involved yourself! Don't just have your administrative assistant search the Web for the research you need for the report you're working on; do it yourself. The benefits far outweigh the time it will take you. You will become proficient at navigating the Web, understand firsthand how frustrating it can be to locate information, and model technology's benefits for your employees. (Believe us, they're watching.)

New Skills to Stay Ahead of the Curve

The demand for skilled workers outweighs their availability in a number of fields, leading to discussions about labor shortages and an "employee's market." To some extent, this imbalance is a normal and natural stage in the employment cycle that results whenever something new debuts. But it began to take wider swings in the later 1970s and early 1980s, when the auto industry couldn't find enough qualified workers to fill its factories and assembly plants.

Companies such as Honda established training programs that taught participants what they needed to know to work in certain areas of the industry and provided jobs in those areas once training was completed. Wages were high and employees enjoyed being wanted. Then the economic winds shifted in the 1980s, and suddenly there were too many cars on the market. Plants slowed production, and companies consolidated operations. People lost their jobs and their skills lost value. Because those skills were so narrowly focused, there was no way to apply them in different settings. Many autoworkers had no other skills, and found themselves on the outside looking in.

Other industries experienced similar difficulties during the tumultuous 1980s, when technology swept across the corporate landscape. Computers became a part of nearly every industry and most jobs. People without computer skills soon found themselves without work. This all gave rise to a new industry: retraining. Many large companies hired consultants to work with employees who were being laid off, to assess their potential abilities and guide them into programs to build skills in those areas. Some companies even paid for the retraining and helped displaced workers find new jobs.

Though these pivotal points seem to arrive without warning, the writing is on the wall, for those who will read it, long before the moment of crisis. The auto industry knew dealer inventory levels were growing—witness the many buyer incentive programs that sprang up. And the personal computer that has so transformed the business world didn't just drop on the scene one day. Its infiltration was slow and steady, starting a good ten years before it became a "revolution." Companies on the cutting edge could see how this new technology might make processes more efficient, and began providing training for employees. These companies and their employees were ready when the technology curve began to break.

FACTS

When personal computers (PCs) first entered the office environment in the 1980s, managers greeted them with skepticism. In those early days, a computer was viewed as an investment that would amortize over five to seven years. No one had ever seen the exponential growth the technology industry was about to exhibit. The ten-megabyte hardcard guaranteed to last "forever" became obsolete within a year. Technology quickly became the largest portion of business expense, after employees, for most companies.

For five or six years, other companies scrambled to find people with the skills to function in this new technoworld. Those that could afford it sent existing employees to training classes and workshops, or hired consultants to provide on-site, customized training. At the same time, they began recruiting employees who had these new skills. It wasn't long before computer proficiency was a requirement for most jobs. People new to the job market had the advantage of seeing a bigger picture than their already employed counterparts. Managers were in the particularly challenging situation of getting their employees up to speed while also trying to learn new skills themselves. Their own needs took a back seat to the needs of employees, and some managers found themselves pushed out of their jobs by ambitious underlings who suddenly spoke the language and understood the potential of the new environment.

Most companies support skill improvement efforts for employees because if they don't, they face the frighteningly real probability of going under. Unless the people who do the work have the proper abilities, they can't do the work properly. Some companies extend this attitude to managers, as they should; others don't, failing to see the value in it or perhaps fearing that they're only giving their managers a better foundation to find work elsewhere. (Yes, this is incredibly shortsighted, but unfortunately all too common.)

As a manager, it is vitally important for you to stay abreast of new developments on two fronts: your foundation skill set and management methods. Some industries require continuing education or recertification to remain qualified; in these, educational opportunities abound because the demand for them is constant and high. Employers in these industries typically support ongoing education in various ways, ranging from tuition reimbursement to paid time off for attending workshops and seminars. Other industries don't have such requirements, so you're more on your own. But don't take this to mean you're automatically left behind. There are many ways you can keep yourself ahead of the curve.

- Read publications for your profession. Sometimes you can get your company to fund subscriptions for magazines and journals delivered to the company. Public libraries carry larger or more general professional publications; college or technical school libraries often subscribe to specialty journals in fields for which they have educational programs.
- Read one book a quarter (or a month, if you have the time) that is related to your career field or interests. Books cover subjects that have at least enough staying power to outlive the typical one to two years it takes to move them from concept to publication.

THE EVERYTHING MANAGING PEOPLE BOOK

- Take one class a year in a subject that relates to your current job or your future goals. Many adult continuing education programs taught through local colleges and vocational schools offer evening and weekend classes or compressed schedules to accommodate people who work.

- Hold debriefing meetings with your work group or department after any of your employees have been to training. Ask employees to share what they felt was useful and what they felt was a waste about the training. Not only will you learn more about what your employees are learning, but you'll also find out what training is worthwhile.

- Ask to sit in on training and informational programs other departments in your company present for their employees, especially human resources. It usually doesn't cost extra to add one more person to the group, and you get to know more people throughout your organization. Also, the group might benefit from your perspective, if it invites you to share it (you might have to agree to be a silent auditor).

What Works for Them Works for You

If it feels altruistically generous of you to work so hard to support training and skills improvement activities for your employees, go ahead and take a minute or so to enjoy the feeling. Then take a few steps back and look at the bigger picture. When the people who report to you improve their skills and expand their knowledge, it's almost impossible for yours to remain stagnant. While it's probably not necessary for your skills to match the skills of your employees as far as work tasks go (unless you're a working manager who has job responsibilities similar to those of the employees you manage), you do need to know enough to know whether your employees need additional training and if so, in what. When your employees grow, you grow.

Today, fortunately, companies place more value on individual work styles and approaches. Managers attempt to understand what employees want, and try to structure the work environment to meet the needs of employees as well as the company. Employees speak out when they're dissatisfied, and find different jobs when that fails to resolve the situation. These were not options for workers in the generations before ours. Today's workplace, however, is all about options, as we'll see in this chapter.

CHAPTER 4

This Is Not Your Daddy's Workplace

W hen most of us were growing up, bosses said what they felt like saying, no matter how unmotivating or hurtful it might be. If they asked you to work late, you did. Plans for the weekend? Too bad. If you didn't like it you knew where the door was. Most people just waited out the tough conditions. Soon enough there would be a changing of the guard and a different boss.

Casual, Flexible, Friendly: The New Workplace

People begin to think about what they want to do and be as adults in high school or even earlier. While once sons followed fathers into their work worlds, now sons and fathers often inhabit very different environments. Fathers might well follow sons—or daughters—into business. For the first time in America's history, there are more women than men in the workforce. Some work because they have no other options; long gone are the days when it was a young woman's role to marry a man who could take care of her while she raised his children. Both stay-at-home dads and career moms are redefining today's workplace.

FACTS

The U.S. Bureau of Labor Statistics reports that 27.6 percent of Americans—25 million—worked flexible hours or shift schedules in 1997, compared to just 15 percent in 1991. Of these, just about the same percentage have children (28.9 percent) as don't (26.8 percent). About 42 percent of managers work flexible hours compared with less than 25 percent of administrative and support workers.

Also redefining today's workplace is its more casual environment. When our middle management fathers left each morning for work, they wore polished shoes, slacks, collared shirts, ties, and sports jackets. A meeting with upper management often required a suit. Women wore dresses and high heels. Even working on Saturdays mandated a tie, although the jacket might come off if no subordinates or superiors were in the office. It wasn't that the workplace was making a fashion statement; it was just the way things were. Dress was a sign of respect, an indicator that what went on in the office was serious work. What you wore to work also signaled your station in the work world. Ties and jackets were the uniform of middle management. Work was hierarchical; it was important for everyone to know who had what status.

FACTS

The move toward casual attire in the workplace gained momentum in the late 1980s when companies began implementing "casual dress Fridays" to build employee morale and reward hard work. The idea was to create a not-quite-a-day-off atmosphere. As it became clear that employees worked no less productively on casual dress days (and in fact, often more productively), casual dress became the standard any day of the week. Some companies now invite employees to participate in "formal Mondays."

Look around your office right now. Do you even see a tie? How about a pair of high-heeled shoes? While some companies maintain formal dress in executive offices, most have gone casual. This reflects the recognition that people who are comfortable are also more productive. It also demonstrates a much-diminished emphasis on status and its inherently divisive qualities, and a redirection to focus on collaboration and teamwork. Many middle managers today are working managers—not only do they manage a work group or department, but they also share in the team's workload. The manager of a training department often designs and delivers training programs as well as provides guidance and support for employees doing the same kind of work. Clothes still symbolize status, of course; that will never change. But the symbolism is far more subtle and less directly related to job or occupation. The man or woman striding down the corridor in jeans and day hikers could be the mail clerk or the vice president.

While some people feel casualness has gone too far, many employees enjoy the freedom and comfort it offers. For managers, the casual office can raise some issues. While some companies have explicit policies that define the workplace environment, many do not. This leaves department and work group managers responsible for setting and upholding standards. How do you determine what attire and behavior are appropriate? Here are some questions to consider:

- *Does the work environment have special safety concerns?* Loose clothing, long hair, jewelry, and even long fingernails can present hazards in work areas where there is moving machinery.
- *Do employees have direct contact with customers or clients?* If so, the rule of thumb is to dress as they dress, within reason.
- *Are employees dressing in ways that are distracting, inappropriate or suggestive, or that interfere with their ability to perform the tasks of their jobs?* Older customers (internal or external) might not consider a young person wearing jeans to be competent or to have the appropriate authority, for example.
- *How do employees want to dress?* A standard that your work group mutually agrees upon is much easier to monitor and enforce than one that "management" imposes.
- *What about personal space?* Many employees like to decorate their offices, workspaces, or desks with family pictures and small personal items. Most companies find that this is not a problem as long as the decor doesn't interfere with job tasks and doesn't offend other employees or customers.
- *Is music appropriate in the workplace?* Many businesses allow employees to play music or have music playing over a loudspeaker system, though some employees find this distracting. Different kinds of music can influence the moods and behaviors of employees as well as customers. Again, consensus is often the deciding factor. Generally people who work in enclosed areas or individual offices have greater freedom to listen to music while they work.
- *Can employees have food and beverages at their desks or work areas?* Decisions on whether to allow eating and drinking depend on what kind of work employees are doing. Sipping coffee or munching a snack is less likely to interfere with job tasks for employees who work at desks and are in contact with clients by phone or electronically than for those who deal with customers in person.

FACTS

Marketers have used music to influence customer behaviors for decades. Music with a hard, driving beat makes people feel excited and impulsive. Such effects influence people to make spontaneous purchases and leave rather than linger—ideal behavior for fast food restaurants. Soft, soothing music makes people feel relaxed and thoughtful. This helps improve mental focus and muscle coordination, and also makes people feel that they want to stay and be comfortable (desired behavior in luxury restaurants, bookstores, and expensive boutiques).

There are some behaviors that are inappropriate in just about any workplace. These include:

- **Profanity.** Swearing is everywhere today, so much a part of common conversation that many people scarcely notice it. But profanity is offensive to quite a number of people, and its frequent presence implies discourtesy and lack of professionalism.
- **Smoking.** Many cities and states have laws restricting indoor smoking to reduce the risk of exposure to secondhand smoke. Some companies have smoke break rooms that are separately ventilated, while others ban smoking on the property entirely.
- **Wearing clothing that is tattered, torn, dirty, sexually suggestive, or derogatory.** T-shirts with slogans often fall into the latter categories. However casual, the workplace is still the workplace. Managers sometimes must explicitly describe what is and isn't appropriate attire.

What employees wear to work and how they conduct themselves can be concerns for managers even when there are detailed policies in place. It's human nature to push the curve of individuality. As much as possible, it's usually more productive to support that curve. Do your employees wear uniforms? If so, why? Some companies like their employees to present a homogeneous image. This makes it clear, to employees and customers alike, that each employee represents the company at all times when wearing the uniform. In such situations, individuality is not as important (for the corporate good) as consistency. Compliance is fairly easy to monitor and enforce. Other organizations such as medical facilities require uniforms because clothing can become contaminated or damaged. In such situations, there is often greater latitude in accommodating individuality—some people might prefer plain colors, others like bright patterns and designs, yet all can be in compliance. And in some work environments, regulations and rules (federal, state, and industrial) dictate attire.

Job Sharing

Job sharing is when two employees share the responsibilities and salary of a single position. This creative approach to flexibility has grown in popularity particularly among new moms (and sometimes dads) who want to work fewer hours but still stay on track with their careers. Job sharing differs from part-time or temporary work in several ways.

The majority of part-time positions fill short-term or narrowly defined needs for a company. Managers tend to view employees who work part time as interested in work as a source of income rather than as a stage in a career path (as might the employees themselves). Benefits for part-time positions in many companies don't become available until the position is at least a .75 FTE (full-time equivalent), which is generally thirty-two hours a week or 75 percent of a full-time position. This saves money for companies, but also reinforces the "not really a career" image of part-time work.

QUESTIONS?

What is job sharing?
Job sharing is when two people share a single position, including its tasks and responsibilities, salary, workspace, and other elements. Usually the division is equal, though sometimes one person might have a larger share than the other.

Temporary positions, also known as contingent jobs, fill (you guessed it) temporary needs. These positions usually last nine months or less. Perhaps an employee is on maternity leave, or customer orders become particularly heavy in response to new products or particular circumstances that create higher-than-usual demands for services. A company will hire employees to work through those specific periods, and then the job ends. There are no benefits beyond wages, and "temps" often feel that they are outsiders in the companies for which they work. Temporary work can be a good way for a person to gain experience or to fill a short-term need, but typically it does not lead to permanent work.

In most companies, the important or career-oriented jobs are full-time positions. It's just too much for companies to invest in training lots of people to do pieces of jobs that are critical to the company's success. But these jobs are also demanding. It might be necessary to meet with clients outside regular work hours, or to travel. These demands are difficult for people who also want to spend time with their families or doing other things.

Job sharing is really about sharing time. In exchange for less time spent at work, job-sharing partners gain more time to be with their families, go to school, or enjoy personal interests such as artistic or athletic pursuits. Job sharing can permit employees to care for children or aging parents, return to college or graduate school, take up watercolor, study piano, train for marathons—whatever is important to them.

While job sharing primarily benefits the employees who participate, it offers advantages for companies as well. Job sharing can help companies:

* Retain qualified and experienced employees who would otherwise quit or move into part-time jobs
* Improve employee job satisfaction and morale
* Maintain, and in some situations improve, productivity and efficiency
* In some situations, save on benefit expenses

Job-Share Arrangements for Employees

Generally, an employee who wants to job-share will approach you with a partner in mind. If your company already uses job sharing, there are probably procedures already in place. If job sharing is new to your company, there are numerous books and Web resources on this topic (Appendix B, "Resources," lists some to get you started). Following are some key points to address when considering a job-share request:

- **Job tasks.** Can the job's tasks and functions be reasonably divided? Will dividing the job create any overlaps or duplication that would not exist if one person did the job? Who responds if there is a problem— the partner "on duty" when the problem arises, or the partner who did the work?
- **Communication.** How will the job-sharing employees communicate with each other? How will they stay in touch with other work group members, if this is important? Is one of the partners the primary contact, or must each person receive memos, e-mails, telephone calls, and other communication?
- **Flexibility and availability.** Can the job-sharing partners trade off if they choose? How will this affect their working relationships with you, with other coworkers, and with clients or customers? Will one partner cover if the other is sick or on vacation? Are both partners willing to attend meetings if other team members or customers want them to be there?
- **Compatibility.** How well do the prospective partners get along with each other? Are their work styles similar? If each does half of a project, will the pieces join seamlessly or will someone else (you!) have to put them together?
- **Pay and benefits.** How will the job share partners share the job's salary and benefits package? (If your company provides benefits for half-time employees, this might not be an issue.)
- **Work space.** Will the partners share space in the workplace? Usually this is the case, since they are two people sharing one job and presumably its accoutrements as well as its responsibilities. Each is then responsible for leaving the workspace and its equipment ready for the other to use. Occasionally a manager has the resources to give each job-share partner a separate desk in the same office or even separate computers, but this is often not the case.

• **Performance evaluations.** How will you evaluate productivity and performance? Are the job-share partners willing to be evaluated on the basis of their work as a team rather than as individuals? Do your company's human resources policies support this?

Ask prospective job-share partners to discuss these and any specific issues relevant to the job they want to share or to your company, first between each other and then with you. Once everyone agrees to the details, put those details in writing and have each employee, and you as their manager, sign the agreement. If you are unsure whether the arrangement will meet your work group's or your company's needs, establish a test period of three to six months (less than this probably won't be enough time to work out any wrinkles so you can get a fair assessment). Include in the agreement the steps you and the employees will follow to measure the arrangement's success.

Job-Sharing Pitfalls and Risks

Job-share arrangements that fall apart usually do so because the division of responsibilities between partners was not clear or because the partners fail to get along. Some people have trouble giving up decision-making authority, for example. If one job-share partner continually reaffirms the other's decisions and actions, other employees will become confused about which one of them to talk to. People who have worked in the same work group for a year or two before entering into a job-sharing partnership are more likely to be successful, although some challenges are difficult to see until they hit you in the face. One partner might be fastidious to a fault, while the other is comfortable with a fair amount of disorganization.

 Sometimes circumstances beyond the partnership cause it to fail. A job-sharing partnership is a lot like a marriage. Sometimes two people who seem to be compatible and get along discover that they have vastly different perspectives when it comes to how things get done.

Can Managers Job Share?

Job sharing can work at nearly any level within an organization. Whether it will or not depends. It's essential for any job-sharing partners to be compatible. When these partners share a management position, that compatibility must extend both downward (to employees) and upward (to upper management). Employees tend to be leery of situations that make them accountable to two different managers. So a key element of structuring a job-sharing arrangement for a management position is to emphasize the position, not just the people who share it. Some managers find that job sharing works best if they divide the work group into members for which each has responsibility. This way, the work group functions as two teams, each with its own leader. Employees know the nuances of the manager to whom they report, and worry less about reporting to someone who doesn't know theirs. The drawback to this arrangement is that neither manager is in the office full time, so one must "cover" the team of the other.

Everything that applies to employees who want to job share also applies to managers who want to job share. Because you are accountable both to the employees who report to you as well as to your superiors, it's critical that you work out every detail of the arrangement before putting it into practice. As a manager, you aren't likely to have the luxury of letting some details work themselves out. It's important that your actions support consistency and cohesiveness within the work group, not jeopardize stability.

Telework

Technology has opened many doors in the work world over the past few years, and one that is gaining in significance is the option to not leave home at all to go to work. This is telework, or telecommuting, which we first mentioned in Chapter 1, "Ideals and Realities." The U.S. Department of Labor estimated that 10 percent of the employees in the private sector, or between 13 and 19 million people, participated in telework arrangements in 2000. The agency projects the number of teleworkers will grow as technology continues to improve. The employee works at a location other than the company's site, usually at home, and is connected to the workplace via electronics—computer, telephone, e-mail, Web site, and even televideo conferencing. Telework is an ideal option for people who are strongly self-motivated and can work productively without continual supervision. Teleworking can improve productivity by removing common distractions such as office socializing. Some jobs don't require the employee to be in a particular location, or require the employee to be out of the office more than in it.

But out of sight can mean out of mind—and that's not a good thing, in love or at work. In the work world, it often means lack of communication, lack of control, and potential disaster. When communication lapses, the benefits of teleworking can become liabilities. Other employees begin to wonder what the teleworker is really doing. They might complain that the work-from-home employee isn't pulling a fair load or has special privileges by not being subject to office policies and standards. Absence allows people—coworkers and managers alike—to create their own scenarios. They begin to envision the teleworker lounging around in pajamas and slippers, enjoying a walk in the sun, or running errands at the mall. It's not easy for employees who have never worked from home or a distant location to understand that teleworkers put in the same amount of hours (and usually more) as they would were they in the office.

ESSENTIALS
If your state has significant traffic problems in urban areas, state law may mandate employers over a certain size to participate in commuter reduction efforts. Look into alternative forms of transportation for your employees, such as carpooling or public transportation, or eliminate commuting altogether by supporting telework options.

Many of the issues relevant to job sharing also apply to teleworking. It's essential for others to know when the teleworker is available, and for the teleworker to be available when expected. Ways to keep teleworkers in the loop include:

- Regular in-person meetings if the teleworker is in the same city. In most situations, meeting once a week is enough to maintain connections and communication.
- Regular conference calls when the teleworker is working from a distance. This at least keeps the person's voice familiar.
- Occasional visits to the office if the teleworker is in another city or state. Even when there is regular voice contact, it helps to keep a face attached to the voice.
- Diligent communication about availability and variations from the schedule. Teleworkers should let their managers and coworkers know if their e-mail is down or they're going to be out for a doctor's appointment—just as they would if they worked in the same office. Likewise, managers need to keep teleworkers informed about schedule changes, shifts in priorities, employee vacations, office meetings, and other matters that teleworkers would know about if they were in the office.

Having employees who telework requires companies to stay current with technology. An employee who is working from a distance is most efficient when he or she has the equipment to support the job tasks. This might mean updating computers and modems, or even improving infrastructure elements such as installing digital phone lines. And of course, not all jobs will support telework. Telework is not a good option when the job requires close and constant integration with the tasks and projects of other employees.

Managers who want to keep productive, creative employees need to be open to finding solutions that balance individual and company needs. Our society is changing, and so is the business world. People have always had private lives, of course, but until the 1980s, companies had functioned as though they wore blinders that kept them from recognizing this. Now things are different. Personal needs are as important as career needs, and people will move around in jobs and among companies until they find what fits. The manager who can be flexible is the manager who will retain top talent . . . and earn the respect and loyalty of employees as well as superiors.

A Safe Workplace

Every employee is entitled to a safe place to work. There are innumerable laws and regulations that define what this means for specific industries and kinds of workplaces. Each manager is responsible for knowing these requirements and assuring that they are met. In general, managers need to be on guard for environmental hazards as well as aspects of the environment that interfere with productivity. This runs the gamut from tripping hazards (boxes, chairs out of place, wires) to lighting. Many companies have formal safety committees that regularly review safety issues and investigate workplace injuries to better understand how to prevent them.

People who feel that the company doesn't care about their safety and comfort are not likely to be productive. And companies that don't pay attention to minor concerns are likely to find themselves paying for major problems.

When employees complain about their work environments, check out the complaints. Improvements can be as simple as rearranging office furniture and equipment to reduce ergonomic stress or installing brighter light bulbs. Many changes employees want are inexpensive yet can result in vast improvements in productivity and efficiency. Involve employees in finding solutions for bigger concerns. Collaborative efforts often produce creative answers, especially when budget constraints or other factors might keep you from implementing the ideal solutions. This also helps all those involved to understand the problems, the possible options for resolving them, and the pros and cons of each. And people tend to be more accepting of remedies that they help to design and implement.

Laws, Regulations, and Rules

Depending on the state and the industry, as well as the level of employee, various laws, regulations, and rules govern the workplace environment. These regulations might be fairly general, or might be detailed enough to include when employees must take rest and meal breaks as well as when overtime can and cannot be required. While as a manager you like to feel that you have some flexibility in terms of how your work group functions, it's essential to remember that there are laws that could supersede your desires. You must stay abreast of these laws! Regulatory influences that affect your workplace might come from:

- U.S. Department of Labor, the federal agency (and its dozens of agencies and offices) responsible for administering and enforcing the nearly 200 federal laws that apply to employment and the workplace
- OSHA, the U.S. government's Occupational Safety and Health Administration, which regulates and enforces a broad spectrum of workplace well-being issues
- State labor agencies, responsible for administering and enforcing state labor and employment laws
- City and county agencies

Your own company likely has policies and procedures to safeguard employee safety and health, too. As a manager, you have some level of responsibility and accountability in assuring that employees as well as the workplace comply. Be sure you know what that level is.

Recognizing and Addressing the Warning Signs of Potential Violence

Workplace safety has been a matter of concern since the beginning of time. Well, maybe not quite, but close. Most safety concerns related to work hazards—falling objects, exposed blades, relentless gears, fires, fumes, toxins, and other dangers. These days there is yet another workplace risk: violence. Our times might have no more negative, angry, frustrated people than any other times in history, but they are more apt to take their feelings out on others. Everyone has bad days, of course. Maybe it's because the pace of our times is so hectic—even frantic—that we feel that we've lost control of our lives. Maybe it's because the line between work and the rest of life has become less defined. Maybe it's a consequence of global warming. Whatever the reasons, angry people are more likely to vent their ire at work . . . and at coworkers.

And whatever the reasons, only motor vehicle accidents claim more lives and cause more injuries than incidents of workplace violence. Sometimes the connection is personal, such as a spouse or significant other who also works at the same company. Sometimes the association is symbolic, such as when a boss behaves in the same way an abusive father used to—but an adult can, and sometimes does, lash back. Most often, there is no link at all: Two-thirds of all workplace violent deaths occur during robberies and other acts of apparently random violence at the hands of strangers. Surprised? Many people are. Many people are also surprised to learn that despite media reports that imply otherwise, workplace killings are down a third over the past four years.

FACTS

Of the 6,000 workplace fatalities that occurred in 1998, 709 (12 percent) were homicides. Of these, the Bureau of Labor Statistics reports:

- Four percent of the victims died at the hands of relatives, usually a spouse or former spouse
- Seven percent of the victims were other acquaintances of their killers, often a current or former boyfriend or girlfriend
- Fifteen percent were killed by coworkers or former coworkers
- The remaining victims died in the process of robberies and other random acts of violence committed by strangers

The potential for workplace violence is frightening for employees and managers alike. However rare actual events are, the National Institute for Occupational Safety and Health (NIOSH) estimates that a million people a year are victims of workplace violence—accounting for 15 percent of reported acts of violence nationwide. "Desk rage" is both a familiar term and a familiar experience to many employees. Experiences range from threatening language to acts of aggression. NIOSH recommends that all companies develop policies for identifying and addressing the signs of potentially violent behavior, as well as procedures for dealing with acts of violence if they occur. Unfortunately, this is not as easy as it sounds. Attitudes and behaviors are often subtle and difficult to discern as "across the line." Studies of recent workplace violence incidents have given psychologists new insights into early warning signs. Would you recognize these warnings in your workplace? Choose the situation you think poses the greater threat:

- The person who slams things around when he's angry or the one who believes federal agents read all of his e-mail messages?
- The person who brags about his bar fights or the one who continually complains about the idiots who make his life miserable?
- The person who has a restraining order against a spouse or the one whose spouse has a restraining order against him or her?

Though it's impossible to know with certainty which people are blowing off steam (a healthy response) and which people are about to blow (decidedly unhealthy for them and potentially for others), in each of these scenarios most experts would put their money on the second situation. Aggressive attitudes and behaviors are often subtle and easy to dismiss, at least in the beginning or at first glance, because they reflect attitudes and behaviors that we all engage in at some point. These become warning signs when they become a pattern that emerges over time. Psychologists say managers should be alert to employees who:

- Are chronically late or frequently miss work
- Speak with contempt of, and show contempt for, authority and people who have positions of authority
- Are paranoid or cynical (believe others are watching them or are out to get them, or that events such as economic downturns, lay-offs, or even computer problems happen because "they" planned them)
- Are hot-tempered, easily fly off the handle, argue when given directions to do something a specific way, or walk out on meetings when others disagree with them

- Talk about how nobody appreciates their abilities, dedication, knowledge, or power
- Delight in the misfortunes of others, laugh inappropriately, or fail to laugh at jokes and situations that others find humorous
- Are awkward in social situations to the extent that they make others uncomfortable or others make fun of them, or create environments of isolation for themselves

If your company has policies and procedures for dealing with potentially violent employees, know what they are and follow them. It's essential to document your observations, including comments and complaints that other employees bring to you. The earlier there is intervention, the better. Many companies have Employee Assistance Programs (EAPs) that can provide advice for managers as well as counseling for employees. Is the employee someone new to your department or company? If so, is the person still on probationary status? Or is this someone you inherited when you became the work group's manager? In either case you need to step in, but the circumstances could influence what you do and how you do it. Some states have laws that regulate how companies may approach, discipline, and fire employees based on how long they've been working in the job or for the company. Generally, you should:

- Research the laws, regulations, and company policies that might apply to the situation so you know what you can and cannot do. Talk with your HR department and your manager so they know what's going on and can support your choice of response.
- Meet privately with the employee to discuss your observations and your concerns. Do this in a calm and nonconfrontational manner. If you are concerned that the employee might become violent towards you, have this meeting where others can see you or have another person (such as an HR representative or your manager) present.
- Explain, explicitly and clearly, what behaviors are problems, why those behaviors are unacceptable, what it will take for the employee to rectify the situation, and what will happen if the problems continue.

- Ask the employee to present his or her perspective, and listen without interrupting or commenting.
- Offer the employee EAP (Employee Assistance Program) consultation or other forms of assistance.
- Notify the police if the employee makes to you, or has made to others, specific threats or threats that are particularly scary.

Rachel was the manager for a group of people who were doing telephone surveys, working on a temporary, hourly basis. Most of them were in between jobs or moonlighting for extra money. The newest hire, Martin, seemed a little scary to Rachel. He came in just as his shift started, kept to himself instead of joining the others at breaks, and rushed out as soon as his shift ended. After he continually rebuffed his coworkers' efforts to include him, the other employees left him alone. One afternoon when Martin had been on the job about three weeks, he and a delivery clerk collided in the corridor outside Martin's cubicle. Martin screamed and yelled at the clerk, calling him names and accusing him of intentionally causing the collision.

ESSENTIALS

The potential for workplace violence is a tricky issue for managers. It's hard to know when and how to take action. OSHA, NIOSH, and many EAPs offer advice, materials, and even workshops about recognizing and handling aggression in the workplace. Take advantage of these resources.

Rachel heard the commotion and stepped between Martin and the clerk. She told Martin to calm down, and he went back into his cubicle. When Rachel saw Martin later, she asked him what had happened—he acted like he had no idea what she was talking about. A few days later, Rachel overheard Martin speaking rudely to an older female employee from another department. When the woman told Martin she didn't appreciate his tone and snide comments, he called her a bitch. Rachel sent Martin home for the rest of the day, and went to the vice president, her direct superior, to suggest the company let Martin go before he caused more trouble. The vice president said he would look into it.

The following week, Martin made a racist comment to a coworker and threatened to hit him. Other employees witnessed the event, and someone called security. The vice president fired Martin on the spot, and had him escorted from the premises. Everyone in the department was pretty shaken up, however, and for weeks worried that Martin would come back to get them. Fortunately, he didn't. In retrospect, Rachel saw that she should have documented Martin's behavior from the first incident with the delivery clerk and established clear expectations for what was appropriate, and the vice president agreed he should have supported the manager's suggestion to let Martin go the week before.

Changing Gender Roles

Today's younger employees (under age forty) inhabit a work world very different from the one that existed when they were born, when men were bosses and women were secretaries. Younger women today have no trouble being leaders, and younger men seem to have no trouble recognizing and accepting women in leadership roles. People who entered or were already in the workforce twenty years ago aren't always comfortable with the equality of roles in today's business environment—men and women alike. Men in their forties and older (and some women as well) may be uncomfortable with women in management positions, either as their equals or their superiors. Younger women who are managers sometimes misinterpret this discomfort, or are unable to adapt their behaviors to help bridge the gap. They might feel older men are disrespectful of their authority and knowledge. (And sometimes these perceptions are accurate; equity in the workplace is still an ideal to pursue despite the advances of recent years.)

A 2000 Gallup poll reveals that while women have greatly extended their presence within the ranks of management, Americans still prefer male to female bosses. Of those polled, 48 percent said they prefer to report to a man, while 22 percent said they prefer to report to a woman and 28 percent said it didn't matter. Women are more likely than men to prefer a female boss (26 percent to 19 percent), but men are more likely to have no preference (35 percent of men, 23 percent of women). In 1975, 63 percent of Americans preferred their managers to be men compared to 7 percent who preferred women at the reins.

Managers, like employees, have biases. It's important to realize this, and to recognize yours—they aren't always what you expect. Arthur was unaware of his biases until angry employees pointed them out to him in a staff meeting. It turned out that Arthur had a clear pattern of promoting only women. The women he promoted deserved to be promoted; that wasn't the issue. What was the issue was that equally competent men didn't get the same opportunities for advancement because of Arthur's bias toward women. This resulted in resentment among the male employees and created considerable divisiveness within the work group. It was during a meeting to address the inability of the group to work as a team that the men's concerns arose. Once his employees confronted him with the evidence, Arthur saw the pattern as well. He realized that he was more comfortable with women, more trusting of women, and felt less threatened by women.

ALERT

There's nothing wrong with employees having a good time together, of course. But it is important to draw a clear line between recreation and work. Discuss business at meetings all can attend, not during activities that some cannot or chose not to attend.

An environment of openness is critical. A manager needs to do things that encourage teamwork and collaboration, and to identify roles and responsibilities to reduce the influence of biases in the group. Sometimes this forces people to work together even when they're not necessarily comfortable. But sometimes this is necessary so they learn to understand, and hopefully respect and appreciate, each other. An environment where ideas are encouraged and respected, even if not acted upon, helps to build a sense of equality.

If desire to foster equality in the workplace isn't enough to motivate some managers, a plethora of laws and regulations are at the ready to nudge them. Discrimination on the basis of gender (sex discrimination) is illegal. Arthur's pattern of behavior was in fact discriminatory, and could have resulted in legal action being brought against him and the company by the men who were denied promotion opportunities. Managers must understand what kinds of behaviors and promotional actions can be interpreted as biased, even when there is no intent to discriminate. Uninformed and insensitive behaviors can lead to serious legal and professional problems, as they nearly did for Lawrence.

A computer consultant, Lawrence had worked with a medium-sized company for several years. Once a quarter, he spent two days at the company's offices, conducting workshops and helping work groups use various computer programs for their projects and tasks. Between visits, a very large company purchased the medium-sized company and retained Lawrence's services. When Lawrence arrived for the next quarterly training sessions, he greeted a familiar employee by complimenting her on the dress she was wearing. She smiled and said, "I have to be honest with you. We have new rules here now. And if you were a coworker, your comments would be considered really inappropriate if not bordering on sexual harassment."

Lawrence was stunned. He hadn't intended to be inappropriate or offensive. "You've got to be kidding," he said.

"No, I'm not kidding," the employee replied. "We have a whole new set of rules here now, including how we can converse with each other socially."

Intentions, good or bad, aside, sexual harassment remains a significant issue in the workplace. One in six employees, the vast majority of whom are women, report that they experience sexual harassment in the workplace. Whether you believe incidents of harassment are real or perceived, it is your responsibility to make it clear that you take seriously workplace rules to prevent it. Male or female, comments made in jest can come back to haunt you. See Chapter 9, "Toeing the Line on Company Policies," and Chapter 10, "Socializing at Work," for more on discrimination and harassment.

Family Matters

There are still a lot of workaholics out there who take on whatever work they have to do and more, but there as many others who insist that work strike a balance with family. This is not only mothers with kids, but also fathers with kids, middle-aged people with aging parents, and even young couples without children who want to balance their careers with their time together.

Much is made of the changing American family. The number of single-parent families has reached an all-time high, as has the number of double-income families in which both parents work full time. While the influx of women into the workforce over the past two decades spurred many of the changes around company expectations, it's important for managers to recognize that it's not only women who have childcare responsibilities. Many men share parenting activities. Their wives might also have full-time careers, they could be divorced dads sharing custody, or they might be single dads with sole parenting responsibility. Fathers need the same opportunities to take time off for sick kids and school activities as mothers do.

It's not uncommon for dads to choose to stay at home with the kids. One woman, a vice president at a large corporation, and her husband made this decision when their children became teenagers. They realized their kids needed a parent at home and available for the many school and after-school activities they participated in. The woman had made sacrifices for her husband's career, including moving to their current location. Then she had a great job opportunity. So they decided that it was his turn to stay at home, and her turn to be the breadwinner.

Family Leave Act

When Bill Clinton became the forty-second president of the United States, his first official act was to sign the Family and Medical Leave Act (FMLA) of 1993. The FMLA allows people to take unpaid time off from work—up to twelve weeks if necessary—to care for a newborn or newly adopted child, a seriously ill family member, or because of their own medical conditions, without losing their jobs. The FMLA does not apply to everyone who works, however. To find out if it covers you, talk with your company's HR department or contact the U.S. Department of Labor (see Appendix B for contact information).

Family-Friendly Policies

Changes in our society, changes in the workplace, and changes in the laws regulating workplace behavior have combined to create work situations for many Americans that are more family-friendly than ever. Companies offer various benefits to support working parents, from childcare referral services to on-site daycare, daycare subsidies, and emergency childcare arrangements. Many companies have opened "Bring Your Daughter to Work Day"—originally an effort to encourage mothers to share their professions with their daughters—to include fathers and their daughters. Many organizations, public and private, provide some sort of open house or similar opportunities for employees to share their jobs with their families.

Another area of growing involvement for companies is in addressing the needs of employees who are caring for aging and ailing parents. Those that offer EAP benefits often include counseling and assistance with decisions about health care and long-term care, as well as time off from work to handle these decisions. An increasing number of companies are also offering employees the opportunity to purchase long-term care insurance as an employment benefit, just as they might buy life or disability income insurance.

Companies realize that the stress of caring for family members affects employee productivity. They also recognize that they can't pretend these problems don't exist in the lives of all employees, from top executives on down. As employers expect more from employees, they understand that they have to give more in return as well.

CHAPTER 5
Work Styles

Work style blends personality, knowledge, skill, ingenuity, and creativity into the package you know as an employee. Each person's work style is unique, although there are common traits that identify general types. Some people are absolutely true to type, but many adopt elements of different work styles, crossing categories. It's important to view each employee as a distinctive individual, even if you think you have your employees pegged.

So why even discuss categories if you should treat each employee as an individual? Because learning to identify commonalities can help you, a manager with several to perhaps dozens of people reporting to you, gain a baseline of understanding about how employees relate to their work responsibilities and to each other. This baseline then gives you the platform from which to further develop your insights into what motivates and inspires each employee to give his or her best.

Channeling Creative Energy

Nearly every job involves some aspect of creativity, from jobs we consider to be creative (such as media or teaching) to those we think of as more mundane (such as accounting or cleaning). Creativity covers the spectrum of innovation, from the ability to see new ways to accomplish familiar tasks to the capacity to envision entirely new processes or products. Although you can find them in just about any job, creative people tend to gravitate toward creative jobs—work that requires them to come up with new processes or products. These jobs are often in fields such as advertising, marketing, electronic media, publishing, design, and architecture. You might define these people as writers, artists, or programmers, or they might have a combination of talents that defies definition. Creative people tend to make managers a little nervous—it's hard to tell sometimes whether they're working or goofing off, and they seem a bit, well, unleashed. Creative types often:

- Appear to have little regard for authority, rules, structure, and routine, viewing these elements of the work world as not applying to them
- Establish surroundings within their work environments that support and feed their imaginations
- Have unorthodox or eccentric methods for stimulating their productivity
- Appear disorganized and to "fly by the seat of their pants" when doing presentations

- Find humor in, or make fun of, just about everything (and might not understand why others don't)
- Work in spurts of intensity that can last for hours, days, or even weeks, then go into a "down" phase where they appear to accomplish very little
- Arrive late or even fail to show up for staff or other general meetings that don't apply directly to their projects

People in creative professions require tremendous flexibility in terms of how they are managed. Emotion, not logic, rules creative ability. The result is often behavior that goes beyond what might be considered standard business behavior. Anger, frustration, elation, and excitement not only exist, but also show. The office of a creative person might look more like a preschool classroom or a toy store than a workstation—and we do mean office here, because solitude is a key element of the creative process. Creative types need to be able to shut themselves away, to get away from the structure of rules and decorum, to give their ideas the space and time to evolve.

FACTS

According to U.S. Bureau of Labor (BLS) figures, nearly 100 million Americans—70 percent of the workforce—work in jobs that provide services. BLS projects that another 19 million workers will join the service sector by 2008, bringing the level of service jobs to 75 percent.

Companies or departments that rely on creative people, such as advertising agencies or media companies, often use brainstorming sessions that to the uninitiated (or those who require structure) might appear to be wild free-for-alls. People laugh, yell, throw things, draw pictures, and tell jokes as they toss about ideas. Political correctness stays in the hall; there's plenty of opportunity later to run the censor filters. The entire mission is to let brains wander freely through the vast seed bins of ideas until some start to sprout. Many companies in creative businesses have lounge areas with pool tables, coffee bars, video games, bean bag chairs, and other diversions to get people relaxed and thinking. Such a lounge creates an oasis from the reality of business (which is of course why the creative professionals are employed in the first place). Once ideas take on viable shapes, creative types disappear into the cocoons of their offices. They re-emerge when they've created something from those shapes that they're ready to share with others or that now needs feedback.

Despite appearances to the contrary, most creative people are highly organized. It's just that the organization doesn't necessarily take the form of neatly labeled files and calendars that record meetings and commitments. Those "seat of the pants" presentations often reflect not lack of preparation but instead a deeply assimilated knowledge of the topic acquired through intense and often extended research or observation—sometimes with a dash of intuition thrown in. This less tangible organization can have the appearance of chaos, but it's not. For the creative individual, it's as close to logical as it gets.

Not surprisingly, too much structure stifles creativity. As a manager, this can be a difficult balancing act for you. On the one hand you have a creative genius (or even a team of creative geniuses) whose ideas generate most of the products that make your company successful. On the other hand, you have the company, which wants to make sure the time it pays for is used productively. Perhaps you are also responsible for managing other people whose work is more traditional and who might believe that anyone who's having so much fun at work isn't working hard enough.

Creativity and productivity are not mutually exclusive, although channeling creativity into productivity can be a significant challenge for a manager. You just need to identify people who are naturally creative thinkers and make sure they have the flexibility—in terms of assignments and environment—to express their creativity. This applies not only to people in traditionally creative professions, but also to people who are just generally creative as well as the people you want to encourage to think creatively from time to time. How can you stimulate and support productive creativity without squelching the creative process? You might:

- Present assignments in general terms, explaining the desired end result but allowing employees the latitude to find their own ways to that result. Establish timelines to keep productivity on track, but don't structure the work process.
- Allow people to express risky ideas without immediately shooting them down. "Let me play devil's advocate" is the surest way to cut creative thinking off at the knees.
- Let people work through mistakes to find their own solutions, and allow time for this as part of the creative process. It takes a lot of coal to make diamonds.
- Learn how to praise someone's efforts without focusing on the result or product you want those efforts to generate.
- Ask employees what you can do to provide a stimulating and supportive environment. You might be surprised at how simple some of their requests will be.
- Sponsor workshops conducted by outside resources. Creative people are always looking to broaden their base of knowledge and expertise. New faces bring fresh perspectives. Employees are sometimes more willing to question and raise issues with outsiders than they are with internal trainers or consultants.

When Roger, the administration manager of a technology company, had to do a presentation about new procedures that were critically important, he wanted to be sure to make a lasting impression on the employees in attendance. So he asked Dave, one of the training department's most popular trainers, to help design a memorable presentation. Roger and Dave met in the "think tank," the training department's conference room. They sat in lounge chairs as Roger explained what information he needed to convey and what he wanted to accomplish with his presentation. Dave listened, took notes, and asked questions. Then Dave got up and started writing ideas on the white board. Each time he started to explain a concept to Roger, Roger shot it down. It was too silly, too boring, too inappropriate—just too wrong, no matter what the idea. It just wouldn't work.

Dave tried several times to tell Roger he was just thinking out loud and that none of these initial ideas was likely to be the final solution but that the process of throwing ideas out would lead to the right one. Dave even tried to get Roger to pop off ideas of his own without judging how effective they were likely to be, but no go. Finally Dave sat down and the two men sat in silence for a few minutes. Then Roger stood up, said he was just going to do the "standard" presentation since that seemed to work fine, thanked Dave for his time, and left the room. Dave was frustrated and a little angry. Why did Roger even ask for his ideas if he already knew he was just going to do it his own way?

All managers must understand and accommodate the different work styles of the employees who report to them. Creative managers need to recognize that employees who desire or need structure might have trouble understanding their expectations. It's important to provide a clear framework for employees to follow.

New approaches are sometimes threatening. Everyone's neck is on the line these days, and managers don't like to take risks that will stretch theirs. Too many people, up and down the corporate ladder, notice. So many take the easy route and, like Roger, stay with the tried and true, no matter how tired that approach has become. This reflects an insecurity that employees pick up on, even if you yourself don't. But it's critical to take risks now and again. Familiarity breeds repetition, which soon becomes complacency and stagnation. No company, no matter what its products or services, can thrive (or even survive) without fresh ideas.

Structure! I Need Structure!

Not all people—nor all jobs—function well in an environment with minimal structure. Some people who are highly creative might not know how to channel their energy into productive tasks with measurable outcomes. Other people have relatively passive personalities that crave direction. Occasionally you'll encounter an employee who needs external structure because without it he or she simply won't do any work at all. Employees who need a lot of structure need a manager who is willing to be more hands-on. Structured people typically:

- Are tidy and organized. Their desks and workspaces are neat and functional. Nearly anyone could step into a structured person's environment and find a file or project.
- Arrive and leave on time, and at the same time every day. If they are early, they are consistently early.
- Have obvious routines that they follow. Other employees almost always know where they are and what they are doing, just by knowing what time or day it is.
- Know what work is due and where in the process the work is, and deliver on time unless circumstances beyond their control intervene.
- Handle complex projects by breaking them into smaller, logical steps. Structured people often keep status and progress logs of their projects.
- Appear disciplined and goal-oriented.
- Seldom knowingly break rules, and might take offense with those who do.

Every company, regardless of its products and services, requires a certain amount of structure. Some functions and departments, such as accounting, are bound to established procedures for conducting their work. People who work in these areas generally (but not always) have work styles and personalities that are compatible with this level of structure. Other functions and departments require structure that supports project timelines and productivity goals. Such structure might be vague and variable or fairly rigid, depending on the work and the employees doing it. Structure might require you to:

- Establish priorities
- Identify tasks
- Identify goals
- Indicate whether tasks are daily, weekly, or monthly
- Suggest the time of day and the amount of time the employee should work on each task or specified tasks

The backbone of structure is clear communication. Employees need to know what they are expected to do and by when. What is more important? What is less important? What happens when there are conflicting or competing tasks? This level of structure is all about prioritizing. Some people are good at establishing priorities, while others need help. Sometimes employees have trouble prioritizing because they are unfamiliar with the department, the company, or the industry. They have no context for the work they do, so they don't know what to tackle first. Such employees tend to simply plow through the day, completing tasks in the order they arrived. Everything becomes critical in such an environment, and as a consequence what gets completed is often frustratingly trivial. The important stuff gets left undone or missed completely.

ALERT

A key challenge for a manager who prefers structure is letting go— but you must. Employees will rebel if they feel you have a "my way or no way" approach. Rebellion against excessive structure often takes the form of passive-aggressive behavior such as remaining engaged in a task without answering a ringing phone.

As a manager, you need to help employees who need structure learn how to prioritize. Once the base structure of priorities is in place, most employees can then build additional structure around those priorities. Generally it's most effective to meet with employees one-on-one, so you can gauge just how much structure each employee needs.

- Start by laying out specific tasks and the small goals that must be accomplished by the end of the day. Be sure the employee has the necessary tools to complete the tasks, and knows how to use them.
- Identify common problems that might arise, and establish a procedure for dealing with them. Some employees find it useful to have a chart or diagram that outlines priorities and procedures, while others might just take notes.

- Meet with the employee at the end of the day to discuss how he or she approached the tasks and what actually got finished. Communication about expectations, and what worked and didn't work, is critical here.

- Establish procedures for identifying and addressing emergencies and unexpected changes in priorities. At first, this might mean having the employee come to you whenever work deviates from the planned schedule. As the employee becomes more skilled in structuring and adjusting priorities, the procedures might shift to general guidelines for when to contact you and when to proceed without assistance.

- Over time and as the employee's comfort with the structure progresses, designate daily tasks as part of the employee's routine, with the employee responsible for making them part of the work week with less monitoring from the manager.

- Be a good model. Show employees how you prioritize your day, and then ask them to tell you how they would, in turn prioritize their own. Then compare, and show them how to make adjustments as needed.

- Follow up to see what works and what doesn't, first on a daily and then on a less frequent (but no less often than weekly) basis.

ESSENTIALS

Revise your plan often! People grow and needs change, and it's essential to keep up with both. What an employee should self-monitor and what you monitor should evolve over time, so that you as manager play a less direct role in sculpting the employee's daily activities.

Sometimes an employee's apparent inability to prioritize reflects an overwhelming workload rather than a structure problem. In such situations you might need to reassign job tasks to lighten the load. This could mean realigning work responsibilities among your current employees, hiring temporary employees to help out, or creating new positions to accommodate a growing workload. Each employee has a slightly different need for structure. It's important for you as the manager to remain in close contact with all employees so you can adjust various elements of structure to support their highest levels of productivity. Ask each employee how he or she feels is the most effective way to structure the workday. By tailoring structure to each employee, you help employees buy into the process. They feel an investment in it because they helped create it.

Careening for a Crash

Some people are just not good fits for the jobs they hold, which raises a number of issues for both employees and managers. We always hope that good hiring practices and regular performance evaluations catch these situations before they become problems, but we also know that even in the most ideal circumstances things sometimes don't work out. The employee might have misunderstood the job's actual responsibilities; sometimes condensing a job description into 100 words or less to fit in a help-wanted ad or position listing leaves out vital details that no one detects during the interview process. Sometimes an employee is desperate to have a job and convinces himself or herself that this is the perfect one. Managers can also find themselves wanting to hire someone for reasons other than compatibility with the job; perhaps the job has been vacant for a long time, or the person strikes the right note on the personality scale and has the desired skills, even though there are signals that he or she is really overqualified or views the job as a stepping stone to more interesting positions. (More on these issues in Chapter 6, "Work Group Dynamics," and Chapter 8, "Evaluating Performance.")

Sometimes an employee has the skills the company needs but a work style that's not compatible. Then the manager has to decide whether those skills are needed enough to accommodate the person who has them—and how to do that. Eve was a brilliant computer programmer. She had the ability to listen to a client's needs, then produce exactly what the client needed. But Eve wasn't much of a team player. She preferred working alone; she wanted to go away to do her work and return with the finished product.

But her department was organized into teams around a structure that encouraged and supported collaboration. When her colleagues confronted her about taking projects on and not telling anyone what she was doing or letting anyone else become involved, Eve swung to the opposite extreme and started delegating everything. She was either on top of her game or at the bottom of the heap—there seemed to be no middle ground, and there was one blow-up after another. Responding to complaints from other employees, Eve's manager began documenting the problems. He sat down with her, identified the difficulties, and outlined a solution for how she needed to fix the problems. Eve agreed to the plan, and for a while everything went smoothly. Eve attended staff meetings, presented her projects to her work team, and even seemed eager to work in collaboration with her colleagues.

FACTS

Managers sometimes misunderstand the scope of responsibilities their jobs entail. You might be a creative free spirit overseeing the work of people who prefer structure, not well-suited for the level of detail managing these employees requires—or the reverse. Be honest with yourself about your work style and your expectations. If you are not a good fit for your managerial duties or are in over your head, you and your employees will suffer. Pursue options that better match your abilities.

The agreement soon broke down. Instead of discussing her ideas, Eve stormed out of meetings. Within weeks, Eve was again at one extreme or the other. Her manager had to make the critical decision of whether to keep her or fire her. The company would sorely suffer to lose her skills (especially if she were to take them to a competitor). But keeping Eve would likely mean losing other employees, and that wasn't a particularly enticing option, either. Finally Eve's manager, after consulting with the company's executives, offered Eve the opportunity to work from home. She received specific assignments and deadlines, and the manager and Eve's colleagues worked out a foolproof system for staying in close communication. Eve came in to the office periodically, usually to meet with clients and sometimes to join team meetings. But mostly she functioned more as an independent consultant.

It turned out to be the perfect solution. Eve was happy, the company was happy, the work group was happy, and clients were happy. There had never been any issues around the quality of Eve's work, just around her style of working. Innovative thinking and the willingness to try something different salvaged a highly productive and talented employee, giving the company a strong competitive edge in its market. It was a win for everyone.

Of course, not all mismatches have such happy endings. In fact, it's a sad reality that most don't. As a manager, it's up to you to be sure you—and your department and company—are doing everything possible to help an employee be successful. This means:

- Providing adequate and appropriate resources, including workspace and equipment.
- Clearly articulating goals and priorities—for the employee, for the work group, and for the company. Put them in writing, so you each have a copy.
- Ensuring that the job tasks are consistent with the job advertisement (and vice versa). The best time to establish that you are all on the same page is during the interview. Then affirm understandings and expectations within the first few days of employment.
- Giving clear instructions when tasks must be performed or completed in a certain way or by a specific time, and monitoring workloads to be sure employees are working to capacity but are not overwhelmed.
- Communicating clearly and regularly with all employees to see how a new employee fits into the work group.
- Carefully documenting problems that come to your attention or that other employees bring to you, and meeting with the employee as soon as you can clearly define that there are problems.
- Work collaboratively with the employee, and with coworkers if appropriate, to find mutually agreeable solutions.

In some situations, you'll find ways to work things out to keep a valued employee on your team. In other situations, the challenges will be insurmountable and you'll have no choice but to let the employee go. If you have done all you can do to give the employee the best possible chance to succeed (including discussing the situation with your superiors as well as your HR department), then you truly have done all you can do.

I'll Save You!

There's little satisfaction in watching someone fail. Even the most cynical managers don't want to see employees fail, if for no other reason than it implies they, too, have failed in some way. This is when your parent hat can obscure your vision. Parents don't like to see their children struggle, and often will do what they can to reduce or eliminate their suffering. Never mind that mistakes are part of learning; we just don't want the lessons to be so harsh. To an extent, this is a good thing. Care and compassion are important ingredients for growing employees and cultivating loyalty. But there comes a point when the parent hat slips too far down on your brow, and caring goes too far.

Where is that point? Well, it can be hard to see until you cross it. How often do you find yourself:

- Taking time out of your day to redo what an employee has done.
  _____ Never _____ Once or twice a week _____ Daily

- Redoing the same tasks for the same employee over and over again.
  _____ Never _____ Once or twice a week _____ Daily

- Missing opportunities to encourage employees to grow by indicating your expectations and how you'll measure progress.
  _____ Never _____ Once or twice a week _____ Daily

- Spending time after hours on work tasks that aren't really yours, when you have other responsibilities or you could be having a life.
  _____ Never _____ Once or twice a week _____ Daily

- Waking up at night worried about how an employee is performing or whether the employee will complete a project correctly and on time.
  _____ Never _____ Once or twice a week _____ Daily

- Defending an employee's incomplete or incorrect work to other team members, your superiors, or clients.
  _____ Never _____ Once or twice a week _____ Daily

- Asking other employees to pick up extra work to cover for an employee who isn't pulling his or her load.
  _____ Never _____ Once or twice a week _____ Daily

If you never do any of these things, you might not be paying enough attention to what's going on in your department or work group. It's normal for managers to have to step in every now and then; even exceptionally proficient employees occasionally stumble. But if you're doing three or more of these things once or twice a week, it's likely that there's some trouble in your work group. Perhaps there's a particular employee who's a problem, or your communications aren't clear. And if you're doing any of these things on a daily basis, it's time for a serious talk with yourself. Something is definitely out of kilter in your work group, and it's your responsibility to find out what it is.

It is important for managers to ask themselves: "What am I getting out of saving this employee? Is it about the employee or me?" Let's face it, it feels good to pull someone out of the wringer. Even if you're angry that the employee got into such a tight spot to begin with, it's a great sense of relief to rescue him or her. And sometimes it's especially satisfying to prove that you've still got "it"—skills, guts, determination, chutzpah—to your employees and your supervisors (as well as to yourself, of course).

ALERT

Employees are adults, and they need you to treat them as such. They need you to offer guidance on how to do things correctly, efficiently, and in keeping with company policies. They don't really benefit from you doing things for them. This teaches them that there are no consequences associated with responsibility.

Mentor or Handicap?

Randall was a brilliant but inexperienced writer, fresh from the journalism program of a prestigious university. His press releases captivated readers, and the news media often ran his stories straight from the releases. He had very tight deadlines, and he met them. Unfortunately, Randall just couldn't seem to get the facts straight. He transposed numbers, misquoted executives, and made things up when he couldn't contact the people who could give him the details he needed. Marjorie, Randall's manager, spent a lot of her time undoing the damage Randall did. Her superiors suggested that she reassign Randall to other tasks in the public relations office until he was more seasoned, but she resisted.

After all, everyone makes mistakes—that's how she learned, and that's how most people learn. So Marjorie had the department's administrative assistant intercept all of Randall's press releases before they were sent out, and she corrected them. It was a process doomed to fail, and it did. Marjorie had emergency surgery and was out of the office for two months. Randall wrote a press release erroneously suggesting the company would post a loss in its third-quarter report and stock prices plummeted. Marjorie's superior fired him.

Marjorie was overprotective of Randall. He reminded her of herself when she was young and enthusiastic about the corporate world. That world eventually stomped the enthusiasm out of her, though, with all of its rules and procedures, and she always wondered what would have happened if she'd been more resistant. She viewed her intercessions with Randall as protecting him from being stomped into compliance, as safeguarding his ability to express his creativity and earn recognition for his talents. She saw herself as Randall's mentor, the guide who would lead him through the entanglements of the corporate jungle. Marjorie failed to see that Randall made different, and more serious, mistakes than she had made when she was a novice publicist. And she failed to see that Randall was not a good fit for the company, and perhaps not for PR writing at all. He had talent, certainly, but he wasn't applying it in ways that would help his abilities broaden and grow.

A mentor helps an employee become better at both his abilities and his job. An enabler, like Marjorie, intends to do that but instead encourages dependent behavior by making excuses and redoing work. This is not a favor to the employee or to the organization. However noble Marjorie's intentions, in truth her actions served only to make her feel powerful. She wasn't so much "saving" Randall as she was salvaging her own ego. Ultimately, her actions were about herself, not about him. And in the end, she was the one who still had a job, although the situation reflected poorly on her as a manager.

There's nothing wrong with wanting to save an employee who is floundering. In fact, that is part of your role as a manager. But make sure your actions are truly helping. Involve HR, and perhaps coworkers or your superiors, depending on the circumstances. Take a step back, push your parent hat up, and evaluate the nature and scope of the employee's problems. Other employees are watching, too, despite any efforts to handle matters confidentially. They can't help but be interested—the situation involves them as well, as members of the work group and also in terms of how they perceive the fairness of events. When working with a struggling employee, it's important to establish:

- Whether the employee wants your help, and is willing to comply with efforts to improve his or her performance
- Clear goals and priorities for the employee, and to make sure the employee understands how those goals and priorities affect the work group or department and the company
- Procedures and steps for the employee to follow to meet goals and priorities—these should be clear and unequivocal, with the employee fully aware that it is his or her responsibility to follow them
- Ongoing communication to address any problems that might arise or difficulties that the employee encounters in completing the assigned tasks and steps
- A process for monitoring compliance and progress, with positive and negative consequences at each step
- An endpoint beyond which the employee will move to the level of independence the job requires
- An understanding of what happens if the employee is unable to make the necessary adjustments

Variations on the Savior Theme

There are two other "savior" variations that are worth mentioning. One is the employee who seems destined to save the day. Ericka was such an employee. She had the ability to find information no one else could uncover, to locate supplies that were out of stock, and to make magic out of ordinary sales reports and marketing presentations. Other employees, her manager, and even managers from other departments turned to Ericka when they had to pull off the otherwise impossible.

For a while, Ericka thrived on the accolades her rescues earned her; she really didn't see anything that exceptional about what she viewed as just doing her job. She was intelligent and innovative, and she liked helping people. As time went on, more and more people began relying on Ericka to find this and do that. Ericka began to resent the assumption that she would always be there to rescue them, especially when it was clear to her that they could easily rescue themselves if they would just put their minds to it instead of running to her right away. Her own job responsibilities began to slip as she became more mired in doing the work of others. Her previously grateful manager now threatened to counsel her if her performance didn't improve. Other employees became angry if Ericka wasn't able to drop what she was doing to get them what they needed. One day she went to lunch and didn't come back. A note on her desk just said, "I quit."

The other variation is the employee who creates a day that needs to be saved. Jeremy was such an employee. A charismatic and energetic sales representative, Jeremy excelled at wooing big clients. He nurtured relationships for weeks, months, and sometimes years. Once he won the contract, though, Jeremy lost interest. The conquest was over, and it was time to move on—in his mind. In reality, however, Jeremy was responsible for following the account through its various stages to make sure the details unfolded to the client's satisfaction.

But Jeremy wasn't very interested in the details, so he ignored them until some crisis arose that forced his attention. Then he swung into action, and he was 110 percent intensity. Here was a challenge only he could resolve—and he did. Time after time, he pulled off rescues that should have never been necessary. When clients became angry, he soothed them with talk about the "system" and all its problems. The other sales reps began to hear gossip about how ineffective the sales department and even the entire company was, and how Jeremy was the only one who could make things happen. They knew that things would happen just fine if Jeremy followed the department's procedures, but he didn't. So it always looked like he was jumping to the rescue, saving clients from the incompetent bumblings of everyone else.

Of course, it was Jeremy who was bumbling the accounts. But because those accounts were substantial, Jeremy's manager was reluctant to discipline Jeremy for handling them inappropriately. After all, the manager reasoned, everything came out okay in the end. It didn't really—turnover among sales representatives was significantly higher than the average for similar companies. Jeremy's "rescues" landed the big accounts, but the company lost good employees who were less than enchanted with Jeremy's antics.

That's Not in My Job Description

Joan's official job was to collect, analyze, and report customer service complaint data. She entered information from customer comment cards into a relational database, then once a month she generated a series of inquiries, summations, and reports. All departments in her company used the information Joan provided to identify problem areas and design solutions that would improve customer service. One month, Joan's manager was presenting the monthly reports at the executive staff meeting, and could no longer answer the questions top managers had about the data and what it indicated. It wasn't her area of expertise. So she decided to ask Joan to attend the next executive staff meeting to present the reports herself. "No way!" Joan said. "That's not in my job description!"

ESSENTIALS Most employees (although not all) welcome the opportunity to stretch beyond the confines of their routine tasks, as long as they don't feel that the real motivation is to take advantage of them somehow. Whenever possible, present additional tasks as optional, and in such a way that employees feel comfortable declining.

Now before you charge what you see as a red flag, take a deep breath. What is Joan actually saying? That she feels put upon, or uncomfortable? It often requires an extended dialogue to figure out the meaning behind the words. In some circumstances, this is the ultimate passive-aggressive behavior from an employee who uses "no" as the ultimate weapon in the battle for power. In other situations, it's an overwhelmed employee's cry for help, a last-ditch effort to stem the flow of work before it completely swamps the boat. Sometimes employees feel that they just do the same things over and over and over, and want a break from what has become tedium. They might want to branch out into new territory, but are afraid to or feel they can't because their existing job descriptions confine them. And sometimes employees will band together to expose the "slacker" in the work group, thinking that if they all refuse the work you'll give it to the one who really deserves it (and discover in the process that the person is overpaid and underworked).

As annoying as it can be to hear "that's not in my job description," it's often a message to you that things are not quite right with at least one employee. You need to:

- Initiate a private conversation with the employee. Invite him to meet with you in your office or in a conference room. Ask, in a nonconfrontational manner, what the employee meant.
- Listen actively and openly. This is not an employee who comes to the point quickly, and may not fully understand the point himself until he talks his way to it.
- Try to understand the employee's framework and background, as much as this is possible. Perhaps he comes from another department or company where the division of labor was clearly defined and no one crossed it.
- If this is a situation of control, see if there are other ways to address the underlying issues.
- If the employee believes another employee is getting away with a light workload, address the matter with the other employee.
- Explain the expectations that you and the company have of this employee and other employees. Sometimes it's necessary to revisit and update expectations, particularly if the employee has worked for the company for several years.
- If you want the employee to do something that truly is beyond the scope of his job description, explain why. Make it clear that you respect and value the contributions he is already making to the work group and to the company. Help the employee to see that there is a benefit for him in taking on the additional tasks or responsibilities.

An employee who stands firm on the boundaries of his or her job description can present a challenge when it comes to fostering teamwork. It's a rare job where there aren't unexpected circumstances or changes that require additional work. The tradition of teamwork is that everyone pitches in, equitably, to get the job done. If you have an employee that you know resists (or refuses) additional tasks, ask this employee to do things that are within the scope of the job description. Most job descriptions define tasks and responsibilities, not the amount of time they require. It's difficult for an employee to legitimately refuse a request to do more of something that is in his or her job description. Just be sure to make it clear whether this is an exception or if there are new expectations about how much work employees handle. Many companies include the phrase "and other duties as assigned" in all job descriptions to avoid the technicality of this battle.

Go Home, Please!

How many hours do your employees put in each week? The standard forty, or more? People who are committed to their professions or who enjoy what they do are willing to spend more than the required number of hours at work. People who are overburdened feel compelled to stay late, even though they know the attempt to catch up will ultimately be futile. An occasional need for extra time and effort is certainly not unreasonable. But the employees who are the first to arrive and the last to leave are headed for burnout. They are the ones who are addicted to their jobs, by choice or by default. And this, like all addictions, will eventually turn destructive.

For years the sales department at the Wacky Widget Corporation had begged to hire a technical writer to write its proposals. Sales representatives should be out making sales, not in the office struggling to write extensive documents filled with technical language they barely understood, the manager pleaded in memo after memo. Finally the powers that be took heed and approved the budget. It was just in time. It was October, when 80 percent of the company's contracts were up for renewal. When Roxanne reported for her first day at work, her manager asked, "Did you bring your sleeping bag?" It was only partly a joke. Wacky Widget's managers in all departments often worked long into the night.

It was an honor to have the CEO thank you, in an elevator crowded with the less dedicated, for having stayed to finish whatever project was the current priority. Although the workday ended at five, no one left before seven. Managers seldom left before ten or eleven. The CEO often strolled through the office around eight, and ordered dinner for everyone who was still there. Everyone sat around the table in the conference room when dinner arrived, eager to exchange chitchat with the main man. This was when information about upcoming projects or problems was most likely to surface first, and managers were reluctant to miss out. So they stayed.

FACTS

In a 1999 Gallup poll, 44 percent of those surveyed considered themselves workaholics, to the extent that work activities interfered with or prevented a life beyond their job. More than half of those who worked full time said they put in more than forty hours a week; the average number of hours worked was forty-six.

When Roxanne started working for the company, it wasn't unusual for two-thirds of the workforce to still be in the office at 8 P.M. Although Roxanne had other interests, she set them aside. "It's just for right now, with all of these contracts renewing," her manager told her. Right now, of course, stretched into the norm, and by Christmas Roxanne had a couch in her office so she could make up lost sleep by napping. In February, she turned in her resignation. In her five months with Wacky Widget, she had worked more hours than she normally worked in a year. The money was good, but the pressure and stress were too much.

When employees are at work too long, they burn out and then they resent their jobs and other employees, as well as their managers, who either haven't rewarded them as much as they thought they deserved or don't seem to work as hard. This kind of commitment isn't dedication—it's insanity. Are you setting the example? Then stop! Right now, today. Take out a piece of paper and write, "Today I will leave work at 5 P.M." Sign it. There—it's a contract. Be gone at five, period. Pack your briefcase and head out the door. Let your employees see you. Do it again tomorrow, because then it will be today again and you have a contract. Facetiousness aside, it is important for you to set the example you want your employees to follow. If you are a workaholic, most of them will be, too. It's fine if you don't have a life beyond work—that's your choice. But don't establish the expectation that your employees can't have personal lives. They might go along with you for a while, but eventually they'll rebel or burn out. Neither is pleasant.

Do you have an employee who regularly burns the midnight oil? It's time to talk:

- Why is the person working so many hours? Does this person have too much work, use his or her time during regular work hours inefficiently, or does not want to go home?
- If there are work-based problems, try to identify viable solutions. If the workload is too intense, how can you lighten it? If the employee has trouble prioritizing, what can you do to help?
- Be supportive and nonjudgmental, yet firm. Make it clear that while you appreciate and respect such dedication, no one expects anyone to stay at work all the time.
- Express your concern that the person might burn out, leaving you in dire need of the skills and talents only he or she can provide. What happens then? Neither the employee nor the company comes out ahead.

While the personal lives of your employees are none of your business, it is your responsibility to be sure they have the freedom to pursue them. No one should feel that a job owns the employee (not even you).

Identifying Your Work Style

Although it's important for you to understand the different work styles of your employees so you can support them, it's also critical for you to understand your own work style. Are you creative? Structured? Wedded to your job? Resentful of the time your job keeps you from other activities? If you're not sure, look around you. What do you see in your employees?

While each person has a unique work style, like attracts like. People tend to be drawn to people who are like them, which is as true in the workplace as anywhere else. All other qualifications being equal, you're more likely to hire someone you feel has something in common with you than someone who is clearly your opposite.

Your personal work style forms the foundation from which you measure other work styles. Yes, it's a bias. But it's where we all start. The key to being successful as a manager is to move beyond square one. Once you understand what your work style is, it's easier to understand differing work styles. As much fun as it would be for your ego, you really don't want a department full of you-clones. You do need different work styles for different jobs and tasks. Someone who excels at innovation is not likely to do well at maintenance. Someone who thrives on detail isn't likely to do well conceptualizing. The only way to appreciate differences is to understand them. Then you can truly manage by building on people's strengths and minimizing their weaknesses. And you can learn from your employees, so you too can grow and evolve.

CHAPTER 6
Work Group Dynamics

A work group is a complex organism that exists as an entity in its own right and also as a collection of the individuals that comprise it. Some groups come together or "click" from just about the first time its members meet, while others labor for months or longer to be something other than separate and competing personalities.

Individual personalities and work styles significantly influence the group identity. The most effective work groups contain complementary, not necessarily similar, personalities and work styles. In such groups, the whole truly becomes more than the sum of its parts. Each person's strengths overlap the others' weaknesses. Creating such a work group is part planning and part luck. It's impossible to know with certainty how people will function together when all you can evaluate is how each functions separately. Just as mixing chemicals produces different results depending on the substance and its quantity, combining personalities and work styles results in varied effects. Indeed, we often talk about the "chemistry" among group members as critical to the group's success. Changing just one member can alter the group far beyond that one member's role and responsibilities—or not.

Effective Teamwork

Sometimes teams form totally around job responsibilities. Certain people in marketing, like the PR group, are a natural team, as is the production control or quality control group in manufacturing. Teams can also be formed that cut across responsibilities. For example, managers can form teams to serve as the departmental education committee, the holiday party committee, to look at a morale issue, to evaluate new technologies, or to help the department get ready to implement a new technology. This is an opportunity to get people interacting in new ways by forming relationships that cut across the usual functional boundaries, especially when those boundaries also separate groups that compete with each other in some way. And by forming new teams whenever possible, managers can help employees learn to adapt to change better because they have to quickly become cohesive and then accomplish something.

Teams develop not only a way of operating, but also of interacting. A culture forms that establishes the group's norms and standards. Each team member has a role; this defines and distributes responsibility. In some groups, one person surfaces as the team's leader, often emerging naturally, although sometimes the manager designates a team lead, if only to serve as the group's primary contact. In other groups, the members share leadership roles and responsibilities. While shared leadership is generally more effective, much depends on the group itself—its goals and purpose as well as the personalities and work styles of its members.

FACTS

Generally, strong individual productivity generates strong group performance. When each member is pulling his or her load, the work gets done. Also, people feel that their contributions are both valued and valuable. Even with one or two weak members, most groups can maintain strong productivity. But the more pronounced the disparities in workload and contribution, the less satisfied all group members become—and then the group's performance suffers even though some individuals within the group are outstanding producers.

What about you? Shouldn't you be the team's leader? Well, yes and no. You are the leader in that you're the one with the authority to make decisions, and usually the one held accountable for the group's actions, performance, and productivity. But in most situations, the manager isn't a team member. It's nearly impossible to be a team member and an authority figure. Teams function most effectively when there is a relatively even distribution of power so each team member feels he or she is making an equitable contribution. As manager, it's your role to stay on the periphery. It's your job to be sure everyone knows his or her role and responsibilities, and that of other members. And you'll need to be available to serve as facilitator, mediator, teacher, mentor, cheerleader, coach, and parent—whatever the group needs.

When teams are working, there is nothing more exciting. But even teams that seem to come together well on their own need guidance and occasionally intervention to help them grow and develop. It's a balancing act that requires constant attention and adjustment. If you as the manager are too involved, then it looks like you're pulling the strings and team members are simply reacting. If you're not involved enough, then it is a constant free-for-all. It's natural to feel pride and responsibility for the group's performance. Just remember that this is about the group, not about you.

Acme Industries was a big, big company. Employees often joked about it being like its own little city; the corporate campus covered several square miles and included a daycare center, health clinic, fitness center, several cafeterias, and even its own security force that patrolled the grounds and facilities. There were many rules and restrictions—some company-wide, others specific to particular departments or work groups. Sheila was the education department's manager. Her department was both a microcosm of and a haven from the company's bureaucracy. On the one hand, Sheila had to enforce corporate rules and policies as well as keep the department on track with corporate goals and objectives. Daily policies such as leave time and working hours had to be consistent with the company's procedures.

FACTS

Do team members have to like each other to be effective? As much as we'd like to think professionalism transcends petty matters like popularity, the reality is that people who like each other get along better. Certainly a work group whose members provide complementary skills can function competently and even productively without friendship to bond them. But when group members consider themselves friends as well as colleagues, they have a heightened investment in the group's activities.

Sheila recognized that it was important for people to feel that they had some control over their work and work environment. Although the corporation was enormous and complex, her department could succeed in meeting its goals only when its members could feel that they were more than just work units. Sheila encouraged both independence and teamwork among her employees, and gave them the latitude this balance required. They had to follow the company rules, but could bend them to fit the needs of their assignments and projects. Team members could work off campus, for example, or order in lunch when work tasks became intense. The department was, in many ways, a haven from the rigid corporate culture.

Employees formed strong working relationships with one another. They had a high level of trust and a strong sense of belonging. They knew Sheila believed in their abilities to handle complex training projects as well as to resolve challenges that might arise within the group. And they knew Sheila was available to them when they needed her—to help with problem solving, to commiserate when stress levels escalated, to be a sounding board for new ideas. As a result, the department excelled in meeting its goals as well as helping the corporation to meet its goals. Absenteeism and turnover were extraordinarily low, and the department maintained a training schedule that would have swamped a less effective team. Sheila praised her department's efforts and contributions, both within the department and in her meetings and contacts with others in the company—her superiors as well as her peers. Her employees knew she, and by extension the company, valued them.

Effective work groups share certain characteristics:

- **A clear sense of mission or purpose and clear goals.** To be productive, group members need to know why they're working. It seems so basic, yet odds are that if you ask ten employees at random why they're working, most will tell you they work to pay bills and have money to spend on the things they enjoy. One or two might say something about enjoying the work or fulfilling a personal dream. Few if any are likely to talk about the department's or company's goals. When a work group knows its mission or purpose (reason for existing) and its goals (desired accomplishments), its members are more likely to focus on activities that move the group closer to completion—of tasks, of projects, of products or services.

- **Mutual respect and support.** It's hard to be innovative when you're never sure how others will react to your ideas. In effective groups, members know that even if coworkers disagree they will focus their objections on the idea, not on the person presenting it. Each member feels he or she has the fundamental right to a level of trust that precludes backstabbing, gossip, and other negative behaviors aimed solely at making someone look bad. Members instead provide positive encouragement and work cooperatively to achieve common goals.

- **Open communication.** Group members must feel comfortable sharing ideas and concerns with each other as well as with you as the manager. Communication exists on numerous levels, from casual chitchat to structured meetings. While each level has its protocols and norms, openness is an essential foundation.

- **The ability to resolve disagreements, conflicts, and problems.** No group (no matter how small, tight-knit, or productive) is going to have all its members get along with each other all the time. The ability of team members to work through their differences to renewed understanding and cooperation is crucial to the group's success. There will be squalls and occasionally storms; conflict is a normal part of human interaction. The most effective groups have processes in place for airing grievances and working out problems.

- **Appropriate external support.** Even the most self-sufficient, effective work groups can't function in a vacuum. They need you and your superiors (often viewed collectively as the company), and sometimes other departments or work groups, to provide the resources required to achieve their goals. Team members need the proper equipment and supplies, an appropriate workspace, adequate administrative support, and suitable environmental amenities (such as lighting and temperature control). It's your role as manager to be sure all of these elements are in place.

System vs. People Problems

Problems within a work group can result from either personal issues or system issues, or both. Sometimes the source of the problem is obvious: The design group can't complete the final drawings because the software update they need to install first is backordered from the manufacturer. The customer call center can't improve call wait times and dropped calls because there are too few lines to handle the volume of incoming calls. The production department is ready to roll, but the templates were cut wrong and the manager had to send them back to the supplier. These are clearly systems problems; the people are ready and eager to do what needs to be done, but they don't have what they need to move forward.

Sometimes the part of the system that's not functioning optimally is its people. The Gizmo Master Corporation prided itself on listening to its customers and using customer feedback to shape new products and services. An important part of the marketing representative's job was to follow up with customers at certain intervals after sales closed. The purpose of these follow-up contacts was to make sure the customer was satisfied and to solicit suggestions for improvements. Often, customers offered good ideas for new products and services. The marketing reps passed these ideas on to the product development department.

The product development engineers were less than impressed. In fact, over time they became angry with the marketing reps. It wasn't easy coming up with the next best-selling gizmo, and the engineers resented the implication that "just anybody" thought he or she could just zip something off the top of their head and—Shazam!—there was the company's next claim to fame. There were computer models and prototypes and lab tests and field tests and focus groups . . . followed by more of the same after revisions and reconfigurations. Then, maybe, an idea might make it into production, if the legal department gave its approval.

Marketing accused product development of failing to come through on the company's promise to listen to its customers. Product development charged that marketing had no understanding of the manpower and other resources it would require to even explore, let alone develop, the ideas customers suggested. Egos clashed, turf collided. Marketing started getting heat from customers because the new products they wanted weren't yet available. Product development started getting heat from upper management because customers were unhappy.

Without intervention, such battles spiral out of control, ultimately interfering with the company's goals. The system clearly has flaws: Marketing is gathering information it is not empowered to use. Policies and procedures, although useful and appropriate in many circumstances, prevent product development from reaching beyond its boundaries. And the people clearly contribute: Marketing reps make promises they can't keep, alienating customers. Product development engineers feel threatened and become defensive.

The two departments' managers shut themselves in a conference room one morning. When they emerged, they had a plan. They created a work group, with members from each department, to bridge the differences between the departments. Over several months, the group developed a new set of policies and procedures that defined the needs of the production department so the marketing reps could solicit customer feedback the engineers could use. The new procedures established a quarterly meeting among selected customers, marketing reps, and product development engineers to discuss ideas for new products and services. The bridge team presented the policies and procedures to a meeting of both departments and worked through a series of revisions until both groups could support them. Six months after implementing the new framework, productivity in both departments was up and customer complaints dropped. By year's end, the company exceeded its sales goals.

Personal issues typically arise from personality conflicts or performance problems. Sometimes people just don't get along with each other. Though we like to believe that adults can put aside their differences to work toward common goals, this doesn't always happen. The challenge is to isolate the personalities that are clashing—not always as easy as it sounds—so they can try to work out their differences. In other situations, people might get along fine (or even too well) but lack the skills or the competence to do the job. In general, ruling out systems problems points the finger at people problems.

Sometimes, it's difficult to tell where the lines are drawn between personal and systems problems. Wacky Widget's customer call center had a telephone tree that routed calls, no matter what time of the day or night, to an extension where a "live body" could answer the phone. The switching circuitry was sophisticated and complex, and relied on computerized records that identified employees as they signed onto their computer terminals. The telephone tree identified them as "live" and routed calls according to a priority structure based on job function.

For months the customer service desk fielded complaints about calls not being answered between 8 A.M. and 11 A.M. on Tuesdays and Thursdays. Technicians checked all the wiring, circuits, and connections. Systems analysts checked all the computer algorithms to verify personnel routings. Finally a consultant from the telephone company helped set up a process for tracing call paths. This narrowed the problem to a phone in the middle of the call-forwarding sequence. Although technicians were unable to find any equipment problems in the office or with the phone, they replaced wiring and installed a new telephone that tracked all calls that rang to it, whether or not they were answered.

Astonishingly, the phone logged no call activity on Tuesday and Thursday mornings, even though the customer service desk continued to receive complaints. So a technician decided to sit in the office and observe. After an hour or so of sitting in silence, the technician asked the employee working in the office if the phone was always so quiet. "Of course!" he said. "I unplug it as soon as I sign in, so I can work without interruptions."

The rest of the story quickly unfolded. The employee was a temporary filling in for another employee who was on maternity leave. Although he had his own log-on ID, the computer station itself was registered to the employee who usually worked there. So when the temporary employee logged onto the computer, the telephone tree routed calls through the office's number because the computer showed it as manned. But the temp using the office was doing special assignments, not filling in for the employee who was on leave. He worked in three different offices during the course of a week, but this was the only one with a direct-ring phone. So he did what he thought made sense to keep calls that he couldn't handle from interrupting his work: He unplugged the phone. System? People? Both!

Resolving Differences

A work group often becomes much like a family. People are forced into relationships with each other that otherwise might not exist, and while they often get along just fine, sometimes there are problems. It's important for you, the manager, to always have your finger on the pulse of your team so you'll immediately know when things are out of sorts. Once a situation escalates it can be too late to salvage the group, at least in terms of restoring it to its previous level of collaboration and productivity.

ALERT

It's not enough to peek in at people a few times during the day to see if things look all right. You need to consistently monitor both output and attitudes. If there are problems with either, deal with the situation right away. Such interventions are not always comfortable, but they are essential.

If there is a team problem, you need to get people to talk. Depending on the nature of the problem, you might meet first with the entire group or with members individually. Once you figure out what's going on, take action. Don't wait for the right time—the right time is now. Intervene with individuals who seem to be having personal or individual performance problems. It's usually also a good idea to meet with the group to talk about the problem in general—its nature, how it's being addressed, when you expect to see things change, what changes you expect to see, and what role, if any, other group members have in resolving it. Avoid naming individuals unless there is no other way to talk about the situation. If you must use names, be sure to focus on behaviors and events, not people.

Put on your parent, mediator, and cheerleader hats—it's time to become a multiple personality. You need to take decisive action, yet at the same time help group members see each other's perspectives. Sometimes the involved member will have to transfer to another department or leave the company entirely. You might need to introduce a new communications process to force employees in complementary but competitive positions to communicate more effectively. The team might need to establish a new approval process to assure that members know about, and have the opportunity to discuss, product or service promises before anyone makes them. And when the problem is system-based, you must be willing to stick your neck out by advocating for employees. These responses build teams and create loyalty, among group members as well as toward you (and sometimes even the company). Who wouldn't want to go the extra mile for a manager who at least tries to go the extra mile for you?

Identifying Performance Issues

Employees with a lot of personal problems or who aren't a good fit with their jobs or work groups end up becoming self-destructive. Signs that this is happening include:

- Not getting work done on time, if at all
- A generally negative attitude
- Yelling and making angry outbursts
- Engaging in passive-aggressive behavior (actions that appear legitimate or helpful but really are not)
- Trying to rally other employees to side with them
- Going from cubicle to office to cubicle, stirring up trouble
- Tuning out or being argumentative at staff meetings
- Showing up late, leaving early, or taking excessively long lunches
- Staying on the phone for a long time, often on personal calls or discussing personal matters with coworkers or customers
- Flagrantly violating or ignoring company policies

As a manager, you need to address the problems. Start by talking with the employee about observed behavior: I saw you do this. I felt this way. What's going on? Sometimes inappropriate behavior at work reflects problems at home—a spouse or child may be ill, a marriage is breaking up, substance abuse. Sometimes inappropriate behavior is a warning sign of deeper personal issues, such as drug use or psychological problems. Many companies offer EAP benefits to get troubled employees the help they need, or have other programs or services. And sometimes, inappropriate behavior is nothing more than someone who doesn't really know how he or she is supposed to behave in the workplace.

Sometimes employees need some guidance on what is acceptable or unacceptable behavior. This is often true of younger employees because of their inexperience in work settings, but also applies to employees of any age who are in new situations. Although the "rules of engagement" are familiar and clear to you, it's your environment. Perhaps the work setting the employee came from had different rules and procedures. Some organizations have the "official" rules that HR distributes at new employee orientation and the "unofficial" rules that actually govern workplace behavior.

ESSENTIALS   Corporate cultures vary widely, and you may need to spell out the rules of your company (both official and unofficial) for people who are new. This might be all it takes to turn a difficult situation around.

Job Performance Counseling: This Is Not Therapy

When we speak of counseling in the context of the work environment, we're addressing the process of formally meeting with an employee to discuss performance issues—and documenting that discussion through a letter or memo that goes to the employee and perhaps to his or her personnel file. In most companies, this is a step in the progressive discipline process. This is not counseling in the sense of "let's uncover what's really bothering you so we can make it better"—this is not therapy. You are not a therapist; you are a manager. You cannot address psychological problems, even if you know enough to see that they are present. Your role is to say to this employee, "There are problems with your performance that we need to discuss." The bottom line is that you want to improve the employee's work-related problems, not fix his or her personal problems.

Often this approach feels cold-hearted and harsh. You are a compassionate human being who genuinely cares about this employee as a person, not just as a productive work unit. And while you can try to focus on the behaviors that you want the employee to change (as you should), you might believe that permanent change will come only when you uncover and somehow address the underlying issues. But that's not your role. Playing therapist (or even friend) can land you and your company in legal hot water. It's a delicate balance indeed, and one that can tip out of control before you know it. Here are five suggestions to help you keep counseling confined to an appropriate role for a manager.

Know Your Mission: Be Prepared

This is a meeting you should schedule and plan. While you want to keep things friendly, this is not a casual chat. It could be the first step to the end of a job for this employee, although you hope it's the beginning of the turnaround you need to see.

- Meet only when you are certain you can remain calm and professional. If you're angry because the employee's problems have caused your superiors to come down on you, give yourself a day or two to cool down.
- Meet someplace that assures privacy. Your office is fine if it has floor-to-ceiling walls and a door that closes (not a cubicle). Otherwise, meet in a conference room or arrange to use someone else's office.
- Have a clear agenda of what you want to cover, and put it in writing if that will help you stay on track.
- Have documentation of the problems you want to discuss—notes, memos, copies of e-mail, work that had to be redone, or whatever other evidence is relevant. Be discreet, of course—have the items in a file folder, not spread out on the desk when the employee arrives.
- Know, at least in general, what you want the employee to do to remedy the situation.

Focus on Specific and Observable Behaviors

If you or someone else didn't observe it, it didn't happen. This is not a meeting about feelings or suspicions. It is about actions and behaviors you can see, hear, or are otherwise tangible—work that didn't get done, assignments done incorrectly, inappropriate e-mail messages, and so on— that are creating performance problems for this employee. Have examples:

- "Here is the memo you sent to accounts receivable about the Robinson account. It has the wrong balances, and you erroneously flagged the account as past due."
- "I've gotten complaints from other departments about the number of jokes you forward by e-mail. Here are copies of messages that people have given me."
- "When we established the timeline for the widgets, you agreed that it was reasonable and would accommodate the kinds of delays that might arise. I've checked with you every week, and you've said you had everything under control. The widget prototype still isn't to manufacturing, though the timeline says it should have been in full production six weeks ago."

What about a "bad attitude"? You might see the crux of the problem as attitude, and that could indeed be the case. But you still need tangible evidence—and usually there's an abundance of it. Yelling at coworkers, badmouthing others, showing up late and leaving early—the signs of trouble outlined earlier in the chapter. Again, be specific. Provide a few examples:

- "On Tuesday you came in at 9:30 A.M. and you weren't at your desk after 2:30 P.M. On Thursday, you got here at 11 A.M. and I watched you leave at 3:15 P.M."
- "Monday at lunch you were overheard saying that the Mitchell project was nothing but a crock and if this company had any smarts it would fire the whole team."
- "Friday afternoon when Fran asked you to sign off on the department time logs, you told her to get screwed."

Unless you've asked other employees if you can use their names when talking to the problem employee, don't name names. Keep the conversation focused on the employee who is in the room with you, and on behaviors rather than personalities. Explain why the behaviors are problems, just to be sure you and the employee have the same understanding (which is not to imply that you must agree).

Listen to the Employee's Perspective

Many employees are surprised when their managers confront them about their performance. Even when you've maintained clear and open communication, the employee might not perceive the situation as serious or as a problem. It's easy for a person to view as reasonable explanations all of what he or she sees as extenuating circumstances. Before you dismiss them as meritless excuses, you owe it to the employee to hear his perspective.

ESSENTIALS
Listen to the employee's side without interrupting. If you take notes, do so unobtrusively. Listen without judgment and without challenging the employee's perceptions. If you have questions, make notes and ask them after the employee has finished speaking.

Sometimes there are issues within the work group or department that at least partially impede the employee's ability to perform necessary job tasks. Antiquated computer equipment, understaffing, inefficient procedures such as multiple sign-offs, and many other factors can be legitimate barriers. Sometimes the employee doesn't know how to do a particular task or step in a procedure and doesn't know who to ask, or is afraid to ask, for help. If such factors are present, it's your responsibility to do what is possible to remedy the situation. If there are barriers you can't remove or minimize, it's not really fair or reasonable to hold the employee accountable for results they impede. It might be necessary for you to modify your expectations or the employee's job responsibilities.

Agree to an Improvement Plan

After you've shared your concerns and listened to the employee's perspective, it's time to move into an action mode. Identifying the problems is the first half of your task; identifying solutions is the second. Although you want the employee to participate in developing an improvement plan, you also want to be sure that plan achieves the goals that are important to you and to the company. Every improvement plan should include these three elements:

- Specific goals for, and descriptions of, the improvements you want to see. "Memos that leave this department must be free from grammatical and spelling mistakes."
- Specific steps for achieving the described improvements. "I want you to run spellchecker just before you save or print any document. For the next two weeks, I want to sit down with you at 11 A.M. and 3 P.M. to review all outgoing memos. We will proof them together."
- Specific methods for measuring performance and assessing improvement. "I ran spellchecker on these memos that I showed you, and each had at least seven errors. By the end of one week, I want the memos we review together to have fewer than three errors each. At the end of two weeks, I want every memo we review together to have no errors that spellchecker is capable of detecting. We'll meet again at the end of two weeks to discuss your improvement."

FACTS

If an employee is having problems at home—with a partner, children, elderly parents, or a health problem—you can lend a sympathetic ear, but you can't intrude into these areas. Recommend that the employee seek outside help. If your company offers an EAP, refer the employee for assistance. If the problem is related to substance abuse, most state employment laws require companies to follow certain procedures for testing, mandatory counseling, and return-to-work agreements. Be sure to follow your company's policies and procedures.

Depending on the kinds of problems that exist and how complex the employee's job duties are, your improvement plan might consist of a few bulleted items or several pages of expectations and directives. Most improvement plans work best when they include an agreement to meet at determined intervals to review progress and make appropriate revisions. If an employee's problems involve numerous job functions, you might want to develop an incremental plan that attacks one problem at a time within the larger structure of more global improvements. Whatever form and length the plan takes, put it in writing. At the end, put a sentence that says, "I understand the requested improvements and agree to follow this plan to make them happen" (or words to this effect). Then sign your name and write the date, and have the employee sign. Each of you gets a copy.

If the employee identifies factors within the workplace that interfere with completing job tasks, establish a plan for you to address those concerns and a time by which you'll get back to the employee with answers or solutions. Every employee has unique needs when it comes to improving job performance, just as each has a unique work style. It's important to establish that this is a serious matter and you are establishing the framework for remedying the situation, yet allow the employee to participate at a comfortable level. When the counseling meeting ends, you both should be able to leave with your dignity and self-confidence intact. After all, the employee really has more of a vested interest in improving than anyone else.

Document

It's fine for you to take notes during your meeting—invite the employee to do so as well. Whether you do or not, take another ten or fifteen minutes immediately following the meeting (after the employee leaves) to write down a brief accounting of what transpired. Be sure to:

- Note what specific examples you used, and how the employee responded.
- Write down the details of the improvement plan you agreed upon, as well as the steps that will be necessary to monitor progress.
- Record any contributing factors from the work environment that the employee feels interfere with productivity, as well as your intentions for addressing issues that involve the employee.

What you do with this documentation depends on your company's policies, the seriousness or complexity of the problem, and your perceptions about how the meeting went. If your company requires or your manager's intuition compels, write a memo to the employee that summarizes the concerns you discussed, the employee's comments and concerns, and the agreement you reached for an improvement plan. To be fair, invite the employee to do the same and be sure that each of you gets copies. If company policy dictates or if the situation is serious, also put copies in the employee's personnel file.

Before you commit your thoughts to writing, consider how your words might sound a few months or years from now, coming from a lawyer's mouth. Be sure your comments are factual and maintain the same tangible focus as your meeting. Laws vary among states, but in many the courts can subpoena any written materials you keep—including notes intended only for your use. If you have any doubts or concerns about what constitutes appropriate documentation, check with your company's HR or legal department.

ESSENTIALS

If an employee is worth keeping, it's worth your time and energy to find solutions that will work for both of you. Consider additional training through classes or workshops, one-on-one tutoring with a more experienced employee, online or video training, job-shadowing—whatever looks to be effective, efficient, and even a little fun.

In general, documentation is a good habit to develop. It records, at the time rather than drawing from memory, the circumstances and events of an employee's behavior and of meetings to discuss problems. A good paper trail can demonstrate your and your company's consistency in addressing performance issues, and can provide irrefutable evidence of your efforts to help the employee change and improve. More often than not, solid documentation deters rather than encourages lawsuits—especially when both manager and employee sign dated copies. This helps protect you and your company against accusations of wrongdoing down the road, when memories have become selective and faded (on all sides). Depending on your company, this could be more than sage advice—it could be corporate policy. Many companies have written guidelines and procedures for managers to follow.

Managers are often reluctant to counsel employees who are in trouble, either because it is emotionally uncomfortable or they simply feel they don't have the time. And it can be both. It's difficult to face another human being and have to say, "You're not doing well." Odds are the employee will be angry, hurt, frustrated, defensive—all powerful emotions. Some managers believe problems will take care of themselves if you just leave them alone. Yes, and sometimes an abscess will heal without antibiotics, too. But it often damages surrounding tissues and leaves a noticeable scar.

So it is with problems you leave to resolve themselves. Other employees become angry, hurt, and frustrated—all those emotions you're trying to avoid—when they see that you're ignoring the distress the problem employee is causing them. Their work begins to suffer, too. They may retaliate by deliberately dragging out timelines, refusing to do anything beyond the minimum required of them, or quitting. Leaving problems to fester poisons the entire work group and can permanently damage the team's cohesiveness and collaborative spirit. Ultimately the situation reflects poorly on you as well; managers stand or fall based on the effectiveness and productivity of their employees.

When Problems Escalate to Disciplinary Action

Most managers hope never to find themselves in the role of disciplinarian. It's uncomfortable for both manager and employee, and nearly always involves other players as well—your superiors, your company's HR department, and sometimes other employees. Disciplinary action is formal notice that the employee's job is on the line.

Writing up an employee for poor performance or other problems on the job is a more serious step than counseling, and in most cases should take place only after counseling has failed to achieve the desired improvements. It is not the same thing as documenting behavior or counseling meetings. In counseling an employee, your objective is to present the elements of job performance that are unsatisfactory and create a plan for improvement; these are corrective actions that demonstrate you're giving the employee a fair chance to change.

In most situations, if you have not counseled the employee, you will find yourself in hot water by moving directly to disciplinary action. There are exceptions, of course—serious mistakes or actions that jeopardize someone's health or well-being could be grounds for jumping to discipline or even immediate termination. (Hopefully your company has policies and procedures that define these actions; if not, work closely with your HR or legal department to respond appropriately.) There could come a point at which you need to suggest the employee find work elsewhere, asking for a voluntary resignation, or to fire the employee. These are drastic steps that require extensive documentation; Chapter 8, "Evaluating Performance," discusses these issues.

FACTS

Many managers are leery of committing adverse performance reports to writing, for fear that what they say will come back to bite them in court. However, attorneys who specialize in employment law generally believe documentation is a company's best safeguard against frivolous lawsuits. Written job descriptions and performance appraisals establish procedural consistency. The paper trail that is likely to cause trouble is the one built solely for the purpose of carrying out a particular action. Documentation should support decisions, not create them.

Handling the Fallout That Affects Other Employees

Phillip came to work one day and dropped a bombshell: He was resigning. He'd had it, he said; what had once been a very pleasant work environment was now a nightmare. He was tired of the complaining and the backstabbing and the lack of cooperation. Jean, Phillip's manager, was stunned. Phillip was the group's most productive member, and without him the department's contact-to-contract conversion ratio would plummet.

As Jean investigated the situation, it became clear that there were two people in the group who were having personal problems that they transferred to the workplace. They seemed bent on ensuring that their coworkers shared in their misery. When asked to pull their parts they refused to cooperate. They went from person to person in the group, complaining about other people, the work, Jean, and the company.

For the most part, it is inappropriate (and often illegal) for you to discuss another employee's difficulties. Even if the work group has become a part of those difficulties, because performance problems affect the entire team, you must keep an employee's difficulties in strict confidence.

Because the team had been functioning smoothly and efficiently, Jean had tuned out of the dynamics of the team. Like some of the team members, she had been lulled into thinking that things were going so well that there was nothing that could go wrong. When things did start going wrong, Jean was oblivious. Other team members could see that she was out of touch, but Jean didn't respond to their hints. By the time Jean realized there was trouble, she was holding a valued employee's resignation letter.

Jean met individually with each of the two problem employees. One agreed to an improvement plan for behavior and performance changes and the other decided to leave the company. Then Jean met with other team members, who finally opened up when they could talk one-on-one. But the damage to the team was irreparable and though it eventually rebuilt and recovered, it never returned to its previous level of cohesiveness.

The problems and performance issues of a coworker often affect other employees, sometimes deeply. No matter how swiftly you might have moved to intervene, they probably think it took too long. And if it did take you a while to catch on to the reality of the situation, other employees are likely frustrated and resentful. How you handle the rest of the work group depends on the nature of the problems.

If this is a big deal—the company lost a major account or other departments became involved—consider a team meeting. One employee's troubles have likely created performance issues for other employees who perhaps couldn't complete their assignments or saw their efforts go to waste. In most cases, it's best to meet without the troubled employee present (although a good idea to let him or her know that the group will be meeting, so there's no sense of exclusion).

As when you met with the employee, plan your direction and comments. Meet in a location where you and the work group can speak candidly and without being overheard. Establish parameters and limits from the start: No bashing, no gossip, nothing leaves the room. Explain that you know about the problems, met with the involved employee, and established an improvement plan that includes measures for follow-up. Then invite the other employees to share their concerns. Keep the conversation focused on processes and outcomes—don't let the focus stray to people and personalities. A certain amount of venting is inevitable, in most situations—just strive to keep the tone from turning belligerent or derogatory. It's important for other employees to believe and understand that you know and care about how the problems have affected them and their work. As much as they might be concerned for their coworker, they also need reassurance that their performance is fine and their jobs are safe. Most people are compassionate and forgiving; if they see that you have responded thoroughly and fairly, the work group will support your efforts. Crisis has the ability to cause groups to pull together or fall apart; if this is a cohesive and well-functioning group, it will rally. If the damage to trust and confidence within the work group is severe, it might take considerable time for the wounds to heal and the group to return to full function.

CHAPTER 7

Communication and Feedback

Most people don't have too much trouble talking. In fact, the trouble is often talking too much. When we think about communication, we think about being able to express ourselves so that others understand both our words and our intentions. Trouble is, most communication actually has little to do with words.

Body Speak: Mixed Messages

Your body is not always your friend when it comes to communication. It has a mind of its own, so to speak—or rather, escapes the influence of your mind, which is busy regulating the words that leave your mouth. So your body is pretty much on its own, and it doesn't always tell the same story as your words. Maybe your eyes wander to the computer screen rather than remaining focused on the person in front of you, your arms cross, and your foot starts to jiggle. Your words say, "You did a great job with the presentation. I've had phone calls from several people saying how much they enjoyed it." But your body's out there on its own, sending very different signals: "Man, is she ever going to leave? There's that e-mail from Sarah I've been waiting for, I have a conference call in ten minutes, and Rob wants that preliminary budget from me by four. And now my stomach's growling!" Meanwhile, there's poor Alice sitting in front of you pouring her angst all over your desk, eager for you to tell her she's doing great, which you are, but not believing you because your body language is sending such different signals than your words. Which message would you heed if you were sitting in Alice's chair?

QUESTIONS?

What is body language?
Body language is the unspoken messages that a person's posture and gestures convey. Crossing your arms, twirling your hair, licking your lips, and slouching are examples of negative body language; shaking hands firmly, making eye contact, sitting up straight, and smiling are examples of positive body language.

We have a tendency to believe that words can lie but the body can't. You can consciously structure and shape the sounds that come from your mouth to convey precisely the message you want someone to hear. We call this conversation: knowing what to say, how to say it, and when to speak. It's a game most adults know how to play, and sadly, play quite well. We become adept at speaking half-truths and little white lies, all told in the name of compassion. And we get so caught up in all of this word play that we fail to notice that our bodies are telling entirely different stories. Body language reflects what we think of as subconscious messages, the content of communication that escapes the intellect's control and manipulation. So we view visual messages as more honest, more revealing of how the speaker really feels. Trouble is, this view is sometimes just as tainted as the words we've come to distrust.

ALERT

Words are only a small percentage of the typical communication process—just 7 percent, in fact. Body language and nonverbal cues account for 55 percent, while 38 percent is the tone of voice. Dialogue that takes place over the telephone is missing over half the content of typical communication!

Gloria was the business manager at a busy medical clinic. Twelve employees reported to her. Gloria really was a warm and generous person, but not many people realized this upon first meeting her. New employees often wondered how it was that she'd gotten a job that required so much interaction with people, since she appeared clearly uncomfortable with them. She stood very rigidly, with her shoulders back and her neck stiff, her arms straight at her sides. Although she smiled when greeting people, she extended her hand slowly as though the action pained her. Her seated posture was no more relaxed; just the angles changed. But when Gloria spoke, she instantly transformed her image. "I'm not as stiff and cold as I look," she usually said in a first meeting, with a voice that was bright and friendly. "It's just these darn rods in my back that keep me from acting like a real human being. But I am one, I assure you!"

Gloria had been in a horrific auto accident when she was a teenager, and her doctors hadn't expected her to ever walk again. With numerous surgeries and indomitable determination, Gloria overcame the odds. But it took continued effort for her to overcome the perceptions of first impressions.

Most people can greatly improve the consistency between their words and their body language by paying more attention to what their bodies are doing when they're speaking.

- Maintain eye contact with the person to whom you're talking. It's okay to look away now and then; you don't want to create the impression that this is a stare-down.
- Closed posture implies a closed mind. Folding your arms across your chest and crossing your legs is a classic defensive posture that delivers the message, "Don't mess with me." Rarely is this a message that's appropriate in the workplace. Let your arms rest on the arms of your chair if you're seated. When standing, many people fold their arms because they don't know what else to do with them; it feels awkward to let them just hang at your sides. Practice standing this way in front of a mirror; it doesn't look as bad as it feels. If you must cross your legs when seated (which is as bad for your circulation as it is for your body language), cross them at the ankles instead of at the knees.
- Sitting across from someone can feel confrontational, especially if you are behind a desk or at a table. Unless there is a reason for you to maintain an image of power (and sometimes there is), sit next to the person instead.
- Don't sigh, play with your hair (including mustache and beard), jewelry, or pens and pencils. Don't practice your origami skills with pieces of paper you find on your desk, or craft paperclip sculptures. Such actions are distracting for the other person as well as for you. Any train of thought is likely to leave without you if you're concentrating on how to transform a memo into a swan.
- Gestures are often space-fillers. Are you waving your hands around to try to paint an air picture of something, or are you having trouble finding the right words? It's usually more effective to use a pencil and paper to sketch out your picture, or to simply pause for a moment to let the right words come to you.
- If you don't usually use gestures, consider adding a little movement to your speech. It's hard to listen to a talking head, no matter how interested you are in the message.

- When you speak, talk at a moderate pace—not too fast, not too slow—and enunciate. Form your words clearly and cleanly.
- Vary the tone and pitch of your voice. Some people drone on in a monotone when speaking formally, either to a group or to an individual, even though their conversational voices are friendly and full of personality. It's as though a little switch in their vocal cords flips and the vocal cords can emit sound on just a single frequency. Unless you're passing out pillows at your meetings, one tone is no good.

ESSENTIALS

One way to practice modulating your voice is to change the outgoing message on your voice mail every day. Strive for a different tone each day, and to sound interested in the caller even though you're not there to take the call.

If you speak frequently in front of groups (including meetings), consider joining a group such as Toastmasters (see Appendix C, "Organizations") to hone your public speaking skills. If you've never had any formal public speaking training, it doesn't hurt to take a workshop or a class. And if these ideas don't appeal to you, try videotaping yourself (be sure anyone else in the room who might also be captured on film has no objections) or talking in front of a mirror.

Listening Between the Lines

The communication cycle is an alternation of talking and listening. The exchanges are sometimes lengthy, sometimes rapid-fire. It's a back-and-forth process, with each participant playing both roles. Too many people view listening as a passive part of this cycle, when in fact it's every bit as much of an activity as talking. The problem is, we tend to spend listening time thinking about what we're going to say next. Or about what to cook for dinner tonight, whether those concert tickets are still available, when the cat's next set of shots is due—anything but focusing on what the other person is saying. You might not really have any interest in what the other person is saying, or could be anxious about making your points when it comes your turn to speak. And it could be your brain's fault—not your mind, but your brain. The brain processes the signals it receives from the sounds that your ears gather and channel to it hundreds of times faster than it can send all the signals necessary to get words to come out of your mouth.

Just as there is more to speaking than the words you utter, there is more to listening than the sounds that enter your ears. Sometimes the real message lies in what's not being said. It's important to listen between the lines to hear the unspoken messages. Pay attention to unspoken signals and nonverbal cues. When an employee says, "Yes, I'd be happy to research that information" but her voice is high-pitched and tense and she crosses her arms across her chest before she speaks, what is she really telling you? That she has enough work already without taking time-consuming assignments, that she's cold and wishes she'd brought her sweater to the meeting, that she can't stand the database librarian she'll have to contact to request the information? You can't know without asking further questions, but you should know there's more to the answer than the spoken words.

Effective listening is an activity that requires your full and focused attention:

- Engage your mind to slow down your brain. Let it hear every word as if it were a delightful chocolate that you want to savor until it melts away, letting every molecule of flavor seep into your senses.
- Beware of the familiarity trap. As soon as the words begin to sound familiar, the search for new information ends. "I've heard this before!" your mind says, and it turns its attention elsewhere. Bring it back! Most listening mistakes occur when you assume something that isn't so.
- Don't cross the line from anticipation to assumption. Anticipating someone's response or next question often helps you shape your end of the communication. But there's a fine line between anticipating and assuming, and assuming will almost always get you in trouble.

- Maintain and keep eye contact, just as when you're speaking. This shows that you're listening and demonstrates your sincerity. It also helps you pick up on nonverbal cues.
- Don't formulate your response or mentally argue while the person is still speaking. You can't be listening to someone else if you're busy listening to yourself.

Listening effectively doesn't mean you have to let conversations roam where they will. You can, and often should, shape the direction of dialogue (at least in a business context). Use natural pauses to ask questions or make comments that redirect the conversation back to its intended purpose. Learn when to set aside that kindergarten rule you've so completely assimilated so you can interrupt smoothly and effectively. Ask structured, open-ended questions to frame the subject yet allow the person to respond freely: "What happened when you opened the box and discovered that all the templates were reversed?"

Daily Interactions with Your Employees

It's amazing how many managers don't interact with their employees any more than they have to. This creates discomfort on both sides. Some of this stems from the way American businesses select managers: Those who excel in the skills of their jobs receive promotions to reward them for their abilities. The result is often managers who are not really people-people. They're skills-people. They're really great as accountants, programmers, sales representatives, production workers, and so on who have done so well in their jobs that they've been promoted to management positions. As satisfying as they find it to be moving up the corporate food chain, they're still uncomfortable—sometimes with being in authority and often with the social expectations that come with the turf. Coming into management on the wave of performance and productivity, many managers get caught up in their own day-to-day responsibilities. They remain focused on doing a good job, failing to recognize that now means helping everyone else do a good job, too. Bureaucracy, paperwork, and managing upwards (office politics) also take their toll, consuming more time and effort than managers and employees feel is reasonable.

Employees need you to stop around every morning (or at the beginning of the shift) and say hello. When you don't, they may assume something is wrong or may feel ignored. And when you don't interact with your employees, you begin to assume that they think and act in certain ways. From these assumptions, you draw conclusions that they are doing, or not doing, certain things. Nature abhors a vacuum. When we don't have information, we make it up. This is true for managers and employees alike.

Consistent daily interaction promotes more than just good feelings; it also promotes effective and collaborative teamwork. When the manager takes a few moments to chat, employees feel better about coming to work and about doing the work expected of them. Small talk matters. When you stop to ask employees what they did over the weekend, how things are going with the kids, or to mention a good movie you saw or your adventures with your new lawnmower, employees feel that you care about them as people and as individuals, not just as cogs in the corporate machine. Not that we need to drag all of our personal problems into work, of course. But we do need to at least remind each other that we are human and have lives outside of work. This is what helps to create bonds.

Is small talk hard for you? That's okay. Communication is a craft each of us must learn. Although the ability to talk seems natural enough, circumstances that require structured dialogue can make otherwise competent adults sputter incoherently. So consider small talk just one of the new skills you must learn to excel at your job as a manager. Each day, make it a point to:

- Stop by each employee's office, cubicle, desk, or work area and greet the employee by name. Use the name that the person uses when contacting you. If the employee's name is Michael, his coworkers call him Mike, and his wife calls him Mitch but he says, "this is Michael" when he calls you, then call him Michael. Or better yet, ask him what he prefers that you call him. Names often reflect a level of trust and equity; jumping to an informal variation (or using a formal variation when others don't) might make the employee uncomfortable.

- Ask each employee one question related to a personal interest. Yes, this might require you to do a little research. Careful listening can help you to build a mental "information file" about each employee. The general question, "How was your weekend?" can elicit an astonishing breadth and depth of information.

- Ask each employee one work-related question. If this is new behavior for you, at first employees might react with suspicion, thinking you're checking up on them (which you are, in a sense) or that something is wrong (which probably isn't). As employees realize that this is now part of your daily routine, they'll warm up. The first sign of progress is when they start telling you about things that are going wrong; you know you're in your groove when they start telling you about things that are going right.

FACTS

In most job settings today, people within one or two corporate levels of each other use first names when talking with or about each other. In some situations, protocol requires using professional or courtesy titles: Dr. Drake, Mr. Johnson, Ms. Hernandez, Sgt. Hamilton, Officer Michaels. Sometimes employees use these titles only in public or when customers are present; in other settings, they use them all the time.

Lewis had toiled long and hard as a computer programmer before his superiors finally took notice and promoted him to manager. The promotion was long overdue, Lewis felt, and he threw himself into his vision of a manager with great zeal. He felt important, and he acted important. Most of the time, he rushed around looking important. Now that he had a real office, he closed the door whenever he was in it. Not sure whether they should knock or just walk in, employees took to waiting for Lewis to emerge—which he did mostly when he needed something or to grandstand about his latest accomplishment (which always happened solely because of his extraordinary abilities, not because of any contributions from the department). When Lewis communicated at all with employees, it was through e-mail or Post-It notes left on their computer screens.

Lewis's behavior turned out to be self-sabotage. With no human bond to him, people in the group short-circuited him. They didn't rally around projects. They did what they had to do and nothing more. They made it clear to upper management and to Lewis's counterparts that they really had minimal interaction with Lewis. Ultimately upper management restructured department lines, which eliminated Lewis's department and job. While Lewis's employees received transfers to other jobs within the company, Lewis got a severance package.

You might get to be a manager because you are a brilliant performer (or a great politician), but what keeps you a manager is how well you rally your troops and keep them performing. It's easy to come into work and go right to e-mail, checking on the status of ongoing projects and plunging into the day's workload. You could end up going the entire day without talking to the employees you manage, even though they surround you. You could . . . but if you want to stay a manager, you can't. Instead, make it a point to go from office to office, cubicle to cubicle, workstation to workstation to make contact with your employees. Don't miss anyone; if you do, people will begin to feel slighted and left out, or that something is wrong. If someone's not there for your rounds, catch him or her later in the day to make contact, however briefly.

Be present without being intrusive. Ask questions, and listen to the answers. Walk around and just listen to employees talk as they work. Don't sneak around—you want people to know that you're there and you're interested. But don't hover, either; you don't want people to feel you don't trust them to do their jobs without constant supervision. You can't know what's going on if you're not there—and if you're not there, people will attempt to resolve problems in their own ways.

Creative Computer Corporation's 600 employees worked on multiple floors in an office complex. Yet everyone knew what kind of mood the CEO was in every day. If he walked around and stopped to talk with department managers, employees knew that the stock market was at least stable and product was moving smoothly through the production and distribution loops. If the CEO stayed in his office all day, only coming out to snap at his secretary, then employees knew something was wrong. The market was down, beta testing revealed an unexpected bug, or focus groups didn't like R&D's latest brainchild. Because almost everyone had stock options, employees feared the CEO's mood affected them directly— and this turned out to be true more often than not. Employees are highly sensitive to routine, and to changes in it. They learn very quickly to read the moods of their managers, and to shape their own moods accordingly. One person's moods can set the stage for a department or even an entire company.

FACTS

In a 1990s study of the reasons people file lawsuits against their doctors for malpractice, not one of the top ten had anything to do with the technical quality of care doctors provided. As often as not, the medical care itself was appropriate; the patient either experienced complications known to be risks or didn't get the result expected. Overwhelmingly, however, survey respondents felt their doctors didn't listen to them and didn't care about them.

Open Doors and Two-Way Streets

When Mark became manager of the assembly group, he established what he believed was an effective open-door policy. He would see any employee about any matter—as long as the employee scheduled an appointment through his secretary and could provide evidence that he or she had tried to resolve the concern through what Mark called "first-level intervention." If the problem was about taking leave time, for example, the employee first needed to talk with the other employee who had already scheduled time off to see if the two of them could negotiate a compromise or with HR if the issue was policy- or benefits-related.

At first, employees welcomed Mark's approach. The group's previous manager only talked to people who were in some sort of trouble, and kept group meetings focused on discussions of work tasks. In contrast, Mark seemed amazingly open. Within the first few months, every employee had scheduled an appointment to talk with Mark. While he was friendly enough in these one-on-one meetings, he kept them just as focused as the previous manager had kept group meetings. When an employee came to Mark's office for a scheduled appointment, Mark expected the employee to present a one- to three-minute summary of the problem and the steps the employee had taken to attempt to resolve it. He had little interest in casual conversation, and no interest in matters that weren't directly related to work processes or results.

When problems arose that employees felt needed immediate intervention, Mark was again friendly but firm: He was happy to do what he could to help, but please schedule an appointment. Not surprisingly, appointments soon dropped off. Mark interpreted this as an indication that the group had finally come together as a smoothly functioning team capable of troubleshooting and problem-solving on its own. But the employees grew increasingly dissatisfied. At least their previous manager had made it unmistakably clear that she had no interest in them and their problems. Mark gave all the appearances of being interested, but in the end was no more so than the previous manager. Requiring appointments to see Mark meant that his "open" door was shut tight to employees unless their needs fit into Mark's schedule. Although Mark believed he was available, his rules and procedures made him inaccessible.

ALERT

People don't just drop their personal lives at the door when they come to work each day. You don't; why would you expect your employees to? Fighting with kids or spouses, traffic hassles, and other irritations may not be directly work related, but they can affect work in a big way.

Managers set the tone for their work groups or departments. Employees need to know that they really can come to you whenever they feel they need to, not just when you determine it's appropriate for them to do so. Of course, this means that you'll find yourself listening to personal problems, family matters, and petty disagreements. But that's all part of being a manager—that parent hat gets a lot of wear.

The open door is both literal and symbolic. If you tell employees they can come to talk with you any time but you work with your door closed, you are sending a mixed message. Most people see closed doors as stop signs. From childhood, we're trained that we don't enter without knocking, and we often hesitate to knock unless the need to talk to the person on the other side can't wait. Sometimes managers close doors out of habit or to block distractions. But are you blocking distractions for you or for others who might see or hear what you're doing? And what constitutes a distraction? Conversation? People walking past? The noises of a busy work group? Ringing telephones? An employee's question? It's difficult to define clear guidelines. Even if you truly want people to just open the door and come in, many will be reluctant to do so. Unless you're working on something that requires privacy, leave your door open. The only way people know you have an open door policy is if your door truly is open.

Productive Meetings

What comes to mind when you think of meetings? Don't feel bad . . . most people can't really express their thoughts out loud, either. Most people will say emphatically that they are not meeting-people, yet the leading complaint in most organizations is that there are too many meetings. What gives? Meetings aren't really inherently evil gatherings that suck the energy and ambition from even the most dedicated employees, although they often seem so. It's just that many meetings are either unnecessary or include people who don't need to be there.

At Acme Industries, there were so many meetings that departments seemed to do nothing else; many employees went from one meeting to another without ever making it to their desks. When someone in marketing wanted to talk with someone in purchasing, odds were that purchasing was having a meeting. When the purchasing clerk called back, the marketing department was having a meeting. And so it went, through the day and from day to day.

The purchasing department met daily at 10 A.M., ostensibly to address back orders and other product delivery issues before they became major problems. Everyone except the receptionist was required to attend these standing meetings, which generally lasted two hours or more. Often, the topics under discussion applied to only two or three employees, yet the entire department had to sit there and listen to what equally often degenerated into petty squabbling. Everyone hated it.

The marketing department met every day at 1 P.M. to brainstorm new ideas and update progress on existing projects. Marketing staff felt they were a great team, and looked forward to their standing meetings as a demonstration of just how much of a team they were. There was a lot of conversation and camaraderie, and no dimension of any idea or project escaped examination . . . and re-examination and cross-examination and further examination. What didn't get enough coverage in the regular meeting went to one of the many committees, subcommittees, and study teams. People often showed up late because their committee, subcommittee, or study team meetings ran over. So the group paused to bring latecomers up to speed. The daily team meeting was scheduled to run two hours, but usually ended only when people ran out of things to talk about. Marketing employees frequently stayed in the office until late at night and came to work even before the cafeteria's coffee counter opened.

FACTS

The administrative department at a large corporation resolved the problem of having daily staff meetings drag on and on by holding true standing meetings in which participants actually stood up for the duration of the meeting. Meetings were scheduled for fifteen minutes. If you showed up late you could only listen, you couldn't speak or otherwise participate. Discussions were brief and decisions were prompt.

Not surprisingly, turnover in both departments was high. People in purchasing grew bored and frustrated. People in marketing burned out. So the managers scheduled more meetings to try to get a handle on what was making people so unhappy. Talk about clueless! Too many meetings both annoy and spoil employees. Meetings eat time, and give employees the impression that they have a voice in everything. If your employees really do, then provide structured, efficient ways for them to share their opinions and suggestions. If they really don't have much voice in department or company decisions, then giving them the illusion that they do will become clear and there will be a lot of negative reverberation.

Managers who can't conduct efficient meetings probably can't manage very effectively, either. A meeting is a showcase for a manager's behavior and leadership skills—and employees watch the performance very closely. Seeing is believing, and perception is reality. When you act like a manager, like a leader, your employees will perceive you as a manager and a leader. Meetings give you an opportunity to establish your leadership role, and following the rules for leading an effective meeting can help establish your leadership image. Meetings can be interesting, useful, and productive. Making them so is within your reach—and is in fact your responsibility.

A good number of meetings are nothing more than time-wasters because they have no reason to exist. If there is no clear reason for a meeting, don't schedule one. Before scheduling a meeting, determine why you need a meeting and who should be there:

- Write down what you expect the meeting to accomplish. Focus on specific, tangible outcomes: to determine who will handle what stage of a project; to present new guidelines for using the company's Internet access; to solicit suggestions about how to accommodate an anticipated supply shortage.
- Make a list of the people who need to be at the meeting, and write down what contribution you expect each person to make. If you can't identify a specific contribution, scratch the person from your list. The only people who should be at a meeting are those who have a specific reason for being there. For those who only need to know the meeting's outcome, use a follow-up telephone call, memo, or e-mail.
- Ask yourself if you could accomplish your desired outcomes without a meeting. Is it important for each employee the topic affects to participate in discussions that relate to the other's involvement? Could you talk with one or two employees in your office or theirs, or convey information by memo or e-mail?

Although many meetings are unnecessary, a meeting can be an effective means of communication for various reasons. If two or more people need to know the same information, it makes sense to get them together so you need to present the information just once. If two or more people need to know different pieces of information about the same topic it might make sense to bring them together—or it might be more effective to speak to each one separately. And if two or more people need to know different information about different topics, it's seldom efficient or effective to bring them together. They'll certainly tune out on topics that don't pertain to them, and could well be so out of contact by the time the information does relate to them that they don't pay attention then, either.

ESSENTIALS

Consider having a different team member chair each weekly department meeting. The week's chairperson can prepare the meeting's agenda and then lead the meeting. This provides good experience for team members, and bolsters the team's collaborative spirit by strengthening the knowledge each member has about other employees' projects and assignments.

Deciding whom to include at a meeting should be as simple as determining who needs the information or to participate and who doesn't based on job tasks and responsibilities. Often, of course, other factors come into play. Call it politics, call it personalities, call it whatever you like—but all managers sometimes feel compelled to include employees who really don't need to be there. Sometimes this is a worthwhile means of preserving the peace and encouraging a sense of teamwork. If all of a department's employees routinely attend meetings with the same one or two employees excepted, there are bound to be hurt feelings. Those employees will feel left out not only of meetings but also of the team and its work. Depending on the personalities involved, you can talk with the few people who don't need to attend meetings everyone else does to explain the reasons and get a sense for how they feel about it. Or you might just decide to include them so they don't feel left out. Sometimes arbitrary factors determine who attends a meeting and who doesn't. These factors might include the meeting's location or time, the size of the meeting room, and other logistical issues.

If your preliminary assessment shows that a meeting is indeed necessary:

- Create an agenda for the meeting. Start with the tangible outcomes you identified, then outline the steps the meeting needs to take to accomplish those outcomes and the amount of time each step should reasonably take. The agenda should include the meeting's location, start time, and finish time.
- Distribute copies of the agenda to the employees who will be attending, and ask them to arrive at the meeting prepared to participate. Include the names of all participants, so everyone attending knows who else will be there.
- When it's time for the meeting, it's time to add a new hat to your collection: that of benevolent dictator. Use the powers vested in you by this hat to start the meeting promptly at the scheduled time, keep it on track with its agenda, and end it at the scheduled time. Most of the time this is your meeting, so you are in charge.

Paul was a nice-guy manager who liked for all of his employees to feel that their contributions mattered—in meetings, to the department, and to the company. At one meeting the discussion turned to the new comp time guidelines, a topic Paul knew was a done deal that upper management would simply implement once the finishing touches were in place. He let the group follow a path he knew was a dead-end. Two months later when the company implemented the guidelines, Paul's employees were angry that the new policy incorporated none of their suggestions. Paul could have averted problems had he handled the meeting differently. He could have said the policy was in its final development stages and any discussion would be more appropriate when it was finished. Or he could have said that although he didn't have any authority to offer suggestions, he was interested in knowing what his employees thought.

As the manager, it's your role to establish clear boundaries and expectations for the meeting. If you have decision-making authority, let employees know what they might influence and what is set in stone. Let employees know what kinds of information and feedback you want to hear. Don't set expectations you can't meet; it damages your credibility. Some managers don't like to give any appearance that their power has any limits. Don't delude yourself. Your employees know exactly where the boundaries of your authority are, even if you're not sure yourself.

If the discussion strays during the meeting, firmly but politely redirect it to the topics on the agenda. This is sometimes easier said than done, and there are many techniques to handle the task smoothly and professionally. (There are numerous workshops and books about conducting effective meetings that present these techniques; Appendix B, "Resources," provides more information.) The most important thing is to respect, and show respect, for the opinions of employees even though the meeting is not the appropriate forum for expressing them. Sometimes you can offer to set up another meeting, or to meet with smaller groups of employees to discuss their concerns. Sometimes further discussion would be fruitless, as it was with Paul and the comp time guidelines, in which case you need to just say so.

Acknowledge group members who attend the meeting, and offer everyone a chance to speak. If a few employees begin to dominate the meeting, intercede to call on silent employees. Pull out your parent hat for a few minutes and let the group know that all members have something to contribute, and all ideas are valid and worth expressing. If an employee is taking a beating in terms of being barraged with questions or criticisms, step in to put an end to it. This is a meeting, not an inquisition. If employees see that those who stick out their necks end up getting their heads chopped off, they're not likely to be willing to speak up themselves, even when the topic concerns them. There is a balance between open dialogue and abuse, and it's your role to maintain it and to protect employees who present unpopular perspectives or information. Likewise, if the group keeps circling for another round of discussion or commentary on a particular topic, pronounce it dead and move on.

Ten minutes or so before the meeting is scheduled to end, it's time to summarize the meeting. If it was an educational meeting, recap the key learning points. If the meeting was to disseminate information, review the essential messages. If further action needs to happen, decide who will be responsible for what tasks. Make assignments, if necessary, and establish timelines and a process for following up. If bringing events to conclusion will require another meeting with the same group, schedule it before breaking up or at least let people know to expect that a follow-up meeting will be scheduled.

How you conduct meetings provides insights into you as a manager as well as into your company's values and operations. Companies in which meetings run rampant and structure is lacking have little sense of direction. Companies with strong strategic plans also have strong strategies for running meetings as well as other operational functions.

In many organizations, starting meetings late is the norm. Sometimes this practice becomes so much a part of the corporate culture that it spills over into other functions. Employees show up late for meetings with other departments, vendors, and even customers. The resulting hard feelings generate indifference and eventually lost business.

Shaping Interactions Among Employees

Meetings are one way managers model the behavior that they want to see in their department. Employees watch the way managers treat them and others, whom they acknowledge and how they acknowledge them. They watch how new ideas are accepted or cut off, and whether one person is told to run with something or whether feedback loops are set up.

Employees figure if the manager acts a certain way, then that is acceptable if not expected behavior. Victoria, the director of a small company, was unpredictable and often abusive. When she was being kind, she could make a criticism sound like a compliment. The rest of the time, she was monstrous. She berated vendors over the telephone in conference calls for not understanding, or not carrying out, her explicit directions. And while she told her employees that she valued their contributions and encouraged their collaboration and teamwork, she was just as quick to lash out at one employee in front of the others or trash-talk one employee to another. No one worried about trying to stay on her good side because she really didn't have one.

Victoria crunched through assistants like they were popcorn at the movies. Few of them outlasted the company's ninety-day probationary period; the record belonged to one young man who walked out at lunchtime on his first day. Finding herself once again between assistants, Victoria hired a young and very talented woman, Amanda. This was Amanda's first job, and she was eager to do well. She was a quick learner, and it wasn't long before she picked up Victoria's nasty ways. When Victoria wasn't in, Amanda stepped in to deliver abuse. The problem was, Amanda didn't have Victoria's experience. At least Victoria's rude comments made sense; Amanda's did not. It was more than many team members felt they should have to put up with, but to whom were they going to complain? They left, in twos and threes. Eventually Amanda tired of working in a job that garnered her no respect, so she left, too (and no doubt ended up as a manager somewhere). Victoria did a terrible job of shaping behavior.

Clarence was just the opposite. He was always respectful and collaborative. He consistently asked employees for their comments and suggestions, in meetings and throughout the workday. He treated vendors like the company's very existence depended on them. Whenever upper management made a decision that Clarence had been unable to influence or that was out of the department's hands, he let everyone know. Then he helped them strategize on how to live with it. If there was a project to be done, Clarence brought people together for the first meeting. He again solicited their ideas. He then identified team members and roles, and how each would contribute and why. Clarence set milestones, making sure each person was able to identify hurdles and concerns. And he helped the department set up a review process to make sure work that needed approval or input from other employees received it.

This structure-by-example provided employees with an institutionalized model for how to behave with each other. As new situations arose, employees knew in general how to behave and respond. Everyone knew, and followed, the standard of behavior in the department. The example Clarence set made people want to be like him.

The Feedback Loop

Feedback is a sort of buzzword that has different meanings in various contexts. In electronics, it is undesirable sound distortion. In the workplace, it is one person giving another person a reaction or response—that sometimes sounds like the annoying whines and screeches we associate with electronic feedback. In communication, all too often feedback becomes synonymous with criticism. When a manager says, "I have some feedback for you," employees often hear, "Let me tell you how you screwed up—again!"

Under ideal circumstances feedback is a loop, a cycle of action and reaction. Neither needs to be big or significant. In fact, when feedback becomes a communication loop, most people don't notice that it's even taking place. It's when feedback is lacking, negative, or devastating that it garners any attention. Of course not all feedback is positive, and sometimes it is downright devastating. But feedback exists along an entire continuum, and most of it should fall somewhere in the center.

Employees always want to know how their managers view them and their work. It's human nature; we are creatures of response. We want to know what others think of us. It helps us to develop a sense of belonging (or not), accomplishment (or not), and confidence (or not). People constantly seek feedback from their managers. Some ask for it directly: "How did I do?" Others are less direct: "What did the client say?" Although conventional wisdom preaches that no news is good news, in the corporate world the reverse is more often the case. Or at least that's what employees think, as they fret and worry because they haven't heard anything from you.

Some feedback should take place in public, such as in a meeting. Take a few minutes to acknowledge an employee who has done an exceptional job. This makes the employee feel good; recognition in front of peers is the highest compliment. It also solidifies roles and responsibilities, and shapes interaction within the group. People feel affirmed in their contribution. Fairness and appropriateness are critical, of course; it's important that you avoid giving the impression of playing favorites. Public praise can backfire if it makes employees whose contributions are less stellar feel less significant. Private feedback also has its place. Stop by an employee's workstation to offer congratulations on a report well written or a project completed ahead of schedule. This individual attention shows that you notice and care about individual effort.

When providing feedback, be concrete. Cite specific, tangible examples:

- "More orders have come in for that new gizmo you designed than for any new product we've debuted."
- "I saw how you calmed that angry woman by getting her out of the waiting room and into your office where she could regain her composure."
- "Josephine Hall is a major client, and your follow-up call caught an error in her order before she noticed it. She called me to say how courteous and professional you were over the phone. She received the corrected order by next-day delivery, which averted a potential crisis."

ESSENTIALS To balance the limited time you have available with an employee's high level of need for feedback, try breaking your comments into smaller bites. Instead of waiting until an assignment is completed to congratulate the employee on a job well done, offer compliments and suggestions along the way.

Work styles come into play here as well. Some (as Chapter 5, "Work Styles," discusses) require constant direction, feedback, and redirection. Others are better left to a general framework within which the employee is free to structure the job's tasks, flow, and progress measures. Consider how each employee works most productively, then shape your feedback to be appropriate within the context of the employee's work style.

Sometimes the employee's work style is the primary factor in performance and production matters. People sometimes have trouble finding their bearings. New employees and seasoned employees for whom these job responsibilities depart from previous experience might be struggling to find a good match between work style and assignments. The feedback you provide can include suggestions for trying different approaches to help the employee find ways to achieve better outcomes. Consider this an incremental process; no one makes major changes overnight. If you see a pattern emerging, divvy up your feedback to cover one facet at a time. If the issue is time management, you might cover establishing timelines this week and prioritizing next week. This is a work in progress, and results won't necessarily be consistent. But be patient. This is the most important kind of shaping, and it's well worth the effort and time you put into it.

Look again at your work style and make sure that feedback is relevant to the employee and how he or she works, not a comparison or criticism because the employee's work style differs from yours. You might like clear expectations and then a wide path to get the work done, without your superiors checking in with you all the time and people telling you what a good job you're doing. And that's fine—it works for you. But it's easy to assume all people are the same way or should be the same way, particularly if you have some employees who are like you in terms of work style. Being among people who share your characteristics reinforces your attitudes and behaviors.

Your perspective and work style might set you up to think that employees who need a lot of feedback are just brown-nosing to stay in good with the boss. Although of course office politics come into play with all people (even you) at times, there's a strong likelihood that these employees are just people who need the sense of structure constant feedback provides. For such people, the manager is the one who defines the work group and its functions, and thus is the most logical choice to go to for feedback. After all, you set the standards, and ultimately it's you who must be satisfied with the results.

Some tips for giving feedback include:

- Comment on specific actions and behaviors. "Barb was very upset that you yelled at her about the delay at the print shop, and that you hung up on her" works better than "Johnson, you're an insensitive boor!"
- Whenever practical, give feedback that is specific yet offers choices. "In reading this report, I didn't get a sense for what the product actually is. Would you please restructure the introduction or add another section to part two?"
- Look for ways to frame less-than-positive feedback in the context of realistic improvement. This is not about sugarcoating; most people resent attempts to cloak bad news in the trappings of compliments. "Customer complaints about delivery delays are up 35 percent this quarter. Let's take a look at the reasons for the delays and then brainstorm some solutions."

As much as possible, praise the entire work group for its collective efforts. This reinforces the team's value and reminds people that teamwork is about performance, not about personalities or stroking egos. Some managers want to be good guys so they give only positive feedback, and this at the drop of a hat. It doesn't take long for employees to figure out that praise is always forthcoming, which diminishes its value. And when feedback that was initially positive is followed by a contradictory message, then the feedback becomes even less valuable. If the news is bad, just deliver it. These people are adults; they know, even if you attempt to hide it from them, that they make mistakes and that life is not all roses and chocolate. When less-than-positive feedback involves just one or two people, deliver it individually and in private. When the message is for the entire group, be direct but compassionate. Don't single out individuals in the group setting; if you have additional specific comments, deliver them in private.

Resolving Conflict

Sometimes differences collide. Each person feels strongly about his or her perspective, and the situation lands in your lap. It's time to pull out your mediator hat and put your communication skills to work negotiating solutions all parties accept and respect. Effective negotiation requires both sides to come to the table with:

- **A common allegiance.** Working toward common goals establishes a connection defined by similarities, not differences. If nothing else, both sides work for the same company and should support the company's goals, which gives them a common mission. When both sides want to achieve the same outcomes, they're often more willing to search for common ground.
- **Mutual respect.** Despite their differences, do the parties respect each other? If so, they will be able to focus on process-oriented solutions and to separate themselves from their disagreement. Respect is the foundation for trust; people must respect each other before they can trust one another to fulfill the agreements they reach.
- **Open minds.** Each party must be willing to both talk and listen, so that together they can explore possible solutions.
- **Willingness to change.** Obviously each party comes to the meeting believing its perspective is valid and correct. After listening to each other and discussing the problems, all parties must be willing to change their positions to accommodate suggested solutions.

Reaching an agreement to resolve a conflict doesn't necessarily mean that each side gets what it wants. Sometimes solutions are collaborative (all parties gain) and sometimes they involve compromise (all parties give up something). Each party must feel satisfied with the solution, or the conflict remains.

When Tempers Flare

People lose it sometimes. Little things add up, tensions and frustrations build. People feel powerless to control or change situations that they believe should be different but exist because you (or someone else or another department or the company) intentionally created the circumstances. Whether or not there is truth to this perception doesn't matter; perceptions are reality as viewed through the ever-changing hues of emotions. Anger is an unmistakable sign that a person has exceeded his or her tolerance for a situation or behavior. It is an intense and powerful blend of emotion and action, which often frightens even the person who is angry. And anger tends to feed on itself; the longer the shouting continues, the more volatile the anger becomes. It's important to defuse anger quickly:

- **Intercede.** Often, just the fact that you become involved is enough interrupt the cycle and start turning things around. You represent a fresh start; there is no pattern of behavior the person feels compelled to continue with you. Even if someone comes storming into your office, there's usually a trail of angry words behind. History shapes the future at all levels; the ability to start over with you lessens the pull of past behavior (however immediate that past is) and to break off on a new path.

- **Remove the audience.** Most people don't spout off in anger if there's no one there to witness the power of their fury. If an employee is yelling and otherwise going off in front of other employees, get him or her into an office or conference room, or ask the other employees to leave for a few minutes. Someone who loses control in front of others feels compelled to maintain or escalate angry behaviors. Paradoxically, this loss feels like a gain to the angry person, who at least for the moment has the false sense of being in control because he or she has everyone's undivided attention. Removing the audience gives the angry person the freedom to back down without losing face and to regain composure.

- **Separate the behavior from the person, and request that the behavior change immediately.** "I want to help you work this out, but first you need to stop yelling." Look away from the person to give him or her a few moments to pull back together, but stay in the room (unless you fear for your safety). This conveys your sense of respect for the person as a human being and your confidence in his or her ability to regain control. By staying in the room, you make it clear that you're willing to do what you can to work things out and also cut short any approach to use anger as a manipulative behavior (more on this a little later in this chapter).

- **Be an active listener.** Let the person fully explain his or her position and frustration, even if you think you already know what the problem is or have heard it before. Ask questions only to clarify details, until the full story is out.

- **Ask what solutions the employee would like to see.** If one or more of the employee's suggestions make sense, discuss with the employee how best to implement changes. "It makes sense to stagger lunch breaks so there are always two people to answer the phones. How do you suggest we decide which people go to lunch at what times?" If the suggestions don't make sense, provide a brief and factual explanation and offer an alternative. "I can see your point about phone coverage during lunch. Assigning lunch breaks is not very practical for our work group since so many people coordinate lunch with seeing clients. What we might do instead is contract with a temp agency to provide two people for phone coverage between 11 A.M. and 2 P.M. Do you think that would solve the problem?"

- **Reiterate any agreements, and establish a plan to follow up.** "I'll schedule a department meeting for Thursday afternoon. You prepare a sample assignment schedule, and we'll present it. Then we'll meet again in two weeks to see how it's working." This formalizes the discussion so the employee knows the discussion was more than just blowing off steam.

FACTS

Childhood bullies often grow up to become workplace bullies. They constantly belittle and criticize others, often targeting one or two people who are particularly intimidated by such behaviors. The workplace bully becomes an especially dangerous individual when he or she is a manager. An increasing number of people leave jobs they love because of bully bosses at a huge expense to companies that must continually recruit needed talent.

If you have any reason to believe an angry employee could hurt you, other employees, or him- or herself, get help. In many cases, this means calling the police. Anger that turns to violence is no longer about anger and is no longer a resolvable situation. Never go into a room alone with someone you fear could hurt you. An increasing number companies have policies for dealing with potentially violent situations; the appendices provide additional resources for addressing workplace violence.

Managing Manipulation

Manipulation is an extreme on the communication continuum. To some degree, we might even consider communication to be a form of manipulation. People listen to each other to identify certain kinds of information, then respond to shape certain kinds of outcomes. While we view communication as a two-way process to meet the needs of each participant, we tend to associate manipulation with unfair tactics targeted toward satisfying the needs of one party without regard for the needs of others. Manipulation can be subtle or overt, and some manipulations are less offensive than others. While it might be mildly annoying to have a coworker invite you to coffee and then have no money when it's his or her turn to order, it disrupts a work group's productivity when a person wiggles out of assignments.

Most manipulators learn their behavior patterns early in life, and receive reinforcement each time they use them with success. They tend to shift into manipulator mode when conventional efforts fail to produce the desired results. Manipulative behaviors target people rather than processes and present generalities rather than specifics. They may include threats, demands, insults, and efforts to make you feel guilty. "I've worked too hard for too long to let you get away with giving me a mediocre performance appraisal. I'm here before anyone else arrives and I leave after everyone else is gone. How can you possibly know what I do all day? You're never here! If you don't give me a better rating, I'll quit!"

These techniques can help you deal with manipulative people:

- Give the person a fair opportunity to present a specific concern or complaint. Always, never, everyone, no one—these are all terms of generality. If you can't put a finger on it, you can't do much to fix it.
- Separate the facts of the concern from emotions and intent, so you can examine them in context.
- Keep your emotional responses in check. If the employee is in tears, hand over a tissue box—without comment. If the employee is yelling, wait for the noise to stop and then speak softly so the person must remain quiet to hear you. If the employee is using an audience of other employees for support, ask the employee to come to your office or give the other employees a coffee break.
- Break issues down into manageable components. Through all of time, armies have used this "divide and conquer" tactic with great success, and it will work for you, too. And if you can engage the employee in the process of identifying components, suddenly the two of you are on the same side.
- If your efforts to focus on processes and solutions fail to influence the employee's behavior, summarize your response in a single sentence and repeat it each time the employee broaches a new tactic. Keep the tone of your voice even, firm, and friendly—which isn't easy because master manipulators will see what you're doing and try to break your resolve. Think of a broken record: The tone and the message just replay and replay.
- Occasionally it's necessary to simply disengage. Again, keep your voice even, friendly, and firm, but tell the employee it's time for both of you to move on to more productive activities. If the employee refuses to leave your office, walk out yourself. The employee will likely storm out in a few minutes; manipulation, like anger, can't exist without an audience.

Anger can become a tool of manipulation as well. Most of us find anger so uncomfortable to be around that we'll do just about anything to put an end to it. Manipulators know this; anger often becomes a staple in their behavior arsenals. Like other manipulative behaviors, anger works only as long as other people let it.

Would You Put That in Writing?

No discussion of communication is complete without mentioning the importance of effective writing skills. Everyone, no matter what position or level in the company, at some point has a need to commit comments to paper. You might need to write a memo, a report, or a performance appraisal. What you say matters; how you say it can matter more. Although writing is a life skill, not just a job skill, many people turn into babbling bureaucrats when they write. There's no reason for business writing to be any more convoluted than talking. In fact, it can be easier to write because you focus just on your presentation. In fact, it's as easy as three steps that you can view as your AIM:

1. **Audience.** Who will read your message?
2. **Intent.** Why are you writing?
3. **Message.** What do you have to say?

Make separate lists to answer each of these three questions. Then use your lists like an outline and begin writing. Write as though your audience is sitting in front of you and you are talking to them. Hold the slang, but stay conversational. Write enough content (your message) to cover your intent—no more. Be sure the vocabulary you choose is appropriate for your audience; steer clear of jargon. When you're finished writing, save your file or set your paper aside. Go get a drink of water, take a short walk, talk to one of your employees. When you return to your desk, read your writing aloud. Are there places where you stumble? Something's not quite right there; choose a different word or rephrase the section. Compare what you'd say in person to what you've written. Keep at it until you can read your writing aloud without pausing or faltering.

Don't let the process of writing intimidate you. It's just another form of communication. Keep these three points in mind as you write:

• You don't have to start at the beginning. The best way to begin writing is to start with what's on your mind. You can rearrange your blocks of words after you get them down on paper (or on screen). Word processing programs and computers make this very easy. Often one idea flows into the next once you get started, leading you through all of what you want to say.

- Nobody gets it just right the first time. Writing is a process of editing and revision. If you don't like the way something sounds, change it.
- Make sure every sentence contributes to your intent and message in a way that is relevant to your audience. The myriad details of last month's focus group might fascinate you, but the employees receiving your report just need to know what problems exist and what suggestions there are for remedying them.

ESSENTIALS Consider this advice from *The Elements of Style*, a staple on writers' bookshelves: "A sentence should contain no unnecessary words, a paragraph no unnecessary sentences . . . This requires not that the writer make all his sentences short, or that he avoid all detail and treat his subjects only in outline, but that every word tell."

Ironically, it's the proliferation of electronic communication that most graphically illustrates the need to address writing skills. How often do you get messages like, "Mtg @ 4. Brg notes lst mtg. Coffee? x2. G2g, l8r." (The translation for those who are fortunate enough not to have seen such cryptic shorthand: "Meeting at four. Bring the notes you took from the last meeting. If you want coffee, stop at Starbucks—and get me one, too. Got to go, talk to you later.") The speed with which we can zip messages across the office or around the world makes us behave as though we must take every available shortcut to save even more time, circumventing the processes that effective writing requires. But for heaven's sake, you're not writing license plates! The instantaneous nature of e-mail makes us feel as though we have to read and write at the speed of electronics. But we don't (and can't), and trying to is often a direct route to misunderstanding. The same guidelines for effective communication on paper apply in the paperless environment of cyberspace.

One additional warning about electronic communication: Because e-mail is so instantaneous, it's easy to fire off responses and comments without thinking about potential ramifications. The fact that most of us delete e-mail messages once we've read or sent them gives the impression that they are temporal communications, existing only in time just like conversations in person or over the phone (and just as private). Wrong! This is a common and potentially hazardous belief. A growing number of companies capture and store electronic messages that travel through the company's networked computer systems. So far the courts have upheld the rights of companies to do this; what you do on company time with company resources belongs to the company and is the company's business.

If you wouldn't write something in a letter or a memo, don't write it in an e-mail message, either. With distribution lists and bulk forwarding, the message you send to your superior "for your eyes only" could end up on hundreds of other computers. E-mail messages have embarrassed presidents and secretaries alike, and are an increasing source of evidence in legal proceedings involving everything from sexual harassment to wrongful termination. That offhand comment you flip off in response to a question about someone's performance could become an electronic ghost that will return to haunt you months or years from now.

CHAPTER 8
Evaluating Performance

With the industrial revolution, we came up with performance measurements like profit and loss. Machinery mechanized jobs. Bosses with stopwatches came in and counted how many times one worker could do the same thing over and over. They did the math and came up with a definition of a day's work.

Some of this mentality remains, enmeshed in the philosophy that if managers set the standards, employees will follow them. To an extent, this is true. Someone with a view of how each employee's job and responsibilities fit into the bigger picture must establish expectations and a structure for measuring performance within that framework. But today's fields and factories are a far cry from their predecessors. The jobs within them, and their tasks, are not easily measurable—marketing, computer programming, advertising, architecture. How do you determine whether someone is putting an appropriate level of thought or creativity into the job? And with people working in teams, how do you figure out what each person should be doing? We are all pieces of a bigger pie.

The Relationship Between Performance and Evaluation

It seems that there should be a clear and definable relationship between performance and evaluation. You should be able to measure, precisely and objectively, whether the employee does the right things in the right ways. The problem is, performance is not precise and objective (and for that matter, neither is life itself). Human interactions are subjective; they involve factors of judgment and perception that exceed the capability of precise, objective measures.

Say, for example, that an employee's job is to make six widgets in an hour. Counting to six is easy enough, but it's also necessary to determine if they are made correctly. Is there a standard of deviation that's acceptable? If so, is it a precise measurement (each widget can be no more than 0.0032 of an inch larger or smaller than the template) or is it a judgment (each widget feels smooth to the touch and causes no splinters)? Must the employee complete one widget every ten minutes, or is it okay for the employee to make all six in the last fifteen minutes of each hour? Can the employee make twelve widgets in one hour, then none in the next hour?

Now suppose it's another employee's job to sell six widgets an hour. Is the standard simply sales, or does it factor in returns? What if there are problems with the phone lines, or the employee calls forty prospective customers but can't convince any of them to actually buy a widget? These are variables beyond the employee's control, yet they directly affect the employee's ability to perform. In the reality of the business environment, objectivity is not as clear-cut as we would like for it to be. And in reality, performance evaluation structures range from nearly nonexistent—a few comments scribbled on the back of a telephone message note—to nearly spreadsheet—the minutiae of a job's tasks itemized and delineated on multiple-page forms. Some take their forms because they must (such as reviews mandated by government or licensing entities), and others because managers and employees alike inherently dislike evaluating performance.

On one end of the continuum are small or family-owned companies that might never formally evaluate anyone's performance. With just a few employees, it's pretty obvious when someone's not pulling a full load. There's no place to hide, no way to blend anonymously into a department or work group. Each individual has unique and important responsibilities; failing to meet them puts the company at grave (and usually imminent) risk. People who work in such settings tend to have strong motivations for being there, and equally strong commitments to the company and its success. Many of them might be family members. Performance evaluation might mean a pat on the back for an extraordinary success or a dressing down for screwing up—if either extreme ever arises in an environment where one is the expectation and the other means the company's demise. Although the evaluation structure appears nonexistent, the performance structure is absolute. Without outstanding performance as the norm from every employee, the company dies.

On the other end of the continuum where many large corporations reside, new employees typically receive a manual that specifies, sometimes even to the detail of what jewelry is appropriate in the workplace, how the company expects each and every employee to behave. There's likely another manual within the department that describes, perhaps to the extent of defining break periods, the employee's job responsibilities and obligations. Each employee knows the precise duties of his or her job. The evaluation structure is rigid, with tasks typically assigned a numeric value along a scale of unacceptable to superior. Simple scales might run from zero (unacceptable) to five (exceptional); more complex scales might rate in increments of tenths along a scale of zero to ten or even zero to 100. Equally strict rules prescribe the consequences for each rating: Less than two means probation, while five earns a 3 percent raise. While the evaluation structure is absolute, there is wide variation in performance. An employee can function at substandard or mediocre performance for a defined period of time without direct consequence to the company.

Most companies are somewhere in the middle of these two extremes, hovering along the center of the continuum. As small companies grow they often add bits and pieces of formality to address specific needs that arise—to deal with the first new employee who doesn't work out, or determine how and when to give someone a raise. Despite the need for their existence, performance evaluations can be a major annoyance for managers and employees alike. Even when there are stringent guidelines, there are employees and circumstances that don't fit within them. When there are minimal guidelines, it's difficult to say to an employee, "Your performance needs improvement."

FACTS

A study conducted in 2000 by the University of Missouri-Columbia revealed that when it comes to what determines happiness, Americans like to feel independent, good at what they do, and close to others. Money and predictability become important factors only in times of uncertainty.

Also, many performance evaluation systems tie an employee's evaluation to salary. Get a good evaluation, get a raise. Get an average or a poor evaluation and the money stays the same. This establishes incentives (or disincentives) for managers to slant evaluations to meet needs other than performance issues. A manager might give a mediocre employee a better than deserved evaluation because the employee needs the raise—often with the hope that the employee will know this and be motivated to do better as a show of gratitude. Such motivation is likely to be short-lived, if it surfaces at all. An employee whose performance is substandard might not know this, and believe the inflated evaluation to be accurate. And since this is the perception of performance that becomes part of the employee's records, it becomes difficult if not impossible to go back later to counsel the employee about performance that really hasn't changed. Or a manager facing a tight budget might decide that no one will receive higher than an average performance evaluation to avoid having to give raises that could push the budget to the brink of layoffs. While the manager might believe this action is justified because it will save the jobs of everyone, employees are likely to feel cheated—they've been giving their best, yet the company views their performance as not good enough.

Just as performance is specific to a job's tasks and requirements, so too is evaluating it. It would be so much easier for everyone if we could devise a universal set of standards. But we can't, and really wouldn't want to. Many jobs require variability and flexibility. People are different in their needs as well. If there's one lesson you should know by this time in your life, it's that "one size fits all" really doesn't fit anyone.

Get Off to the Right Start: Hiring Right

In an ideal world, a job description defines the basic expectations that you and your company have for employee performance. This message runs consistently through advertising, interviews, and performance evaluations. How closely reality matches the ideal varies widely. One effort to close the gap lies in the myriad federal and state laws that regulate employment. Designed with the best of intentions (usually), such laws attempt to balance the rights of employees with the needs of companies. Most employment laws attempt to define how a company or manager can:

- Establish job requirements
- Interview applicants
- Make hiring decisions
- Treat the employee on the job with respect to salary, work conditions, disciplinary action, and related factors
- Terminate employment

Laws typically mandate that companies define job responsibilities consistently and explicitly. Laws also require companies to treat employees in certain ways, and may regulate such factors as benefits packages and work hours. (Chapter 9, "Toeing the Line on Company Policies," talks more about laws and regulations that apply to the workplace.) Depending on the industry, the company's size, and the amount of bureaucracy, these requirements may be more or less flexible. Beyond laws are corporate policies—the internal regulations that tell managers what they can and cannot do when it comes to hiring, evaluating, promoting, and firing employees. It is always important to start with your HR department to make sure you are acting in a responsible manner from the perspective of the law as well as complying with internal policies. Key questions to address include:

- Must you interview and consider internal applicants before seeking external applicants?
- If internal applicants meet the job's basic requirements, must you hire them?
- Do union contracts include stipulations and procedures for considering potential employees?
- Do requirements differ for replacement employees to fill vacated positions and employees being hired into newly created positions?
- Do requirements differ according to the job's classification (hourly, salaried, exempt, nonexempt, permanent, temporary, full or partial FTE)?
- How can (or must) factors such as race and gender affect your selection process?
- Can you decide to hire someone with less experience or fewer qualifications because that person shows an eagerness and aptitude for learning, or must you accept the candidate whose actual skills are the strongest?
- Can you go through the entire interviewing process and decide that rather than hiring any of the candidates you want to post the job again?

There are a lot of topics you cannot ask about in an interview. Among the obvious should be age and religion. Also high on the taboo list are birthplace, marital status, children, sexual orientation, or anything that might allow you (intentionally or unintentionally) to make a judgment based on class, background, lifestyle, or other factors not related to the job's requirements. Be sure you discuss all of these factors with your HR representative and understand, fully and completely, your legal obligations. Failing to do so can have serious consequences for you personally as well as for your company.

If the employment process truly were as simple as following all the laws and rules, there would be no need for employment attorneys. But that's a growing field, which tells us that laws and policies aren't enough. Jobs are about more than skill sets. Jobs are about the people who fill them, no matter how much companies might want to diminish that factor. Most jobs actually have two sets of requirements: those related to expertise and experience, and those related to personality and work style. Requirements related to skill sets appear to be fairly clear-cut and easy to establish. This is probably true for jobs in which the tasks are highly structured or even rote. If you need to hire someone to operate a punch press in the production department, it's easy enough to determine whether an applicant has the knowledge and skill to do this. Because the job itself is highly structured, the person's personality and work style are less relevant to performance. If you're hiring to fill a position in the sales department, the situation is far more subjective. Work style and personality are significant factors; the job involves forming relationships (however short-lived they might be).

ESSENTIALS

In the words of poet John Keats: "Don't be discouraged by a failure. It can be a positive experience. Failure is, in a sense, the highway to a success, inasmuch as every discovery of what is false leads us to seek earnestly after what is true, and every fresh experience points out some form of error which we shall afterwards carefully avoid."

Michael was the manager of a software company's marketing department. His work group spent a lot of time together, and its productivity depended a great deal on how well employees could work collaboratively. It was crucial that new employees had both the appropriate job skills and the right "mesh" with the rest of the group. There was little room for frail egos or high-and-mighty attitudes, and Michael could smell either all the way from the lobby. His department needed people who were talented yet genuinely humble. They spent much of their time in meetings or on the phone with clients and prospective clients. They had to be people-people, and they had to be good listeners.

The company's HR department confirmed resumes and conducted preliminary interviews, then forwarded to Michael the applicants who met the job's technical qualifications and the company's basic requirements. One "test" Michael incorporated into job interviews was to drone on and on about a particular subject to see how the applicant responded. This gave him a sense of how the person might respond to a client who did the same thing. An applicant who maintained eye contact, nodded and smiled, and appeared to remain interested even when Michael began to bore himself earned an invitation to tour the department and meet with the group. An applicant who checked his watch, fidgeted in his chair, interrupted, or whose eyes glazed over was not likely to make it to the next round of interviews.

It was also important to Michael that the people he hired have diverse interests. His department supported a wide range of clients and projects. So he also engaged applicants in dialogue about events in the news. He broached topics of interest to the local community, to see whether an applicant could pick up the threads and weave them into a conversation. And he asked both work-related questions and more general-interest ones, just to see how he felt as he and the applicant talked. At this point, intuition guided many of Michael's reactions. Was this a person he wanted to spend time around? Was this someone he wanted to mentor or nurture? Was this someone who would get along well with the department's existing employees and clients?

The final step in Michael's hiring process was to have the applicant meet with a number of his employees. He usually scheduled a formal meeting in which three to five employees sat down with the applicant to describe their work and ask the applicant questions. Michael also tried to have several informal connections take place, to get "first impression" feedback from employees as well. Before making a final decision, he reviewed all the factors and responses, and compared them to what he knew were his personal biases. One of those biases was about attitude. Michael felt it was nearly always a better decision to hire someone who was eager and cooperative but a little short on practical experience than someone whose experience was astounding but who had an arrogant attitude. When Michael was satisfied that he had a balanced and quantifiable perspective, he consulted with HR one last time and then made a decision.

There are aspects of Michael's approach that appear arbitrary. It encompasses intangibles on Michael's end, such as his ability to select employees that his experience tells him are good choices for the work and the department. These are inherent dimensions of subjective judgment. But if you look closely, you'll see that Michael's approach incorporates a great deal of consistency as well. Michael follows the same pattern of questioning in each interview. The challenge for all managers is to balance the book and the story. The book—laws, regulations, policies—follows a strict structure. The story—personalities, work styles, potential—exists within and at the same time extends beyond the book. While it's crucial for you to go by the book as far as laws and company policies go, it's also essential for you to make decisions that are consistent with the story of your department (its needs). There has to be a happy medium between finding the best person to advance the interests of the company as well as to be a positive fit in the group.

FACTS

Consistency and realistic latitude should coexist in company policies. There are times when following the rules to the letter is counterproductive. Granting exceptions demonstrates an understanding that individuals sometimes have differing needs. Establish a process for considering exceptions that looks at the specific circumstances, the benefits for the employee, and the benefits for the company. If you decide to deviate from policy, explain your reasons for making the decision and emphasize that this is an exception, not a new way of interpreting the policy.

This isn't to say that you should only hire people you like, or that your employees must approve of new members to the team. And not all jobs require close interaction among employees. Use sound and rational judgment. It's more important that a computer programmer knows your company's network and applications inside and out than be able to carry on a conversation about the political environment in the Middle East. It might even be acceptable for this person to be a bit on the antisocial side, as long as he or she possesses the highly specialized skills the job requires—computers don't engage in dialogue—and isn't toxic to others. You might not want to go for coffee with this employee, but he or she will make a positive contribution to your department or company.

Interviewing is a craft. You won't excel at it right away, but you can become quite skilled as your experience grows. There are many books and workshops that focus specifically on interviewing; if your job involves more than one or two interviews a year, invest in some training. At the very least, take an HR specialist or manager to lunch and ask for tips and suggestions. In general, in your interview you should:

- **Describe the actual job activities.** Explain what a typical day in your department is like, and what kinds of successes and challenges employees encounter.
- **Describe the work environment.** Is it collaborative or independent? Do people get individual recognition, or does the group sink or swim as one? Is there a lot of overtime, and what compensation is there, if any, for putting in extra hours?
- **Ask the applicant for examples that demonstrate his or her abilities and skills in particular areas.** If building relationships with prospective clients, ask the applicant to describe two or three similar experiences that relate to your circumstances.
- **Press for specifics.** If an applicant says "I like that kind of environment," ask how it is similar to or differs from work environments the employee has experienced in the past. If the employee says he or she has done "something like that," get details. Just how, exactly, was the applicant's previous experience "like" the requirements of the job?

- **Turn on your bunkometer.** Listen for grandiose claims or statements that don't make sense. If in doubt, question. Again, press for specifics. Back-pedaling and convoluted explanations should send that needle soaring into the danger zone.
- **Keep your comments neutral and your opinions to yourself.** Unless you know without a doubt that this is the person you intend to hire, don't give the impression that this is the case.

Setting Measurable (and Reasonable) Standards

A job's measurable standards should begin with the job description and extend into the details of the job's performance requirements. The more effectively you establish this in the job interview, the greater clarity new employees will have about your (and the company's) expectations. It also lays a trail, in documentation as well as in practice, that demonstrates your (and your company's) consistency in defining, monitoring, evaluating, and reporting performance standards. This is important first and foremost because it establishes a solid foundation for new (as well as existing) employees, making clear the path that leads to success with the company. It also establishes a solid foundation for you (and your company) in the event that things don't work out as anticipated and you end up defending your actions and decisions in court. The employee who gets the job as well as the candidates who don't could potentially have grounds for legal action if you have acted inconsistently or inappropriately in the context of hiring procedures and protections provided under the law.

Employees have rights. In most states, you cannot arbitrarily fire an employee. And even if the law doesn't prevent you from doing so, common sense should. The decisions you make regarding an employee's job status—to promote or not, to give a raise or not, to fire—are not decisions to make without careful deliberation. Employees (prospective, current, and former) can sue. They can claim you discriminated against them or failed to provide equal opportunity. For your company to defend you and itself against such an allegation requires more than "well, he just didn't fit in" or "she didn't work hard enough." Those are subjective perceptions that, without quantifiable or subjective substantiation, are nothing more than vague and obscure opinions. And you know what they say about opinions. . . .

ALERT

Without specific and measurable performance standards and appropriate evaluation processes in place, you're setting yourself up for the starring role in "The Manager's New (Nonexistent) Clothes." What clothes? If no one else can see them, you're naked. And that doesn't look good in court.

Performance standards and measures, like clothes, are often a matter of perspective and judgment. The Tell Us Everything Corporation (TUEC) does qualitative research. Some clients like the company and its employees and some don't. TUEC's work is all—to use the technical term—touchy-feely. An employee can be the best interviewer in the business, but someone who doesn't like her hairstyle or the way she pronounces "tomato" can decide not to be a client anymore. Conversely, an employee could be a contender for world's worst interviewer, yet have an enormous following among clients because he's a fun guy to go out with for beer and pizza. Sometimes clients like TUEC's services but run out of budget and disappear. How do these factors, over which neither individual employees nor the company as a whole has any influence, enter into TUEC's performance measures?

After much struggle and discussion, TUEC's managers came up with a way to measure effort (the actions an employee takes to attempt to win or keep a client) as well as results (the count of new and retained clients). Performance standards called for employees to:

- Follow up with clients by sending thank-you notes when a project ends and periodically telephoning to keep in touch
- Constantly improve and update their skills through classes

- Mentor each other on new skills
- Attend professional meetings and meet people
- Do one cold call per month to a prospect
- Locate a couple of potential companies to do business with every month
- Schedule a lunch with one ad agency planner each month
- Attend two conferences per year, and do a presentation at one
- Join local associations and attend their regular meetings
- Take on one pro bono project each year
- Develop a specialty area in terms of the kinds of clients each employee typically works with

By establishing these measures, TUEC acknowledged that what clients think and do is beyond the ability of its employees to control. But employees could put their best efforts forward in terms of staying up-to-date and in terms of communicating and sales support. This established a performance standard of doing everything possible to maintain customer satisfaction and to bring in new clients within the recognition that winning wasn't always possible. TUEC also established a structured reporting system, so that each employee provided the same kind of information in the same format. This helped the company keep better track of efforts and results in terms of which were effective and which were a waste of time and energy.

Managers discuss these standards when they interview job applicants, so employees coming into the company know these actions are among their responsibilities. And while TUEC couldn't ask each employee to bring in a specific dollar amount of business, it could and did establish company goals. Managers don't evaluate employees directly on these goals, but tie annual bonuses to the company's success in achieving them. Rather than creating divisiveness and competition, as individual accountability might, the emphasis on a collective goal encourages collaboration and teamwork.

It is possible, not to mention important, to have performance standards in all jobs even if performance is difficult to quantify. Sometimes you need to take a step back to look beyond the apparent tasks of the job to assess what factors are within the employee's control. It's neither fair nor wise to hold people accountable for actions and results they have no power over. Within the factors employees can control, identify and describe specific behaviors. Rather than expressing the concept of "follow-up," identify the task: "Send thank-you notes to clients after projects are finished." This distinction makes clear the precise action you expect an employee to take and that you will measure. Measures should be reasonable and realistic, of course— and unfortunately these are often moving targets as circumstances change within companies and even within industries. Advances in technology might ratchet up expectations; it's important to communicate such changes to employees who might find themselves suddenly behind the curve.

FACTS

Union contracts often define performance standards, measures, and evaluation procedures. In most situations, you cannot change any of these (and often other) elements of the job without a written amendment to the contract. Whether or not the employee wants or agrees to the change is irrelevant; actions that violate contracts can have serious and far-reaching consequences. Every manager should know what union contracts affect the employees in his or her department. Check with your HR department if you're not sure about yours.

Work styles come into play here as well. If you're a workaholic who doesn't see a problem with taking home a couple of hours of work, or going into the office for a couple of hours on the weekend, you risk establishing this as a performance standard among your employees— formally, informally, or simply by example. Yet your employees might not agree with your version of a work ethic. You might need to modify your expectations to be sure you don't transfer your standards in this regard onto them. If there is no reason for your employees to work on weekends, that shouldn't be the standard.

Encouraging Employee Participation and Buy-In

People are most likely to accept and comply with performance standards if they have a role in establishing them. In many companies and industries, certain standards are carved in stone—either set by regulation or outside authority, or inherent in the work. Hospitals, colleges, universities, and other kinds of organizations are subject to quality expectations established by accrediting bodies. Without meeting these, they cannot remain in business. Standards that apply to the organization trickle down through all levels, becoming imbedded in job descriptions as well as performance evaluation procedures. Within these standards, there may or may not be room for variation, depending on the industry.

When the Tell Us Everything Corporation embarked on its mission to establish performance measures, department managers met to formulate basic goals. From these goals—to keep current clients and add new clients to allow the company to grow at a certain pace—managers went back to their departments to talk with employees about how the department and each employee could contribute. This helped determine what employees did control, what was within their ability to control, and what was not within their control. From this discussion, departments developed goals. Managers then asked employees to identify what they could do on a daily, weekly, or monthly basis. And from this discussion, employees and managers together established the individual behaviors that would support the goals.

Take the "keep current clients" goal. Managers asked employees, "What makes for a happy client?" The list included a well-trained interviewer, a good kick-off meeting, daily progress updates, debriefing after the project, a well-written report, a follow-up call about the report, and a thank-you note when everything was wrapped up. These became the performance measures employees agreed they should and could meet. Then managers and employees broke each behavior into specific actions—sending a thank-you note became a sequence of events from writing the client's name and address on the envelope to signing the note, sealing it in the envelope, and taking it to the mail room or post office.

Not all employees enjoyed the process, of course, or even thought it was necessary. Some dragged their feet, while others outright refused to participate. But in the end, the other employees convinced the skeptics that the process was both better than the existing system and worth a try. People left the meetings feeling like they were controlling their own outcomes rather than having them dictated. And even goals that were dictated, like growing the business, became somewhat controllable because employees had input into how they could reasonably contribute.

In addition, each employee was responsible for coming up with two or three personal goals. These could contribute to professional growth as well as support department and company goals. An employee might set a goal to complete a specialty training program, undergraduate degree, or graduate degree. This would clearly benefit the employee, but had benefits for the company as well by making the employee more promotable or, at the very least, more knowledgeable. This was the sugarcoating that made the process palatable for even the most resistant employees. While some skepticism persisted, everyone was willing to at least give the new approach a try. In some companies, it might be useful to divide the department or team into groups, each of which tackles a specific company goal, department goal, or job responsibility. If the process represents a major overhaul, consider starting with a task force that comes up with the initial take on what the standards should be.

Even when it appears that there is little latitude for employee participation, there are usually small areas open to influence. A hospital must require employees in patient care areas to wear certain clothing and protective aids to safeguard them against exposure to infectious diseases. Allowing employees to choose clothing in various colors, patterns, and designs that are appropriate for their units encourages them to establish a dress code they can live with because they developed it. Performance standards, while somewhat bureaucratic, are also a way of ensuring both the perception and practice of fair treatment—which is something managers and employees alike desire. Employees are more likely to buy in if they are also responsible for enforcement.

Implementation and Adjustment

When TEUC implemented its new performance standards and measures, there was a numeric value associated with each behavior—one client lunch, one cold call, two conferences. After a few weeks, many of these quantifiers began to feel arbitrary and artificial. Some weeks an employee could easily make five cold calls, while another week was so busy putting out fires every day that there was no time for anything else. People began to feel anxious about failing to meet a particular performance measure, which distracted them from the functions of their jobs. Employees admitted, somewhat sheepishly, that the new measures looked better on paper than they worked in reality.

ALERT

Whatever system your department or company uses to set performance standards, as manager it's your job to make it work. If employees suspect that their participation has been an exercise in futility, it's all over for collaboration and teamwork. This is an invitation to frustration, disappointment, and office politics.

After agreeing that the standards were fine but attempting to quantify them was not working, work groups met and divided the standards into clusters: client initiatives, client follow-ups, reporting standards, and new business presentations. Then the groups clustered the small tasks within these larger categories. Each employee in the group took responsibility for one category, which included developing ways to monitor the activities within it. Each category's responsible person was then accountable for reminding other employees of their roles in that category's activities, providing whatever assistance others needed, and reporting on the category in group meetings. An unexpected outcome of this adjustment was a phenomenal increase in the sense of commitment people felt. New leaders emerged and existing leaders grew more confident. Buy-in grew; people who had not taken their responsibilities seriously or had disappointed other employees felt chagrined. Managers seldom had to intercede to redirect a work group; employees felt empowered to go to one another for assistance or to encourage those who were lagging to get it in gear.

There's more to meeting performance standards than personal satisfaction. Salaries, as well as any bonuses, generally depend on how employees meet the performance standards. Some companies assign a percentage value to each standard or standard category, such that they add up to 100 percent. While sending follow-up notes might be worth just 2 percent, this function is essential to client satisfaction that, in turn, can be 25 percent of the total points. This kind of a system gives weighted importance to key functions, yet makes all activities essential to the whole.

Using Performance Measures to Support Individual Growth

Employees are not at jobs simply because they have nothing to do all day or because they want to save the world. They want to grow, or at least to make more money. And they want you, their manager, to show them how they can do this. Any performance evaluation process should include short- and long-term personal goals. These goals, perhaps more so than department and company goals, change and evolve. For each employee, consider:

- What steps does the employee need to take to grow in the department?
- What reward can the employee expect for achieving such growth?
- Where can the employee expect to go next in his or her career?
- What are the employee's prospects for a few years down the road?

Of course, it's essential to have the employee participate in formulating personal goals, since manager and employee will need to agree to these goals. It's also important for you to help employees identify where their strengths seem to be, where those strengths can take them, and how they might change or improve their options by taking certain training courses or learning special skills. (Are you wearing your mentor hat?) If you can't help an employee honestly define his or her next career goal, you're showing the employee a brick wall. With employees whose abilities shine, this is an easy as well as enjoyable part of your job. It's exciting to watch people grow and develop and reach their potential. But some people choose career objectives that their skills and abilities don't support. As a mentor, you can help such employees find paths that are better aligned with their talents—or find ways to successfully pursue the directions that interest them. This is not easy work. Vagueness can't be an excuse for not wanting to think or for evading discussing painful issues.

FACTS

According to the U.S. Bureau of Labor Statistics, an employee's salary represents about three-fourths of the company's direct compensation costs for having the employee on staff. Benefits (such as insurance, paid time off, and retirement plans) account for one-fourth.

Evaluation Structures

A formal evaluation structure, regardless of the form it takes, benefits managers, employees, and companies. (Hold the groans, now.) Say your star employee makes a huge mistake that costs the company big money and has your superiors all over your case. It's a major screw-up, and everyone in the department knows about it. Yet will you remember it six months from now when it's time to do that employee's formal performance evaluation? If you do, to what level of detail? The reality is that memories quickly fade, even (or perhaps especially) bad ones. You might swear at the time that you'll never forget, but you will.

And if that's not problematic enough, other employees will remember—but not the real story. Employees talk, and as they do the details change. (Remember the childhood game of telephone?) It's not that people intentionally misrepresent the facts. They might have had limited knowledge in the first place, just a piece of the whole picture. So they fill it in, because we all like stories with details and endings. And memories fade—even theirs. What people can't quite remember, they create. It's human nature.

A well-designed performance evaluation system includes processes to document such experiences at the time that they happen (and ideally to address them with involved employees at the time they occur). This prevents, or at least minimizes, the likelihood that these experiences will return to haunt you. And most managers don't like playing the bad guy. A performance evaluation system provides the documented support that you need to present your perspective or defend your position. From morale to legalities, a formal performance evaluation structure benefits everyone.

ALERT

Some companies do not want managers to deviate in any way from the standard. Be sure your company gives you the latitude to augment standard procedures. What matters most is to set the standards and then follow them.

The most traditional structure features an annual review, usually on the anniversary of the employee's hire date, with supplemental quarterly meetings. Some companies review salary and performance at the same time, while others separate them. Be sure you know your company's policies; your mistakes could cost employees money. What structure your company uses isn't nearly as important as the fact that it has a structure of some sort in place. There are any number of approaches, methods, and systems; if your company doesn't have one yet, Appendix

B lists some resources for learning more about various performance evaluation systems.

Some managers use the company's structure, and then supplement it with their own approaches. Many systems use a numeric rating structure that assigns a point value to a scale of performance measures, such as from one (poor) to five (exceeds expectations). If your company does, you might want to add a bulleted list that highlights the employee's accomplishments and strengths, as well as identifies specific areas for improvement. This meets the company's needs, and also provides a level of detail that's useful to the employee. Employees become frustrated when they don't receive feedback. They get especially frustrated when the company has standards that they know the manager is not following. And if there is the potential for more money, the manager becomes an unacceptable stumbling block.

Regular communication—daily or at least weekly—is the most effective way to both monitor and shape employee performance. It remains your most effective tool as a manager. Don't save things, good or bad, for a formal evaluation meeting. Nothing you say or the employee says in a formal meeting should come as a surprise to either one of you. When you do meet with an employee to discuss performance, follow the guidelines in Chapter 7, "Communication and Feedback," to listen and talk effectively. Remember to:

- Establish ground rules: "I will tell you my assessment of your performance for each measure, then give you an opportunity to share your perspectives and comments. I ask that you not interrupt me, and I promise I won't interrupt you."
- Stay focused on the topics at hand and keep digressions to a minimum. Present examples of observable behaviors to support your comments. If issues surface that warrant further discussion, schedule another appointment to address them.
- Take notes, and encourage the employee to do the same. Offer the employee the opportunity to add his or her comments (on a separate page) to the evaluation packet that becomes part of the employee's file.

- Present improvements from a positive perspective as much as possible. "You've done a great job developing a system for monitoring report status. Let's take a look at some ways that you can streamline your work flow to be more efficient."
- If there is bad news, it shouldn't be news to the employee. He or she should know, or at least suspect, that there is a problem. Be direct in presenting the problem, and have a sense of what action you intend to take in response.
- Involve the employee in developing an improvement plan. Specifically identify steps and measures as well as a timeline for change.

Timely Follow-Up

In concept, performance is ever-evolving as the employee's skills and knowledge grow and expand. Every employee's performance has room for improvement. Although your company might have formal evaluation meetings just once or twice a year, change (whether to correct a problem or foster growth) requires regular follow-up and monitoring. You should establish the shape and form of this follow-up during the evaluation meeting, or at a subsequent meeting if that's how you set things up. What are the employee's obligations and commitments? What are yours? Is the employee going to work with you to establish priorities, present you with realigned priorities, or rely on you to present priorities? Be sure the improvement plan establishes:

- A schedule of regular meetings to assess the employee's progress toward improvement
- Suggested improvement actions (expressed in terms of observable behaviors)
- Clear expectations for what each follow-up meeting will cover, and what the employee needs to bring or provide
- Exactly what improvements you expect to see (expressed in terms of observable behaviors), and when you will be satisfied that the desired improvements have taken place
- Consequences for failing to improve

If the employee raised concerns during the evaluation meeting that require your action, give the employee a timeline and sense of structure for expecting responses from you. As the manager, you are responsible for making sure that follow-up occurs, both in terms of the desired behavior changes as well as the meetings or discussions to monitor or confirm the changes. If you don't care enough to follow up, why should the employee care enough to follow through?

Follow the Structure

Some managers simply hate paperwork. Marge was one of them. It didn't matter why the paperwork was necessary; she just hated it, and avoided dealing with it at just about all costs. Her employees generally admired this attitude; it positioned her as somewhat of a rebel, making her seem to belong more to them than to upper administration. Clarence was one of those employees. In the two years he reported to Marge, he hadn't had a single performance evaluation. He didn't work any less hard as a result; in fact, he put a lot of time and effort into his work because it felt less bureaucratic than the typical corporate environment. Of course, Clarence didn't get a raise during this time, either, since the company linked raises to performance. But he didn't really mind; he was well paid already, and he believed all it would take was a good word from Marge and he could circumvent that part of the process, too.

Before he got around to asking Marge to do that, the company adopted new policies and procedures that forced Marge to do a formal performance evaluation for all of her employees. She did so, but with intense resentment. To his surprise, Clarence discovered that Marge wasn't entirely happy with his performance. She perceived issues in several key areas of his job responsibilities, and asked him to propose an improvement plan. Because of his relatively low measures on the formal evaluation, Clarence received a mediocre raise. He felt betrayed and stabbed in the back. Yes, he could see that he had tripped himself up in certain things, but that wasn't really his fault since no one (like Marge) had told him he was on the wrong track. Clarence lost all respect and affection for Marge. She hadn't been there for him, in her parent and mentor roles, to give him the negative feedback he needed and suggest improvements to help him change and grow. Clarence resigned.

Some managers present long, rambling memos that are incredibly positive but read more like a horoscope than a performance evaluation. These presentations lack focus and detail, leaving employees wondering just what exactly was being evaluated—their great attitudes and awesome potential? The lack of standards and appropriate feedback leaves employees directionless.

Firing an Employee

No manager enjoys the prospect of firing an employee. Firing someone is the most serious consequence for failing to improve. Before you come to the decision that you need to end a person's employment, you must be sure in your heart of hearts that this is the right thing to do. Then you must be sure that you have complied with all relevant laws, regulations, and company policies and that all of the paperwork is completely in order. There are laws that govern firing, even in hire-at-will states. Most companies further establish strict policies that require extensive documentation affirming that you have followed those policies. Work closely with your HR department, if your company has one, to be sure you do things right—for your sake as well as the employee's. This is a decision from which there is no turning back.

Plan the meeting to fire the employee according to your company's policies and procedures. Some managers prefer to conduct a firing at the end of the workday, so the employee can collect his or her things and leave without everyone else watching. Will a security guard have to escort the fired employee back to the office to gather his or her possessions and then out of the building? Does an HR representative supervise the packing? As humiliating as these requirements might seem, they are often necessary safeguards for the company to prevent theft or sabotage. If the employee has valued work saved on the company's computer network or on a company computer, back up all the files the night before you intend to fire the employee as an added protection. Before the meeting, rehearse what you intend to say. Practice speaking clearly yet nonemotionally. When you do meet with the employee:

- Have an HR representative or your superior present as well. This bolsters your authority and lessens the likelihood of emotional pleas or outbursts.
- Keep the conversation short, to the point, and unemotional.
- Review the conversations and documentation that support the decision to fire the employee. It is not necessary or advisable to invite the employee's comments or perspective. The time for that is long past.

ESSENTIALS Expect the meeting to become emotional, certainly for the employee and probably for you. Regardless of the reasons for the firing, this person is someone you know. Be prepared to deal with the gamut of emotion from anger and sadness to pleading and tears. You might need to sit in the room with the employee until he or she regains composure.

If you've done your job as a manager, the firing shouldn't come as a total shock to the employee (although the finality of it might be temporarily stunning). You've counseled the employee about his or her performance issues or whatever are the problems that have led up to the firing, and you've given the employee plenty of opportunities to fix the problems. Keep your cool and stick with the "script" you've rehearsed. If it is necessary for someone to escort the fired employee from the premises, be sure that person is ready and waiting.

As soon as possible after the terminated employee has gone, assemble the other members of the team to give them the news. Keep the reasons for the employee's termination to yourself; such information is confidential. Chances are, the other team members knew this was coming and they know better than you do why this was the only option. Sometimes, however, you need to reassure other employees that this was a matter specific to the fired employee; it's natural for them to feel some fear and apprehension about the security of their own jobs. Other employees may want to talk about how they feel, but it's generally better to focus on how duties will be reassigned, what the plans are for hiring a replacement, and other such details. The key is to move on. It's important to treat people with respect after they've been fired, regardless of the reasons for firing them. Those who remain will watch how you handle things, and their perceptions will affect their attitudes, performance, and loyalty.

CHAPTER 9

Toeing the Line on Company Policies

olicies define a company's responsibilities and obligations to its employees and its customers, and vice versa. Policies exist for both legal and practical purposes. Some policies explain how the company complies with certain laws and regulations. Some policies delineate procedures and expectations. In most situations, you inherit the policies you must comply with and enforce.

Most employment laws and company policies are in place to define and ensure fairness in the ways the company treats its employees. Some are harder to figure out than others and even appear to be confusing, counterproductive, and contradictory—laws and policies alike. You might appear to be in compliance when in fact you're not—a situation that can create problems for you as the responsible manager as well as for your company.

Fairness: Concepts and Perceptions

Fairness is an underlying theme throughout this book, but is such an important topic that it needs focused attention. Fairness is, after all, the core message of the Golden Rule: "Do unto others as you would have them do unto you." We all like to be treated fairly. Does this mean we expect to be treated the same as everyone else? Only when that means it makes us special! As much as we want to be treated the same, we also want to be treated as individuals. Fairness is a tough standard because of its subjective nature. What you like and dislike often become significant factors in defining what you consider to be fair. Some fairness standards make sense when we talk about them but become convoluted and complex when we try to put them into practice. Most people agree that everyone should have the same opportunities to pursue their interests and aptitudes. The water gets deep and murky, however, when we try to figure out just that means.

Every American child knows, upon entering kindergarten, that he or she could grow up to be president. Or a brain surgeon or an astronaut or a fighter pilot or a fashion model . . . the list is endless. We enculture our children in this belief as the ultimate standard of equity in this country: You can be anything you want to be, as long as you work hard enough to get there. It's a grand and glorious ideal. But when it comes to reality, the circumstances are very different. By fourth or fifth grade, most youngsters know that in the country's history, not yet four dozen individuals have held the nation's top position. Hundreds might become brain surgeons or astronauts or fighter pilots or even fashion models—still slim odds in a workforce that numbers better than 60 million. Hard work, though incredibly important, is not always the passkey. Not everyone has the aptitude to become a politician or a scientist or a professional athlete. Other standards come into play: grades, test scores, economic and financial circumstances, competition. By high school, few young people truly believe their opportunities are endless. Most are expected to know what they want to do and to already be shaping their lives in those directions. And they are conforming to the external forces that are shaping their lives.

FACTS

Competition for promotions is often intense. Sometimes there are hard feelings after the manager makes a decision, and it's natural to want to help those who didn't get the promotion feel better. This is fine, as long as you can do so without violating the privacy of the promoted employee. Keep discussions focused on the unhappy employee and the issues with his or her performance compared to the job's performance standards, not to that of other employees.

Most people believe this dynamic represents a corollary to the fundamental concept of fairness. Equal opportunity to compete is fair; acquiring a position for which you are not qualified is not. To be a star quarterback, you must throw the football harder, more accurately, and more consistently than everyone else who wants to be a star quarterback. To be a physicist, you must excel in mathematics. To be sure, the underlying attributes that make these capabilities possible have little to do with determination and hard work. But achieving these potentials has everything to do with them—within a framework of fairness. When the doors of opportunity remain closed to someone no matter how talented and dedicated he or she is, for reasons not related to ability and resolve, we consider that unfair. And in many situations, the law considers it discrimination. Fairness becomes an issue, and often discrimination, when people are denied the opportunity to be hired or promoted on the basis of factors not related to their qualifications or abilities.

Some people work harder and make more significant contributions than others—from kindergarten through college and into the workplace.

It's important for you as a manager to encourage and reward employees who can and are willing to contribute the most toward meeting the work group's goals. Indeed, it's your responsibility to do this—you're accountable for those goals, and this isn't kindergarten (or college) anymore. High performers need constant challenge to keep them interested and motivated. They need new responsibilities, recognition and praise, and higher salaries. At the same time, it's important—and essential—for you to make it clear that you are committed to providing opportunities for all employees who report to you.

But what is fairness? In kindergarten, fair is pretty simple. Everyone gets a turn, everyone tries the same tasks, and everyone gets attention from the teacher. Some kids excel and the teacher praises them. The teacher also praises, with equal enthusiasm, the efforts of the kids who don't excel. In kindergarten, effort counts just as much as achievement. By college, the scales tilt. You might study harder than you've ever studied before and still fail the test and get a bad grade. Fair? It's the same test everyone else took—some passed, some didn't. Maybe geology isn't your thing, but you can do calculus in your sleep. How fair is this? After all, everyone else is better than you in one, and you're better than everyone else in the other. But your perception is likely to be that geology class is unfairly hard, and you could find it hard to believe that others feel that way about calculus class.

The same goes for the work world. Some people simply have more aptitude than others. You might want to be a novelist or an astrophysicist, but unless you clearly have abilities and aptitude, these doors aren't open to you. Is this fair? If you have the abilities and aptitudes, you probably think so. If not, you likely don't. What makes it fair overall is that you have the opportunity to compete, even if you're eliminated in an early round. This is pretty much the concept of fairness that applies in the workplace, in its simplistic form. Just as in college there are tests and grades, in the workplace there are performance standards. The more clear the guidelines in either setting, the more fair the outcomes feel.

When a senior project manager's position in their department opened up, Craig and Patrick were among the current employees who applied for it. Each had been with the company for six years; Craig was hired into the department and Patrick had transferred from another department two years ago. After interviewing all the candidates, Jennifer selected Patrick. Craig stormed into her office demanding to know why; he had been in the department longest, and felt he deserved the promotion more than Patrick. "You've always favored Patrick!" Craig accused. "You talk about projects with him after everyone else has gone home, and you let him go to classes the rest of us can't go to!"

Jennifer asked Craig to have a seat, then excused herself and left the room. When she returned ten minutes later, she had a file folder and a notebook in her hand—Craig's department personnel file and the department's performance standards. She opened Craig's folder and spread the papers on the desk in front of him. "These are your performance evaluations since you've been in the department," Jennifer said. "Look them over, and tell me if you see anything there that surprises you."

Craig looked at the forms he'd signed and dated. In the company's scoring system, he rated a three on a five-point scale in nearly every area—consistently meets and occasionally exceeds expectations. In one area, "works cooperatively and collaboratively with coworkers," he received a two—needs improvement. And in one area, "customer satisfaction," Craig consistently received a rating of five—exceptional performance. He thought his performance evaluations were pretty good, and he said so. Jennifer handed Craig the notebook, open to the job description for senior project manager, and asked him to read out loud the first numbered item.

"The successful candidate will demonstrate exemplary skills in collaboration and teamwork," Craig read. "If an internal candidate, he or she has consistently received fours and fives in performance standard three."

Performance standard three was the ability to work cooperatively and collaboratively with coworkers, Jennifer reminded Craig. "And despite your strong qualifications in some other key areas, the standard here is clear and your performance doesn't meet it," she said.

Once Jennifer was able to demonstrate to Craig that the department's performance standards had guided her decision to promote Patrick, she was able to discuss Craig's career potential. She pointed to the company policy that said the company would pay, in full, any tuition or fees for training and education directly relevant to an employee's job. Every employee could select and attend workshops and classes; Craig had never requested to do so, even though the department's bulletin board had postings of upcoming programs. Jennifer also pointed out that Patrick was typically in the office early and stayed late; she viewed this as showing initiative. She reminded Craig that the same open-door policy that allowed him to be talking with her right now applied to other employees and other situations, including Patrick and his interest in the department's projects beyond the scope of his involvement. And lastly, Jennifer returned to Craig's performance evaluations.

"Each evaluation includes my suggestions for your improvement and growth, both as an employee and for your career," she said. "You also provided suggestions of your own. But as you can see, when we've reviewed these at the next evaluation to assess your progress and success in meeting the goals you committed to, you haven't come through."

One aspect of Craig's misperceptions lingered for several months, however: the doubts and concerns his allegations created among his coworkers. Some sympathized with Craig, believing he should have been promoted instead of Patrick. Others felt Craig's complaints were way off base. The resulting "divided camp" mentality within the department showed in the productivity reports. Employees who previously had been all too happy to help those whose workloads overflowed suddenly became too busy themselves, and the entire department suffered. Craig's understanding of Jennifer's reasons for selecting Patrick and his acceptance of the decision were much slower to make the grapevine rounds than had been his outburst when he first received the news.

ESSENTIALS   Take time to thank the person in the mailroom, your secretary, or the department coordinator. It's easy to praise the people who do the most obvious tasks, but don't forget about all the others who work to make those tasks possible.

In every work group, each employee brings certain strengths. Such diversification is essential, even when job functions are similar. Some are always going to shine behind the scenes, or in a supporting role, while others will always have a more visible role. Unfortunately, the one in the visible role gets a lot of attention, not only from the manager but also from clients. This often leads to more opportunity, responsibility, and money. In the workplace as well as in life, the more visible continue to be perceived as also deserving more. But lose a few of the background players and see how quickly your productivity takes a dive. What happens when the bookkeeper gives notice—on her way out the door? The office manager quits, or the technical writer? Watch how quickly the so-called stars start to flounder—usually with you right along beside them. Managers need to constantly reinforce with employees that they are all working together and that each person is contributing. These techniques can help you stay appropriately focused:

- When trying to explain a situation of apparent inequity or favoritism, focus on the employee who is complaining, not the one (or ones) that he or she is complaining about. It's not your responsibility or your place to defend your actions regarding other employees; those are between you and them, and revealing too much information can result in complaints (often justified) about breaching confidentiality. When an employee does come to you with an accusation of unfairness, address it completely and thoroughly.
- If you don't know the details, schedule a meeting to discuss them after you've had a chance to research them. Going into a discussion about why someone else got promoted without knowing the circumstances is like scuba diving without checking the air gauge on the tank. It won't be long before you're in serious trouble.
- Be kind, yet direct and factual. Speak in terms of observable behaviors and measurable results. Refer to the specific performance standards that might apply.
- Focus on the person's strengths and how he or she can improve them. Even when the issue is a deficiency or weakness, identify it in such a way as to support whatever strengths lie within it. "You did a

great job with the Robinson account, bringing it in on time and under budget. This shows that you have the ability to manage multiple job functions concurrently. However, the client felt you focused too intensely on the budget and not enough on the client's needs. Let's talk about how we can improve your communication skills."

- Ask the employee about his or her goals—with your department, with the company, with his or her career. Where would this person like to be in three, five, and ten years? Structure a formal improvement plan, with the employee's full and equitable participation, that supports those goals to the extent possible.

FACTS

The Equal Employment Opportunity Commission, or EEOC, is the federal agency charged with overseeing compliance with federal laws and regulations aimed at supporting fairness and preventing discrimination in the workplace. These include Title VII of the Civil Rights Act, Americans with Disabilities Act, Age Discrimination in Employment Act, and Equal Pay Act. EEOC receives about 80,000 charges, or complaints alleging discrimination, a year. Roughly 10 percent of those are charges of sexual harassment and 14 percent are harassment of other kinds.

Equity or Entitlement?

Fairness is a standard that can appear arbitrary. Some employees believe that their knowledge or expertise creates an exception to the standard process, entitling them to jump to the head of the line when it comes to salary and promotional opportunities. Other employees are certain to disagree, and to view both this perception and any actions that might support it, as blatantly unfair. When an employee truly does bring a special and highly valued talent or ability to your department, of course you must recognize that in some way. Nonetheless, you must also recognize the roles and value of your department's other employees. As valuable as one person might be, your department cannot succeed in meeting its goals without the full cooperation and collaboration of all its members.

Nowhere is this delicate balancing act more obvious than in professional sports. The newspapers overflow with stories about the astronomical salaries of talented young stars, many of whom have little experience going into the professional arena but who appear to have potential the team simply can't live without. Talent, of course, isn't everything. Few football fans would argue that the stellar salaries paid to quarterback greats such as John Elway, Dan Marino, and Steve Young are unreasonable; after all, these stars led their teams through winning season after winning season. But many question the wisdom and inevitable consequences of bringing untried young quarterbacks such as Ryan Leaf and Rick Meier at salaries that most seasoned veterans don't even dream about. Yet talent leads many young athletes to believe they are entitled to such riches and rewards. In sports that have salary caps limiting the amount of money a team can spend overall for players, such high-cost players can prevent the team from keeping or acquiring other valuable players.

The business world is no different. When "star players" come into the company at inflated salaries or with other benefits that other employees don't get, it's difficult to maintain any sense of fairness. And when entire companies build around such inflation, it doesn't take a crystal ball to see that eventually the balloon will pop. From the oil magnates of the early twentieth century to the dot-commers of the early twenty-first century, the struggle between equity and entitlement continues to play out in the workplace. As Calvin Coolidge astutely observed, "Nothing is more common than unsuccessful men with talent."

FACTS

In 2000, approximately 10 million Americans were millionaires; 60 percent of them acquired their wealth through tech-related ventures and investments. This compares with approximately 100,000 American millionaires in the 1960s—and fewer than 30,000 in the 1930s.

Equity and Potential

As a manager, it's your role to help employees identify their potential (put on your coach or your mentor hat). The first step is to ask the employee what he or she wants to achieve, and what route appears likely to travel in that direction. What obstacles exist? How can the employee overcome them? Are the employee's perceptions of ability and potential the same as yours? If not, why? Opportunity is a significant element of equity. Fairness is not getting everyone to the same place, but rather helping each employee get to the place he or she wants to be. This means both opportunity for growth as well as recognition. How can this person best contribute, now and in the future, as an individual? Opportunities come alive for people when you, as a manager, take the time and interest to assess their interests and work with them to realize them. Such opportunities are not always obvious or what they seem. To help cultivate an employee's potential you could:

- Send the employee to several work-related seminars and conferences each year.
- Invite the employee to accompany you to a meeting or event in an area of interest for the employee that he or she otherwise wouldn't be able to attend.
- Incorporate a discussion of future goals and objectives into every formal performance evaluation, including follow-up from the previous evaluation.
- Ask each employee several times a year what you can do to support his or her career aspirations. Pay attention to goals that change; goals should change if the employee is making any progress toward meeting them.

Remember, equity is your guiding light in this. Ongoing training or continuing education is often required for many technical and professional staff, though could be easy to overlook when it comes to support staff. While a course in computer code might hold little appeal for an administrative assistant, a class in creating PowerPoint presentations might. Every now and then, if your budget allows, let employees attend workshops that aren't directly related to their jobs but that interest them for some reason. A technician might enjoy a class in graphic design, or a sales representative might like to go to a seminar on construction methods. Some choices might seem a bit far afield, but most people will choose options that appeal to their longer-term goals.

Franklin worked for a research company that did quantitative and qualitative research. His job was on the qualitative side; he excelled in talking with people to explore their feelings about events, issues, and products. Franklin quickly ascended to the top rung of management in the qualitative group, but then grew frustrated when he couldn't seem to climb any further. He appeared to have hit a ceiling—while others around him continued to rise in the organization, he was stuck. So he went to talk with his manager, Bill. The top people in the company, Bill explained, were proficient in both quantitative and qualitative work. They understood the full circle of the company's scope of business, and could function comfortably anywhere within it. While Franklin could take classes, it wasn't likely he would ever be competent on the quantitative side of the house—numbers and analyses just weren't his strong suit. He didn't have a "feel" for statistics like he did for listening, Bill said; Franklin was purely people-oriented.

Bill went on to explain that he didn't view this as a negative. To the contrary, he saw considerable opportunity for Franklin to continue advancing within the qualitative side of the company. He told Franklin some of the changes the company was planning to implement over the next few months, and talked about how he saw Bill as an integral part of the new scheme. It was hard for Franklin to hear that he really didn't have a shot at any of the company's top management positions, but he appreciated Bill's directness and thoughtful assessment. And Franklin realized that the changes Bill presented were actually more along the lines of what he wanted to do with his career. The discussion turned around Franklin's perception of unfairness. Bill was committed to developing Franklin's abilities and aptitudes, which in the end would serve him much better than being promoted into a position he would come to hate within a year.

And here we come back to work style. Most people like to be around people who are like them. We enjoy similarity in our social lives and in our corporate culture. This culture tends to reward people who mirror its beliefs and behaviors. Those who are out of sync with the dominant culture often feel left out and unfairly treated. Huffdigger & Boast was an up-and-coming advertising agency known for its prestigious clients. Started by a pair of ambitious marketing majors who had graduated in the top 2 percent of their Ivy League college class, the firm cultivated an image of cutting-edge sophistication. It sought out super-polished Ivy-Leaguers who fit the mold. These preppies were the "face" of the company and they got the key positions. Everyone knew this was the structure, but few people were unhappy about it. Even those who worked in the background had opportunities for promotion to high levels within the company. The "faces" even joked about living in glass houses. Was the structure unfair? If anyone thought so, it was the "faces" who were always on display.

Sometimes remaining fair across work styles means separating out the accomplishments, both real and potential, of employees from your own values and standards. You might be pretty loose when it comes to the structure of your workday, content to work late all week and then take Friday afternoon off. Yet you might have employees who insist on leaving right at the stroke of five, regardless of what activity engages them when the workday officially ends. As frustrating as this is within the context of your work style, it's important to shift your perceptions into the employee's work style. If this person is incredibly productive during the workday, then it's only fair for you to acknowledge this. You can't expect your employees to behave like you do, or only reward them when they do. Fairness means being able to respect and reward people for what and who they are, not what you want them to be.

Fairness: Laws, Regulations, and Policies

Employment laws are numerous and complex, existing at the federal, state, and industry levels. Some apply to organizations that employ over a certain number of employees, while others affect everyone who works. Workplace laws and the regulations derived from them change as legislatures pass new laws and agencies develop new regulations. It is your responsibility as a manager to be familiar with the laws and regulations that apply in your state and industry, and to your company. We can't stress this enough; not knowing is no excuse.

Laws, regulations, and policies affecting the workplace typically cover issues of safety, health and welfare, and fairness. (See Chapter 4, "This Is Not Your Daddy's Workplace," for discussion about safety and health and welfare.) They are no more stringent than in the area of fairness. Fairness is an uncomfortable topic for many people because it includes gender and race, all those things we don't even want to think about, let alone talk about or have to defend. But often, a manager must do both.

ESSENTIALS If you don't know your state's employment laws and regulations, look into one of the many professional organizations that sponsor workshops and seminars about employment laws and related issues. The important thing is to educate yourself about these laws and stay up to date on any changes.

Although you might look around your company and see a diverse, relatively happy workforce, it's important to remember that the laws that have made this possible didn't come about just because some legislator had a wild hair. The workplace has a long and ugly history of unfair practices. It's likely you have experienced unfairness at work yourself. Laws came into effect to protect employees from unfair (targeting a single person) and discriminatory (targeting a particular group of people, such as by race or gender) practices, although they have by no means eliminated them.

Managers sometimes look on these laws as intrusions into the workplace that keep them from doing their jobs. Yes, employment laws do sometimes protect employees who shouldn't receive protection. There are people who will take advantage of every little loophole to avoid doing the work they were hired to do. Every manager (and probably every employee) knows such a person. Yes, there is often a lot of paperwork involved in what used to be simple, even word-of-mouth processes. It used to be, a generation or two ago, that a handshake sealed employment offers and a boss's good mood meant a raise. No more—

there are letters of intent and contracts and fair labor standards and . . . you get the picture. It's a different world.

The reality is, it's a world that is by and large much better off than the one of a generation ago. The unpleasant truth is that we have all these fairness laws and regulations because there is such an extensive history of egregious wrongs: People working in dangerous conditions for next to no money, with no help from the company if they became injured or even killed on the job. Jobs available—or not—purely on the basis of race or gender. The laws and regulations that structure the modern workplace became necessary to create a workplace that is equitable to all.

Many behaviors once viewed as "the way things are" are no longer appropriate in the work environment, and might indeed be against the law. Use common sense. If you wouldn't say or do something in front of your parents or your children, don't say or do it to your coworkers, either.

The Risks of Playing Favorites

Favoritism is generally a personal matter. A manager likes someone, so he or she gives that person breaks. Sometimes favoritism is obvious; other times it's subtle. In every case, however, favoritism divides. It pits employees against each other (not always consciously), forcing them to compete for your attention. No one likes to feel left out or passed over. Experiencing these feelings as adults often surfaces unpleasant memories of similar situations from childhood. It's one thing to compete for something and lose because the winner is truly better. It's quite another to lose because you didn't have a chance in the first place. Sometimes favoritism arises from a genuine desire to do something good for an employee that then evolves into a mentor-turned-monster scenario. Often favoritism exists as a form of office politics, with employees jockeying for position in the kiss-my-shoes line.

Are Those Your Biases Showing?

Now the vice president of finance at her company, Dorothy had worked her way through the ranks. She had started as an office assistant in the payroll department twenty-five years earlier, working part time to help pay her way through college. When she completed her undergraduate degree in accounting, she joined the company full time and worked in various departments in the finance division. Through the years she earned her CPA and her MBA, each of which opened new doors for her. When Dorothy was promoted to director of accounting, it was a time when women in upper management were rare. She was often the only woman in management meetings, where she often had a difficult time convincing her male counterparts that she wasn't there to serve coffee.

As one of the few female managers in the company, Dorothy made it her mission to help promising young people, often women, achieve professional success. She handpicked her supervisors based as much on potential as on experience, and often brought them with her to meetings with other managers and with clients. Dorothy believed this gave the assistant a chance to see the inner workings of the company, better preparing him or her for promotion. By the time Dorothy became vice president, she had amassed a cadre of loyal followers, mostly women, who appreciated her efforts to take them under her wing and provide opportunities that otherwise wouldn't have been open to them. She also had acquired a reputation of being biased toward women, and several men in her department filed a complaint.

Dorothy believed she had been providing extra support and encouragement for what she perceived to be an imbalance in the corporate world. She didn't see her actions as biased; she saw herself as a mentor to people who needed a guiding hand with their careers. She didn't feel she singled out women for this guidance, and pointed to several men whom she had mentored as well. But perceptions are reality. Those who didn't benefit from her "extras" felt left out. Although Dorothy's intentions were commendable, her actions ended up bordering on discrimination. Her company responded to the bias complaint by implementing a formal mentoring program involving all of the company's top executives. A committee established written application and participation procedures, and handled the selection process.

It's important for managers to recognize that while people are not equal, every employee is entitled to equal opportunity. It's equally important to recognize the role your personal biases, however subtle, influence the perceptions others form about your actions and behaviors. When you're making decisions about an employee's performance, capabilities, and potential, ask yourself:

- How much of this is the employee and how much of this is me?
- Does this employee deserve the benefit of a doubt? An extra push?
- Under what circumstances am I making this decision? Is this decision based totally on merit?
- Whom else have I considered? What made me decide in favor of one employee versus another?
- Why am I deciding this way? What are the observable behaviors and quantifiable factors?
- Do I like or not like this employee?
- How are my biases affecting my decision?

FACTS

Between 1990 and 1998, the U.S. Justice Department reports that job discrimination lawsuits tripled, from just under 7,000 to just over 21,500. Furthermore, 65 percent of the more than 43,500 civil rights lawsuits involved employment matters such as bias and discrimination in hiring, promotion, pay, and firing.

We're not suggesting you list your biases and send them in a memo to HR, of course. That would accomplish little benefit to you or the company. Our biases are our own. But by acknowledging them, to ourselves, we can take a step back and think when we are in uncomfortable situations. Your biases are a natural part of you. You don't need to, and probably don't, like all of them. They're most likely to sneak in on you when you're reacting on autopilot. When you're aware that this can happen, you're more likely to take the extra time to separate your biases from the situation and the action you need to take. The outcome might be quite different.

Crossing the Line: Discrimination and Harassment

There is a point at which biases become discrimination and even harassment. The line of demarcation is often hazy and hard to find—until you cross it. Generally, you've done so when:

- You draw automatic assumptions about individuals based on nonindividual factors: "She's upset because she's a woman and women get emotional."
- You hire or promote certain employees for factors not related to job abilities or performance, such as race, gender, or physical attractiveness
- You fail to hire or promote certain employees for factors not related to job abilities or performance, such as race, gender, or physical attractiveness
- People act uncomfortable around you, or complain to others about your actions

Federal laws that protect employees from discrimination in the workplace have spawned volumes and volumes of regulations and procedures. The key guiding laws include:

- The Fair Labor Standards Act, passed originally in 1938 and modified numerous times through the years. The original FLSA established the forty-hour workweek, set a minimum wage, and placed restrictions on child labor. Its numerous revisions established equal pay for equal work and procedures for calculating compensatory time given in lieu of wages.
- The Equal Pay Act, originally passed in 1963, and which further clarified the concepts of equal pay for equal work, specifically prohibiting companies from paying women less than men for performing the same job tasks.
- The Civil Rights Act, originally passed in 1964. Title VII of this federal legislation makes it illegal for companies that have fifteen or more

employees to discriminate in hiring, pay, promotion, and firing on the basis of race, color, religion, gender, or national origin.

- The Age Discrimination in Employment Act, passed in 1967, which makes it illegal for companies with fifteen or more employees to discriminate against people who are age forty or older.
- The Americans with Disabilities Act, passed in 1990, which established requirements for companies that employ fifteen or more employees to provide "reasonable accommodations" for individuals with disabilities.

Each state has its own set of laws and regulations, many of which are more restrictive or explicit than federal legislation. Sexual harassment laws, relative newcomers to the discrimination scene, evolved as a result of U.S. Supreme Court rulings that found it to be a variation of gender discrimination and thus covered under Title VII of the Civil Rights Act. (For more about sexual harassment and related issues, see Chapter 10, "Socializing at Work.")

QUESTIONS?

What does exemption mean?
Exemption means you're not protected under federal law from practices otherwise regulated by the FLSA, such as work hours, paid overtime, and equal pay for equal work. State laws might provide protection, however.

Are you exempt from the requirements of the Fair Labor Standards Act? You might be if you meet the following guidelines:

- You are salaried (without overtime pay or reduced pay for days you miss work).
- You have "hire and fire" authority.
- You direct the daily activities of two or more employees.
- You make your own decisions about how and when to do the tasks of your job.
- You spend 80 percent of your time engaged in management activities.

Discrimination is a complex issue; we can only scratch the surface in this context. What looks like discrimination in one situation might not be in another. What you need to know as a manager is that behaviors that imply or reflect bias lead to perceptions of discriminatory actions. It's your responsibility to understand what constitutes discrimination from a legal perspective. There are dozens of books that deal specifically with issues related to discrimination in the workplace; Appendix B, "Resources," lists some titles you might find helpful.

The most important weapon your company can employ to fight workplace discrimination is a strong (and enforced) policy that defines discrimination and outlines the procedures employees should take when they feel they've been the victims of discrimination. As a manager, it's your first responsibility to be sure you do not behave in ways that are, or could be interpreted as, discriminatory. Second, be on the alert for situations of discrimination and harassment. Your failure to take action can make you just as liable as the person committing the harassing or discriminatory actions.

All too many discrimination defenses start with "but it was just a joke!" What you find funny, someone else might find offensive. When it comes to telling jokes in the workplace, the real punch line could end up knocking you right out of your job.

Proaction on your part can save a lot of grief down the road. Make it a point to:

- Pay attention to coffee room chatter. If you hear stories that arouse your suspicions, contact the involved employee later and speak with him or her in private about what you heard.
- Encourage employees, regularly at department meetings and individually when the need arises, to report situations of bias and discrimination in accordance with your company's policies and procedures—whether they are themselves the victims or have knowledge of the situation.

- Investigate all complaints that come to you, if this is among your responsibilities. Be thorough, and be sure you follow your company's guidelines and policies—especially when it's time to turn everything over to your company's lawyers. If such investigations are not part of your responsibilities, be sure the appropriate HR representative conducts an investigation.
- Squash the pejorative jokes; nothing in the workplace is "just kidding." This includes forwarding questionable jokes by e-mail and telling questionable jokes even when you think your audience will find them funny. How do you know what's questionable? One manager uses the "mother" method: If you wouldn't tell the joke to your mom, you shouldn't tell it to anyone at work.
- Document, document, document. We can't emphasize this enough. A paper trail is your only proof of concern and action. Make sure it's one you can follow.

Workplace Privacy

An issue of increasing significance in today's workplace is that of personal privacy. When communication was limited to telephone or in-person conversations, we had a sense that our discussions were limited to those participating in them. There was also a sense of immunity; if no one else heard the conversation and it later became an issue, it was one person's word against another. This created some ugly scenes, to be sure. But for the most part, there were few ramifications. The electronic age changed all that. Now there are as many ways to "spy" on communications as there are to engage in them. Many people feel that telephone conversations, e-mail, and Internet use are matters that don't concern the company. Companies are increasingly taking the opposite view. Many monitor all forms of communication, ostensibly as a dimension of quality improvement activities. It's important that you know what your company can and cannot do in this area.

The federal Electronic Communications Privacy Act limits the level to which a company can intrude on telephone calls and voice mail. In general, companies can monitor only business-related calls and messages.

In reality, it's often difficult to distinguish. A good guideline is to encourage employees to limit personal calls to and from work phones. Not only does this prevent issues of privacy from arising, but it also improves productivity.

E-mail is another area where employees (and maybe you) have the delusion of privacy. Not so, as we discuss in Chapter 7, "Communication and Feedback." Think of what would happen if that e-mail message you're writing about someone wound up being sent to that person. Scary thought? Don't send it. Don't even write it. E-mail messages have been and continue to be used by both sides in discrimination and harassment lawsuits.

The Importance of Consistency

Consistency and fairness are really like conjoined twins. Separate them, and one will likely die—or at the very least, fail to thrive. Make consistency in the ways you deal with employees as much a pattern in your daily activities as getting out of bed, brushing your teeth, and reading the newspaper with your morning coffee. When you make your daily rounds to connect with your employees and see how things are going, stop at every office, cubicle, or workspace. You might stay longer at some than others, but don't stay longer at the same ones every day. If you have things to discuss with one employee, ask that employee to come to your office.

Go ahead, go to coffee or lunch with your employees. Go one at a time, or with small groups. Just be sure you extend an offer to each employee to join you for a break at some point within a reasonable amount of time. Again we remind you that perception is reality. Spend twenty minutes with one employee and three minutes with each other employee, and you can bet everyone in the department is watching the clock. The perception of unfairness that you're building gives the illusion that you treat some employees better than others. In its infancy, this is favoritism. Later in the game, it becomes bias and then discrimination. It's not a path you want to follow.

It is easy for managers to buy into the special needs or requirements (or perceptions of them) that certain employees seem to have. Maybe one employee commutes from a long distance, so when he constantly shows up late, you don't say anything. You know this employee is also a high performer who typically stays late. Another employee is not such a high performer, and you know he lives three blocks from the office. When he comes in late, you come down on him. Logically, this makes sense and may even seem fair at some level. But chances are, the other employees will not agree.

Be consistent about enforcing the basic rules and procedures. That is the essence of being fair. It might mean modifying the policy, making the start time flexible, with the understanding that late start times have to be approved and communicated to everyone else, and the late starters have to stay late as well. Interestingly, it is these kinds of situations that often make employees more frustrated than one person getting promoted over another. It's often obvious to the work group that one person is gifted in a certain area or exhibits leadership potential. But it adds insult when certain employees constantly get away with ignoring general policy. Equal enforcement is consistency.

CHAPTER 10

Socializing at Work

One benefit of having a job is that you spend time with other people. As much as these people might frustrate, annoy, and even anger you, they provide a venue for social interaction. This is necessary, this is good, this is how it should be. Humans are, after all, social creatures. Most jobs require a certain amount of socializing—at the very least, talking among coworkers to collaborate or talking to customers.

At what point does socializing become dysfunctional? It's another one of those issues where the line can be hard to see until you cross it. But once you've crossed over, it can be disaster.

Hello, Is Anyone There?

Early in her career, Kathleen worked for a totalitarian boss who allowed no talking at all among employees unless to ask questions or share information that was strictly business-related. Employees could talk about personal matters in the break room or at lunch. Kathleen swore that when she became a manager, she would have a "human" department. So now that she was, her department continually buzzed with conversation and laughter. Sometimes it got so loud that other managers came over to ask that employees settle down. Kathleen thought they were being a bit uptight; what was the big deal, as long as people were getting their work done?

FACTS

To discourage the "rumor mill" that exists in most companies, some managers use a system similar to a suggestion box to collect questionable information, then investigate and post responses on a bulletin board or e-mail them to employees. Other managers appoint an employee committee to handle these activities. If you're worried that this could lead to breaching confidentiality or leaking proprietary information, consider that some form of information is already out there. The truth is seldom as damaging as rumors are.

But there was the problem: they weren't. Customers were complaining that no one was answering the phone; indeed, at times you couldn't even hear the phones ring for all the chatter and noise. Other departments started complaining, too—they weren't receiving reports and information on time or sometimes at all. Kathleen held a department meeting and told her employees, with obvious reluctance, that they needed to curtail their conversations and focus more on getting their work done. Everyone agreed to do so, but within a few days the noise was back to peak levels.

Finally Kathleen's superior called her upstairs. The meeting was her last action as the department's manager.

It is possible, and desirable, to set reasonable standards for socializing in the workplace. Most people are willing to settle down to work after greeting each other in the morning, and will keep personal conversation to an acceptable level throughout the workday if this is the standard you establish by policy as well as by example. Work should be fun—just not so much so that no work gets done. Here are some tips about socializing:

- Encourage socializing that is friendly and supportive. Use positive language in your dealings with employees to set the tone and example.
- Discourage gossip and rumors. Establish a "rumor central" where employees can bring rumors to find out whether they're true.
- Support collaborative efforts among employees on projects that warrant more than one participant.
- Encourage employees to consult one another to share knowledge and expertise.
- Provide opportunities for people to just talk, such as when the workday first begins or for a few minutes before meetings start.

Personalities and Politics

However focused you might like the workplace to be on job skills and performance, many aspects of going to work have more to do with personalities than abilities. Relationships form the foundation for effective teams—people working with other people. There is a synergy that exists in the most successful teams, a peculiar and dynamic blending of individuals and personalities that makes the team as a whole more than just the sum of its parts. The resulting relationships bond people by commonalities (the negative flip side of which is competitive divisions, and sometimes "enemy camps," within the work group). At this level, what matters is whether people like or dislike each other.

A sort of "relationship language" evolves after a time. People learn to get what they want from each other through indirect methods—husbands wait until their wives are in good moods before they tell them that they spend too much money on something, teenage sons mow the lawn and then ask to use the car. In family and social settings outside the work environment, these tactics have a give-and-take nature to them that causes us to view them as "playing games." In the workplace, we call them office politics. The motivations they reflect are personal—a desire for individual gain, a need for individual attention, a longing for recognition and reward. Because satisfying the motivation often comes at the expense of someone else, we tend to perceive office politics as manipulative and self-serving. Although we all profess to abhor office politics, everyone who works with other people becomes engaged in them to some extent.

At work, everybody wants something—more money, more status, more power, whatever. In the workplace, some people just want to come in and do a good job. They expect to be recognized and rewarded and given more responsibility. Why is this such a problem? Because people are human. They are naturally competitive. They may do a good job but they worry that they are not recognized for their contribution, so they try to do that little bit of manipulation that will maybe assure that others notice their contributions. An employee might drop in on the manager, alone, and casually mention an achievement or ask for advice on something. This self-gratification doesn't usually hurt anyone else, unless the person is taking credit for work someone else did.

A more damaging variation on this theme is the employee who uses the forum of a meeting to ask another employee an embarrassing question. More insidious is the employee who requests a confidential meeting with the manager to, out of sincere dedication and as much as he hates to have to do this (not!), alert the manager to certain people who are not pulling their share of the workload or are incompetent or are overqualified or who need remedial help or . . . Then there's the employee who consistently ignores assignments her manager gives her, but gushes, "Gosh, I wish someone had suggested this to me earlier!" when her manager's manager assigns the same project.

And technology has given people new ways to polish the apples they want others to notice. An employee can send out a grandstanding e-mail that gives the impression she is managing the project instead of the team member who really is, and copies everyone in the department or—oops!—the entire company. E-mail has become the latest weapon in political agendas, replacing drinks after work and standing outside in the rain to grab a smoke as the ideal venue for pitching an idea or kissing shoes. Who gets copied in and who is left off the list is the ultimate political move—checkmate!

Managers need to be constantly on guard for office politics. Communicate with all of your employees. Don't jump to conclusions about who is doing what—get all sides of the story. And beware of your own need for strokes. Office politics proliferate in part because managers themselves have hungry egos.

Office politics—whom you know, how much you support the ideas and pet projects of your superiors, what relationships you cultivate and which ones you discourage—often play into promotion decisions, at least minimally. A leadership personality is important for a manager, and that encompasses the ability to schmooze. Job skills matter too, of course. It's important to make sure the right people know your thoughts and see you shine.

This is reality—for you and for your employees. Make sure they each have this same opportunity to showcase successes and achievements for you. Just be sure you know whether that apple-polishing employee is advancing the goals of the team and the company or feeding the beast. Take the time to ferret out the true objective before you come to a conclusion. When an employee attempts to communicate with you at the expense of the team leader or coworkers, send the employee back to the group to communicate appropriately. Sometimes the employees doing the most communicating have the most time to do so because the real performers are too busy doing the work.

Office Parties

The office party—a wonderful way to let employees relax and socialize together in a less stressful environment than the workplace. Right? Sometimes. The occasional office party does help people get to know one another in a context other than coworker. Just as they might wear hiking boots and jeans in the woods or business suits in the office, people tend to adopt certain behaviors for specific environments and circumstances. Seeing each other outside the usual wardrobe can break down barriers and encourage greater cooperation in the workplace. Someone you consider to be arrogant or uptight in the office might turn out to have the same interests and hobbies that you do, once you're able to relax and get to know each other.

A party can be a reward for a job well done, something the company gives to employees to show appreciation for their extra effort and hard work. This makes people feel special, and also reinforces the value of teamwork. People get the chance to mingle and get comfortable with each other while someone else foots the bill. We all like to feel that we're getting something for nothing. Parties can lose their charm when they get out of control, however. This can happen when:

- Parties become so frequent that they no longer feel special. Employees can begin to resent that the company has enough money to throw away on entertaining every Friday evening, but not enough to give them raises or upgrade software or cover whatever other expense has been put on hold.
- Parties become the sole expression of appreciation that the company provides. Everybody loves a good party, but once in a while it's nice to get a reward that's clearly personal, such as a day off with pay.
- Parties serve to further divide, rather than unite, a work group or department. The hope and intent for an office party is to bring people together. If a work group contains great diversity in personalities, a party can magnify rather than minimize differences. Sometimes diversity in age presents challenges as well, as younger and older employees might have vastly different tastes and interests. Parties that cater to one group make others feel left out.

- Employees feel obligated to attend, even though doing so interferes with other plans. This is especially the case when employees are expected to bring their spouses, or to bring their families to holiday celebrations.
- Alcohol flows too freely. According to several studies, 70 percent of companies serve alcoholic beverages at office parties and 60 percent of employees drink enough to become intoxicated. Most office parties feature beer and wine, if not cocktails. Drinking is a social activity for many adults, and most people expect it at adult functions. Problems arise when people drink too much, then say or do things they will regret (or that others will wish they hadn't).

When MegaBig Software grew large enough to have more than a handful of people working for stock options and dreams, its founders decided working there would always be a party. So there was a party every Friday evening, in the cafeteria. There was an abundance of imported beers, expensive wines, and gourmet food. For the first few months everyone went to the Friday party, if only to grab a beer and a free meal. Then people started straggling in as they got off work, coats on, staying just long enough to put in an appearance before looking at their watches in mock disbelief and dashing out the door mumbling something about other commitments. They had lives outside work, and decided to enjoy them. Besides, it was a bit hard to relax, even with a drink, in an environment where earlier in the day or week they'd had a brainstorming lunch—it really wasn't "getting away" when the flipchart pages still hung on the walls. Before long, just a small group of the same employees showed up. They drank themselves into raucous revelry. It wasn't unusual for the cleaning crew to find a half-dozen or so people crashed on the floor the next morning. Other employees felt out of place and unwelcome if they dared stop in for a drink or a bite to eat, and the feelings carried into the workplace. Instead of bringing people together across boundaries, the weekly parties created new borders that separated groups and reinforced cliques.

Parties are more relaxing when they are less frequent—no more than quarterly in most situations—and are held off-site. If it's been a rough day or week, the last place people want to be to unwind is the office (even the cafeteria). People are creatures of habit, and tend to follow the same patterns of behavior in their environments. A work group at a party at the workplace will sit together, likely in the same seats they take at meetings or lunch, depending on the party's location. It doesn't do much to break people from their routines if they end up sitting with their usual group at their usual table.

For all the reasons people expect to find alcoholic beverages at parties, alcohol is a problem. Employees often like to have a drink or two to unwind and loosen up. It's hard to feel comfortable in new settings, especially when the socializing appears contrived and your coworkers are not people with whom you'd ordinarily go out. Because it's good to be able to relax, many companies hold parties at locations that serve alcohol. This gives the impression that it's not really the company that's supplying the drinks, and makes people feel more comfortable about drinking. They relax and have fun, and that's what parties are all about . . . until someone gets out of control.

Holiday parties are often the worst in this regard. For whatever reasons—the holiday spirit, perhaps—people seem more inclined to let their hair down, so to speak, at holiday parties. Most people are already in a good mood, and might have exchanged gifts or had relaxed workdays already. Festive holiday decorations transform even the most mundane room into a party delight. Warm spiced wine, hot buttered rum, and eggnog are sweet and wonderful, belying the alcoholic punch the drinks pack. If someone hangs mistletoe, you can be sure it will be a night many people will want to forget. If the holidays are all about excess, holiday parties are often right in sync. Drunkenness becomes extreme. People do highly embarrassing things that would appall them if they were sober, including saying things to their managers and going home with each other. The repercussions last for weeks.

Increasingly, there are consequences for such actions. Managers and employees have a tough time returning to pre-party behaviors and relationships. Something said as a drunken jest lingers to hang like smog between coworkers. Managers might lose the respect of their employees; employees might lose the trust their managers had in them. People end up asking to be transferred to different jobs or quitting altogether. More frightening and severe consequences can arise if an employee leaves the party drunk and drives, getting into an accident on the way home.

ESSENTIALS

Consider holding your office party at a restaurant or other off-site location that can provide full-service catering. With professional bartenders mixing and serving drinks, it's easier to moderate the amount of alcohol employees consume. It's also easier to have the bartender, rather than a manager, cut someone off who's had too much to drink.

It's certainly not your job to babysit employees at parties; after all, they're adults and can make their own judgments and decisions. But if you knowingly allow a drunken employee to drive away, you could end up holding the accountability bag. A court could find you and your company partially responsible for whatever damage the employee did—including taking someone's life—because you had failed to intervene. You, as a manager, are a representative of your company at any company-sponsored event. To keep parties from getting out of control as a result of alcohol consumption:

- Serve lots of good food. Not just snacks and hors d'oeuvres, but real food that people will want to eat. Breads, pastas, and pastries help people feel full, which lessens the inclination to drink more. Food also slows alcohol's absorption into your system.
- Clearly define the hours the party will start and end. Stop serving alcoholic beverages at least thirty minutes before the scheduled ending time and bring out the coffee instead. It's not that coffee does anything to counteract the effects of alcohol; it doesn't. But it is a recognized social signal that the drinking is over.
- Consider scheduling the party as a happy hour, starting immediately after work and ending two or three hours later. This lets people socialize for a while, have a drink or two, and then go home or otherwise get on with their lives.

- Encourage employees to bring their significant others to office parties. This tends to curtail both excessive drinking and wild behavior. Some companies designate the first few hours of the party for employees only, then welcome significant others.
- If you see someone who clearly has had too much to drink, speak to whoever is serving drinks to switch the person to nonalcoholic beverages. If it's a no-host or honor bar, try to encourage the person to stop drinking alcohol, or ask the person's friends to intervene.
- If people consistently drink too much and then act boorish, consider jettisoning alcohol altogether in favor of a coffee and dessert bar.

Have a reason for having a party. Some managers plan parties and events in part because they have nothing better to do. They like to have other people around them, and since work is their lives, they make it their social lives as well. Employees who might have lives outside work will quickly resent this kind of intrusion.

What if a drunken employee says something rude to you at a party, or otherwise acts up? No easy answers here, sorry to say. You have to decide whether to make an excuse for drunken behavior or have a chat with the employee—or both. Alcohol changes behavior by blocking inhibitions. Drinking doesn't make people say and do things that are counter to their basic values, generally; it just silences that little voice of warning. Your decision on how to handle the situation depends on what the employee said or did, and who else heard or saw it. You're likely to remember the incident more vividly and for a longer time than the employee who was drunk. And this discussion begs the parallel question: What if you get drunk and say or do something rude to an employee? You could face serious consequences. It's one of the ironies of the system that as a manager you remain a representative of your company no matter where you are or whom you're with. The best advice: Don't do it in the first place. Then you don't have to worry about how to fix it.

Afterhours Events

In the hit television show of the late 1990s, *Ally McBeal*, the quirky cadre of lawyers gathers at the bar conveniently located on the ground floor of the law firm's office building for a little R&R after work. It appears they do this every evening, every single one of them. They drink, gossip, dance, and pair off. Watching the show, it seems these high-powered professionals spend as much time socializing as working together. They have no lives beyond the office building. Reality? Of course not. Television is noted for its ability to compress life into one-dimensional wafers. But drawn from reality? Perhaps, or at least from a vision of reality that suggests this is how life should be. Work hard, party harder.

While office parties are nearly always afterhours events, other activities that are less formally organized often draw employees together in what are at least intended to be social settings. Many such events imply that your presence is expected, if not outright required. These could be Saturday softball games, Sunday afternoon picnics, evenings at the dinner theater, comedy club, or circus. Employees can grow to resent these events, feeling that they are compelled to attend, uncompensated, when they'd rather be doing other things. There's typically an element of office politics that comes into play when afterhours events get out of hand. People sense, often rightly, that unless they are there they will become the focus of gossip. In some companies, the only people who get ahead are those who always attend the same events the boss attends.

FACTS

Not all afterhours events are purely social. Some companies sponsor community contribution days, on which employees donate their time and talents to service and charitable organizations. This might be a day spent serving lunch at a homeless shelter or building a house with a volunteer organization such as Habitat for Humanity. When community giving is involved, many employees feel a sense of satisfaction and contribution that overcomes perceptions that managers might be taking advantage of them.

The frequency of afterhours events is usually more of an issue than the events themselves. People feel they already give too much of themselves to their jobs; continuing to encroach on personal time is a ticket to disaster. Less is more when it comes to using such activities as teambuilding opportunities. Even events that have strong community contribution components are better scheduled occasionally rather than frequently. If you are planning an all-day event, try to schedule it on a workday or give people some sort of compensation for coming, such as the afternoon off the day before. When employees already work long hours, requiring attendance at afterhours functions makes the event feel like it's just more work. Plan something special, and do it well. And again, keep in mind that even when you're having fun you're still representing your company. Stay on your best behavior.

Workplace Friendships

The more time people spend at work or involved in work activities, the more likely it is that the workplace will become the primary venue for social activities. Their friendships and even romantic relationships start and thrive, borne of work relationships. This is especially true in jobs that demand long hours, intense focus on complex projects, or frequent travel. Friendships can make work more fun, which often increases employee satisfaction as well as productivity. Work friends enjoy spending breaks and lunch times with each other, and sometimes extend their socializing beyond the office. Most of the time, these friendships and their consequences are positives for employees, the department, and the company as a whole. Having a strong system of support through workplace friendships can help employees weather the inevitable downs and hard times of work life, making such experiences more tolerable. Such a network of friends can even keep employees in jobs when they might otherwise feel inclined to leave.

Every now and then, however, friendships turn sour. This can have far-reaching ramifications for the involved employees as well as other team members. It didn't take long for coworkers and peers Robin, Chris, Carol, and Brad to become friends. They had similar interests and tastes, and often met for lunch and sometimes for drinks after work or for dinner. They became the bedrock of the department, a solid team their manager and their coworkers knew they could count on to shift effortlessly into high gear when challenge reared its ugly head. The four friends incorporated their work friendship into their lives outside work, introducing each other to nonwork friends to create an even wider circle.

ALERT

It is difficult for a manager to supervise and evaluate an employee who is also a friend. And other employees might suspect favoritism. In most situations, friendships between managers and subordinates are more likely to survive when they keep a low profile in the workplace.

One weekend Robin and Brad had a falling out. Unlike previous disagreements that they patched up after just a few days, this one grew into a feud. It splintered the circle of friends, and the work team's productivity plummeted. Robin left the team and joined another, creating havoc in both. The feud between her and Brad intensified, and became the source of much office gossip and speculation. Brad grew increasingly dissatisfied with conditions in the department and surreptitiously contacted a headhunter to explore opportunities with some of the companies that had been interested in him before he took his current position. Still friends with Robin, Carol and Chris let slip a comment about Brad's actions. When Brad came to work the next morning, no one would talk to him. When he opened his e-mail, he discovered why. Copies of a half-dozen e-mail messages between him and the headhunter in which Brad had candidly and bluntly described his dissatisfactions with his coworkers, the department, and the company had been forwarded to just about everyone.

It's not just friendships that turn sour that can divide and disrupt a department or work group. Being out of high school doesn't mean you're free from the influence, often detrimental, of cliques. In high school, cliques frequently formed around star athletes or cheerleaders. In the workplace, it's not always so easy to see the core of cliques; many form around outside interests. These could be hobbies, social activities, and even religious activities. Sometimes what starts as a friendship develops into a clique when members exclude rather than welcome others from floating in and out of the circle.

QUESTIONS?

What are cliques?
Cliques are groups, usually small, that form around specific interests and then exclude those who do not share those interests. Cliques at work can be particularly damaging to other work groups and the department because they interfere with the usual social formations that are essential to effective teamwork.

The yearning to belong is a basic human need. We need other people in order to survive as well as thrive. In primordial times when survival consumed every waking minute, numbers meant safety (not to mention food). But like the fight-or-flight response to potential danger, this driving need to belong failed to fade when it became less critical to survival. Just as a near collision on your drive home from work will give you an adrenaline jolt that leaves your heart pounding and your muscles quivering, the suspicion that you're being left out of the group—or worse, have been exiled from the group—becomes nearly unbearable.

Unfortunately, managers don't have all that much control over how work friendships form or whether cliques develop. As long as employees are doing their work, not skipping up and down the hall with their friends or hiding behind closed doors, then there's no reason to interfere. And truth be told, most people don't want managers monitoring these relationships. It's very intrusive and makes teamwork nearly impossible. But you do need to keep your eyes open. Don't hide in your office or pretend you don't know what's going on. Knowledge is power, whether or not you use it to take action.

There are, of course, times when you must intervene. It's time to step in when you notice that:

- Employees spend more time socializing than working. They can't possibly be doing what they've been hired to do if they spend the entire workday in gossip-and-giggle mode.
- One group keeps others from being successful by undermining their efforts, or keeps information from other people and groups. This is a clique, and its actions are counterproductive.
- Office politics turn vicious, and rumors and gossip abound. A bit of chitchat is not a bad thing. People are curious and often legitimately concerned about each other when they talk about situations and the other people involved in them. When talk turns destructive, it's no longer conversation—it's sabotage.

If you do see that friendships and socializing are interfering with productivity or preventing some employees from doing their work, you might need to distance people from each other. You can split a work team into smaller groups, and assign them different projects. You can also take steps to promote new, positive working relationships by realigning project partnerships. And you can model an appropriate balance between socializing and working in your own behavior. If your employees see you standing in the doorway chatting about the guy in accounting who's dating the senior vice president's daughter, they will believe it's okay for them to do the same thing. As trite as it sounds, actions speak infinitely louder than words. As a manager, it's your responsibility to make sure an environment of fairness exists in your department.

When Coworker Relationships Turn Romantic

Sometimes one thing leads to another, and before you know it there's a story that would make any manager blush. But we'll keep things publishable. (You don't need a book for these stories, anyway; just look around your office or company.) When people spend most of their waking hours together, it's natural for them to want to get to know each other better as people, not just as coworkers. This is especially true when a work group completes a particularly difficult project that has put team members through unusual stress. People bond when they share survival, whether in a catastrophic event or an intense work challenge. There's the thrill of everybody working together as coworkers and comrades united toward a common goal: company success. Days, nights, weekends—everything goes into it. There is hard work and dedication all around as employees rally for the cause. When it's all over, when the project is finished, it's natural to look at the person sitting next to you and think: "We did this together. Together. I wonder what else we could be doing . . . together?"

The odds of a work friendship blooming into something more increases with the level of chaos. High levels suspend reality and put personal lives on hold, two of the key ingredients necessary to brew disaster. High-tech wonder company or conservative corporation, it happens everywhere: coworkers date. Sometimes hours are long and the tasks are boring. Sometimes it's a fast-paced but isolated environment such as a hospital (it's no accident that so many successful soap operas are set in hospitals). Sometimes it's a bureaucratic company where day-to-day life is a drag or people have boring jobs and no goals. And sometimes it just happens. Two people see each other across a crowded room—even a room turned into a maze by the cubicles that cordon workspaces into territories—and sparks ignite the fires of passion in each of them. Sometimes these two are both legally available (unmarried or divorced); just as often at least, one is not.

FACTS

Surveys suggest that as many as 40 percent of employees have dated coworkers at some point; many people view the office as an ideal opportunity to get to know someone with relative safety. If things work out, the explorations move to activities beyond work. If not, no harm done. Right? Not always. Failed relationships are a leading factor in sexual harassment claims and lawsuits.

Dating between coworkers is not against the law, although it might violate company policies intended to minimize the potential for claims of favoritism and harassment. When such policies exist, every employee should know about them before accepting a job offer; violating the policy can have serious consequences. Companies are more likely to strongly discourage romantic relationships among employees than to outright prohibit them; there's a fine line here between regulating workplace behavior and interfering with personal lives.

Dating within the department is seldom a good idea, even when the involved employees are discreet. Disagreements and arguments are inevitable even in the best of relationships, particularly during the "growing pains" stages. It's almost impossible, from a human perspective, to simply drop these at the door when coming to work. Rather, it's equally inevitable that lovers' quarrels between coworkers will spill over into work functions. Other employees might feel the need to choose sides to defend one partner or the other. Dating between employees who work in different departments is less likely to be disruptive, as long as the departments don't interact with each other.

When coworkers begin dating, it's important to be aware of potential conflicts and to watch for signs of favoritism or even competition. It might become necessary to transfer one employee to a comparable position in which there is less direct contact with the other employee. Nothing is more demoralizing for other employees than to look down the hall and see two coworkers prancing along with smirks on their faces—especially when the relationship somehow places those other employees at a disadvantage. You might need to step in to review decisions that involve the happy couple, such as overtime and off-site assignments. Even if all is on the up-and-up, other employees might perceive the dating duo to be getting choice assignments or evading unpleasant ones.

Dating between managers and their subordinates is almost always a bad idea. It's impossible to escape the scrutiny of employees, regardless of how discreet you think you are. It's equally impossible to avoid perceptions of favoritism while the relationship is hot . . . and discrimination or harassment if it fails. The greatest risk is for managers who date employees who report to them; even if company policy doesn't prohibit this, it's poor judgment. How can you fairly and objectively evaluate the job performance of the person who shares your life and knows your deepest secrets? Certainly you can't control personal attractions, and many people are happy together because something drew them together. If you find yourself attracted to a subordinate:

- Start by considering the end. Where could this relationship lead, and what are its possible consequences? Can both of you accept them?
- Remove yourself from a position of authority over the person whom you are dating. Transfer the employee to a different work team that reports to another manager, if he or she is willing, or request a transfer yourself. It might not seem fair, but someone's career trajectory will need to change or both could easily fade to nothing.
- Conduct yourselves with discretion, but don't for a moment let yourself be deluded into believing that no one else knows about your relationship. Someone does, if not everyone.
- Don't sneak around, especially at work. If anything, the onus is on you to go out of your way to avoid situations that make it look like you're sneaking around.

ESSENTIALS

Make sure you know your company's policies and corporate culture regarding interoffice dating and particularly managers dating subordinates. Some companies permit dating among coworkers of relatively equal status, but frown on or prohibit dating between managers and subordinates.

Work-related dating can be risky even when it doesn't directly involve other employees. Claire was an account manager in the sales department who wasn't especially competent. She was often abrasive and rude toward other employees in the department, although sweet as could be with clients. Her performance evaluations were poor, and her manager had worked with her to structure an improvement plan. Then Claire started dating one of the company's main clients. Her behavior toward both her coworkers and her superiors turned vicious. To demote or fire her, however, meant the company might lose the client's business, which would be a significant blow. Finally a high-level executive got wind of the relationship and intervened with executive management at the client's company, which assigned a different administrator to its account. Claire's power base evaporated, and within a few weeks she resigned.

Let Me Call You Sweetheart

Sometimes dating between coworkers leads to what appears to be a good thing. Two people in different departments meet in the company cafeteria and the rest, as they say, is history—they start dating, they fall in love, they announce their union to their respective work groups that then celebrate with a joint after-hours event. The happy twosome comes to work and leaves for home together, shares a parking space, and names the baby after the company president. It's a match made in . . . well, maybe not heaven, though it certainly appears magical enough.

Okay, hold the phone. What happens when these two departments, however different, need to interact? One can't criticize or otherwise be objective about the other department when a spouse works there. And what happens if, heaven forbid, they end up working in the same department? Can you say, "Take cover!"? Couples fight . . . it's part of life. When spouses work for the same company, the normal battles of relationships spill over into the workplace. What starts as an argument about breakfast cereal could end up costing a major account . . . or a job.

Rhonda and Patrick met when each was running an errand to the copy store. She worked in advertising, he was an industrial engineer. Their departments never interacted and the company had no policy prohibiting dating or marriage, so they felt safe in pursuing their relationship. They eventually married. All went well until the company went through a period of restructuring and downsizing. Both kept their jobs, though the advertising department had to cut half its staff. As a result, those who remained had to pick up the slack, which meant considerable overtime. Patrick worked out at the health club with Pete, Rhonda's manager, and after a few weeks decided enough was enough. So Patrick called Pete and asked him to excuse Rhonda from the mandatory overtime because it was creating problems in their relationship. Pete refused, and chastised Patrick for imposing on him in such a way. Rhonda's workload eventually stabilized and she returned to a regular workweek, but her relationship with Pete remained strained. After a few months, she resigned.

Policies prohibiting employees who are married to each other from working in the same department or even in the company at the same time are more common than policies against dating. In legalese these are called anti-nepotism policies, and their proscriptions typically also apply to employees who are related to one another in any way. Some companies promptly fire one or even both employees if coworkers do marry in defiance of policies prohibiting it. Such policies should explicitly state what behaviors are not allowed, what is necessary to invoke the policy ("rules of evidence"), and what consequences the employees face. As with all policies, consistent monitoring and enforcement are essential.

FACTS

Company policies prohibiting employees who are married to each other from working in the same department or even anywhere within the company could run afoul of the law in states that make it illegal to consider marital status in employment and other decisions. The results of court cases involving these issues are mixed, making it difficult for companies to know whether their policies will help or hinder their efforts to maintain an equitable employment environment.

Of Love and Lust

While there's often an aura of magic and romance that surrounds two people who fall in love at work (at least in the beginning), lust-driven affairs spawn nothing but gossip and disruption:

- At a retreat for executives, the CEO heard something in the middle of the night. He looked out the window and saw the CFO running out of the VP of Customer Service's bungalow in his underwear.
- The VP of Development was having an affair with one of the technical writers. They started sending obscene e-mail to each other.

One of the techies intercepted a message, which immediately went around the company.

- A department head had an affair with another department head. He was married. She had a drinking problem. She verbally attacked him at a company party (you gotta watch those after-hours parties) after he broke up with her.

- A female manager at a very large company basically went through the company, sleeping with one superior after another. Unfortunately, stereotypes generally arise from an element of truth.

- On the drive to an off-site company meeting, an employee stopped at a fast food restaurant for a quick snack. Standing in front of her were a sales manager and a customer service representative (each married to other people), holding hands.

Managers can't sit around and gossip, of course, but they do need to be in the know about what gossip is going around. Often, you can't do anything or even confront the people involved because doing so would be career suicide at best and could result in charges of sexual harassment. But if you observe specific behaviors that affect job performance and productivity, either individual or work team, it's your responsibility to bring it up. You don't have to say, "I know you're having an affair." (In fact, you probably shouldn't.)

Instead, express what you've seen and how it affects the department—as you would handle any performance issue. "I and several of your coworkers have seen the two of you holding hands in meetings and working in one office or the other with the door closed. The other members of your team tell me you two frequently miss team meetings, and I'm hearing considerable gossip about your behavior. Three of your projects are behind their timelines, and I've received calls from other departments about them."

By remaining focused on how the behavior affects job performance, you can steer clear of personal issues that really aren't your jurisdiction. Consult with your HR department before meeting with the dating pair, to be sure you fully understand your company's policies and procedures regarding such matters. Because so many sexual harassment claims involve coworkers who once dated each other, it's important for you to view such a claim as a potential outcome of the situation. Document, document, document!

Sexual Harassment

Unwanted social or sexual advances that create an unpleasant work environment or place pressure on an employee are illegal, a violation of the Civil Rights Act, Title VII. Monetary penalties for those found in violation—individuals as well as companies—can be stiff. Career consequences can be severe. Sexual harassment takes many forms, and involves women pressuring men as well as men pressuring women. Unfortunately, what constitutes sexual harassment is not always clear-cut. Decide whether these incidents do:

- A key executive asked his department coordinator to meet him at a restaurant for a drink to talk with her about how things were going. He presented the invitation as a reward and a way to talk uninterrupted by the chaos and frenzy of the workplace. He just happened to make the reservation at a hotel restaurant. During dinner he casually mentioned that he had reserved a hotel room for the night and asked if she would like to join him.
- A new director, a single man, immediately wanted to get to know the employees in his department (he had been brought in from outside and was also new in town). So he asked a couple of the single women if they would like to have dinner with him and help him get acquainted with the area.
- A female manager and a male subordinate were traveling together on business. She picked him up at his apartment to go to the airport. It was summer and very hot, so he was wearing shorts. Twice in the car she told him that he had great legs. He changed into slacks when they got to the airport.

If you pegged each of these incidents as sexual harassment, give yourself a pat on the back. Harassment is generally in the perspective of the victim, regardless of the intention of the overture. The new director in the second story, for example, was dumfounded when he learned that the women he invited to dinner complained to their manager. He viewed his actions as cordial and gentlemanly. It made sense to him to ask single women to join him because he felt they would have the freedom to do so. Bad judgment all the way around! Even as he was defending himself, he could hear that he sounded just like a scenario in a sexual harassment training workshop—which is exactly what he became.

Sexual harassment is a complex area of law, policy, and behavior. Companies can define it in different ways, which doesn't necessarily mean they'll find the courts on their side if an employee files a lawsuit. It's important to realize that much depends on how the person who complains perceives the behaviors. The most insidious sexual harassment is often the least obvious—the male manager who stands just a little too close to female employees, makes comments that can be interpreted as suggestive, compliments female employees on their clothing or perfume. Or the woman manager who does the same with male employees—men are victims of sexual harassment, too, although not as often as women. Chapter 9, "Toeing the Line on Company Policies," presents other information about sexual harassment, and Appendix B, "Resources," lists books and other sources that provide more detailed information.

CHAPTER 11

Check Your Baggage at the Door

I n many ways, the workplace resembles a family. Because of this, people tend to carry "baggage" to work with them—emotions and reactions rooted in other aspects of their lives. Our experiences with other people shape our personalities—sometimes through bumps and bruises.

People remind us of other people that we've known. Look around your workplace. Do you see people who remind you of your mom, dad, brother, sister? The guy you dated last summer, or the girl who broke your heart freshman year of college? Your neighbor or your barber or your favorite clerk at the grocery store? These impressions guide your responses and reactions, even though the "new" people are different from the "old" people. Knowing that this is how the human mind functions helps you to break free of the pattern when it's clear that it doesn't apply. That pushy boss probably isn't really just the same as your overbearing father, even though they might sound and even look alike.

Sometimes these similarities are helpful. If you've developed healthy and effective ways to deflect a domineering dad's authoritarian ways, you can adapt them to dealing with a dictatorial boss. This crossover becomes hazardous, however, when the ways you've learned for dealing with your father are dysfunctional—as is often the case when personalities and behaviors are extreme. Then, applying home tactics to the workplace can backfire. Work is not home, after all, and the boss is not your father.

What Punches Your Buttons?

Much of the time, the behaviors and responses we carry from setting to setting and person to person are subtle enough that we might not even recognize what we're doing. It's important to learn to recognize your own patterns of behavior, and to take note of what triggers them. While those near the bottom of the corporate ladder are often quite adept at hiding their reactions, it seems that the further up the hierarchy you go, the less constraint you encounter. Some managers seem to believe that it is not they, but everyone around them, who needs to adjust. People in positions of power often feel that they shouldn't have to be self-aware because those around them should be aware of them. But not knowing what pushes your own buttons ends up interfering with objectivity and fairness.

Let's take a look at a few scenarios in the following sections. In situations such as these, employees lose and so does the manager. Do any of these scenarios sound at all familiar?

Managers who don't know their hot buttons leave themselves vulnerable to manipulation. And employees who work for these managers can't get the structure, support, and guidance they need because the manager is always reacting to triggers that are not related to the circumstances at hand.

One Bad Experience

As an accounting intern, William has a very bad experience with an aggressive, sometimes abusive, female boss. Some of the other interns are bothered by her, but have learned not to let her get under their skin. Others simply ignore her, or quake and quiver but get the work done. But she gets to William, who never does figure out how to deal with her. No matter what he does, he always ends up feeling that it wasn't enough or he was wrong. He doesn't know how to ignore her tirades or how to confront her about her behavior, so he just takes what she dishes his way.

Later in his career William takes a position as accounting manager for a small company. There are some women in the group he manages who exhibit some of the same general characteristics as the woman who had been his first boss. They are straightforward and don't mince words. He immediately comes down on them, rather than understanding and even appreciating their no-nonsense attitude toward getting the job done. He is the one who loses. His behavior earns him a reputation for being a chauvinist, and the group's productivity dives when the women leave.

Tunnel Vision

Loretta has an obsession about timeliness. She is almost neurotic about getting everywhere early. She manages a group where people certainly get to work, but not always at the split second the day begins. Instead of looking at this objectively and recognizing the good work these employees do, she criticizes them. She nags at them for every little thing—though never talks to them about timeliness. She considers their lackadaisical attitudes toward the clock an affront to her authority. They consider her to be so focused on details that don't matter that she's willing to sacrifice their good work just to force them to toe the line—her line.

Mr. Sensitivity

Russell is a very nurturing kind of guy, really sensitive to other people's feelings. His employees feel they can come to him with any problem and find a compassionate ear. Most of the time this is a good thing. But Russell's employees have figured out that he also loses his objectivity when an employee becomes emotional, such as when an employee comes in and bursts into tears. Russell immediately wants to make it better, and even starts to criticize management or other employees when talking to this employee. He becomes desperate to make everything better. Some employees take advantage of him by appealing to his soft side, while others don't hear the honest criticism or firm guidelines that they need to hear. Still others, who are not so aware of feelings, consider him weak.

That's Not Really Why You're Angry

Anger is a secondary emotion. It is a cover for something else, and a way of keeping other, scarier, feelings away. We get angry when we feel afraid, sad, threatened, insecure, disappointed. We often express anger when we feel out of control, because anger elicits a response when other efforts may fail to do so. In this regard, anger can give a false sense of control. Anger is uncomfortable for others to experience so they often do whatever it takes to put an end to their discomfort—which often means placating the angry person by giving what the person wants.

Everyone gets angry, and everyone has gotten angry with the wrong people for the wrong reasons at the wrong times. For most people, such situations represent the culmination of feelings they can no longer control. The actual event that sends them over the edge is often something minor and might not even be related to the reasons they're angry. Carolyn, an administrative assistant in the accounting department, blew up when Stephen, an accounts payable clerk, stopped at her desk to tell her the break room was out of coffee. "I've had it! Get your own damn coffee!"

she screamed at him. "I'm not the only one in this department who can walk two lousy blocks to the store to buy a package of fine grind! It doesn't take a college degree! Just go get it yourself!"

John, the department manager, heard Carolyn shouting and came out of his office to see what was going on. He asked her to take a walk with him. Once they were outside the building, he asked her what had happened. Still agitated, Carolyn repeated her exasperation that everyone in the department seemed to believe buying coffee was her responsibility and hers alone. "I don't even drink coffee!" she said. "Nowhere in my job description does it say that it's my job to buy the coffee! No one notices anything else I do, but when we run out of coffee, everyone comes running!"

FACTS

According to projections released by the U.S. Bureau of Labor Statistics, all of the ten fastest growing occupations require some level of education or specialized training. Leading the list are computer engineers and computer support specialists, which are expected to more than double in the ten-year period from 1998 to 2008. BLS also projects that pay in these fields will grow the fastest as well, increasing by as much as 117 percent in the same period.

John immediately agreed that it was not Carolyn's job to buy coffee. It wasn't even a job responsibility at all, for anyone. It was a pattern the department slipped into because she had once been willing to do it, he noted, but it certainly wasn't an aspect of her job. John assured Carolyn that he would post a memo asking the coffee drinkers to decide how to maintain the coffee supply. As they walked and talked, it became clear to John that Carolyn was very frustrated because her job was not giving her the opportunities to advance that she had anticipated it would when she took it three years ago. In her career plan, she was to have been an accounting clerk by this time—but here she was, running to the store to buy coffee. "I know just as much as the other clerks, probably more, but no one notices that I'm the one who corrects their statements and records," Carolyn told John. "There have been three openings in receivables in the past six months, but you've selected someone else each time."

John explained that the department used educational requirements to screen applicants, and that Carolyn didn't have an undergraduate degree with a major in the any of the desired fields. He agreed that she did have exemplary knowledge of the department and its functions, and said he would check with HR to see if there was a way to flex the education requirements to accommodate Carolyn's degree in communications. John also reminded Carolyn that he had an open-door policy because he wanted people to come to him with their concerns. If she had come to talk to him when the job openings were first posted, he could have talked to HR then. As it was, there weren't any vacancies now, and he didn't know when one would surface. John and Carolyn agreed to meet in one week to discuss what John was able to find out from HR.

Carolyn also confessed that things weren't going well at home and that she was planning to file for divorce. But she was worried about her ability to support herself, and didn't believe she could do that on her present salary. Because she was at the top of the salary range for her position, thinking about being on her own put her in panic mode. "I guess I just felt you as my manager should know what a good job I do, and be willing to make an exception for me without my having to ask you to," Carolyn said. "I'm not comfortable coming to you to say, 'look what a good job I'm doing.' You give me good performance ratings, so I didn't think I should need to remind you."

Carolyn's anger had nothing to do with poor Stephen, who simply happened to be in the way when she erupted. Being asked to buy coffee did have some involvement; Carolyn perceived that to epitomize the inability of her manager and her coworkers to recognize her capabilities. Beneath these surface manifestations was the real issue: Carolyn felt unappreciated and unfairly overlooked when it came to promotional opportunities. This aroused nagging doubts about whether she truly was qualified for the job she wanted to have; if no one noticed how good she was, maybe she wasn't really that good. So she tried even harder to get John and others in her department to notice her work and recognize her abilities—she left Post-It notes on people's desks whenever she corrected paperwork they submitted that was incomplete, and joined in on discussions about department procedures and accounting matters. That no one picked up on these attempts to gain recognition further fueled both her frustration and her self-doubt.

As Carolyn's manager, John should have had a better understanding of Carolyn's career goals. Career planning was a key part of the company's performance standards and evaluation process. Each employee met with his or her manager every six months to review progress toward stated goals and objectives. If Carolyn was vague in these meetings, John should have pinned her down at least to be assured that he understood what she hoped to accomplish during her employment and in her career. When Carolyn hit crisis mode, however, John reacted swiftly and appropriately. He:

- Removed Carolyn from the scene. When someone bursts into outrage in front of other people, it's nearly impossible to back down without losing face. Since frustration and fear are among the core emotions that ignite anger, a person in outburst mode is not going to willingly validate them by surrendering. Removing an angry person from any audience removes the need for the person to continue raging. It also provides an opportunity for the person to regain composure and dignity.
- Agreed with Carolyn that her feelings were valid. This put them both on the same side, giving them common ground from which to work toward a solution.
- Stayed focused on the issues. While John didn't support Carolyn's behavior, he didn't criticize it, either. He directed the discussion to tangibles—Carolyn's disappointment and frustration about not being promoted, and the company policies that impeded her efforts. This allowed John to present possible solutions.
- Gave Carolyn time to recover. By taking Carolyn outside of the office and the building, John reduced the likelihood that any of Carolyn's coworkers would see her so out of control.
- Concluded the discussion with tangible actions and a follow-up plan. Without making promises he might not be able to keep, John told Carolyn exactly what he would do to try to resolve her frustration and when they would meet for further discussions.

Although angry employees are a key concern for most managers, angry managers are just as often a key concern for employees. Employees are unfortunately convenient when a manager blows a gasket—and again, often for reasons not at all related to the reasons for the anger. Managers, like employees, sometimes carry problems from home or other dimensions of their lives into the workplace. A fight with your spouse or kids might start your day with a sour outlook. Because you know you have to go to work and deal with all the pressures there, you try to stay calm and collected at home so you can at least leave with the delusion of peace and harmony. But when you get to work, an employee says or does something that triggers those feelings you've swallowed, and back up they rush. Before you know it, you're dumping all over this employee whose only offense was to be in the wrong place at the wrong time saying the wrong thing.

FACTS

Stress affects everybody. There are many pressures in today's world, both at home and at work. Your company's EAP (Employee Assistance Program) can be a good resource for employees and managers alike. Most EAPs provide short-term counseling to help people find solutions to their problems. Many EAPs extend consultation services to managers and supervisors, offering advice and recommendations about workplace issues. Such interventions help managers deal with stress and the factors that cause it, and can head off problems before they become serious.

Managers often have high expectations for their employees, then become frustrated, disappointed, and angry when employees fail to live up to those expectations. That's because these expectations are as much about the manager as they are about the employee. When employees excel, their managers look good. Employees also often feel grateful to their managers for providing opportunities and encouragement. All of this strokes the manager's ego. When employees fail to meet expectations, managers feel hurt and let down. How do we often express disappointment? With anger! In these situations, it's usually the hapless employee who bears the brunt of this expression, which of course doesn't help matters any. In reality, the employee might not have been aware of the manager's expectation in the first place—though we all like to feel proud of the accomplishments of those we've mentored and encouraged, it's awkward to directly express the desire for the employee to do well so we can feel good about ourselves.

Sometimes a manager over-identifies with an employee. Perhaps the employee reminds you of yourself in an earlier stage of your career, or is at risk for going down a path that you know will be a mistake. You want this person to do well or even better than you have done. So you invest in this person—you provide opportunities, recognition, support, encouragement (and probably expect similar investments in return, either from the grateful employee or from one of your superiors who notices your selfless commitment to advancing this employee's career). Their perceived failures become our failures, even when the perception of failure is misguided. Such expectations are often unrealistic and become distortions. You might interpret an employee's unwillingness to work day and night as an attack on your values and authority, rather than seeing it for what it is—just the person's work style.

It's not always easy to see that you're doing this, and it's even harder to stop when you make the recognition. Managers are people, too, and they don't like to fail (especially in front of others) any more than anyone else. Check in with yourself to be sure your expectations are appropriate:

- Constantly ask yourself: Is this about them or me? Be honest. It's not always a bad thing for your expectations to be about you even when they involve others, but it is essential for you to know when this is the case.
- Establish boundaries, framed by specific job requirements, around your expectations. Performance evaluation standards and job descriptions, as much as they feel intrusive and bureaucratic, can help save you from yourself. Let them guide your expectations, and save your stomach lining and your heart.

- Tune in to your emotions and emotional reactions. If you feel anger boiling just below the surface, take a walk or close your door until you can regain control. Don't engage when you're angry; there's nothing wrong with walking away from a situation until you can deal with it calmly and rationally.
- Identify the real problem. Are you angry because the employee failed to complete an assignment and now others can't complete their assignments, or because you were planning to showcase the project at this afternoon's staff meeting and now you can't? Then address the real problem.

Managers can get away with a lot of abusive behavior toward employees, or at least think they can. They can close the door and say what they want and get away with it—for the short term. But the toll in loss of morale and even legal issues at some point catches up. Employees learn quickly to read the moods of their managers. When managers have problems at home or are feeling pressure from other departments or their superiors, employees learn to anticipate venting and tirades. Some duck for cover behind work projects that take them out of the office, while others get angry themselves.

FACTS

Sometimes managers use anger as a way of turning employees against the company. A manager may not like the direction of the company, for example, so he incites anger in his employees, hoping that he can hurt the company by hurting them. This gets everybody angry and unites the work group in battle. Although employees are often unaware that this is what's going on, they are likely to suffer the consequences in terms of lost opportunities and bad reputations.

When a manager loses control, and particularly when the loss unleashes anger toward employees, the consequences can be severe and far-reaching. When you feel anger rising within you that you know is going to splash all over some employee, take a deep breath and ask yourself:

- Is this employee the source of my anger?
- If so, why?
- If not, who or what is?
- Am I really feeling angry, or am I disappointed?
- What, realistically, can the employee or I do to remedy the situation?
- Can I talk with the employee about this without losing my cool?
- What is the worst that can happen if I just walk away from this and address it later?

If you can't talk to the employee without losing your temper, don't try to talk now. Do whatever you need to do to cool off. Then before you approach the employee, write some notes to yourself that explain the problem as you see it, what adverse consequences occurred as a result, and what solutions you propose. Stick to this "script" in your conversation to help keep yourself calm and focused.

When Personalities Collide

Families evolve and grow through marriages, births, and adoptions, sometimes bringing people with disparate interests and personalities to live together when, were they strangers, they wouldn't even greet each other in passing on the street or in the store. Workplaces are similar. The people within them aren't necessarily together because they choose to be. They are together because the work they've chosen puts them together. They spend more time with each other than with the people they have chosen to be in their lives, such as significant others and non-work friends.

Just as family members don't always get along or even like each other, neither do employees. Although we often think that and act as though our coworkers should also be our friends, this isn't always the case—and in fact it isn't necessary. Yes, work is a social setting. But an ulterior purpose drives it: work. People don't gather around the water cooler at work just to exchange greetings and stories. Well, they do, of course, but they do so because they're at work for other reasons. Would the people who are your friends at work be your friends if you didn't work together? Certainly they could be, but odds are that the answer is no.

Friendship and liking one another at work are important to many people. So important, in fact, that some will take or leave jobs on the basis of the other people who work there. You probably know who these people are in your workplace, and as a manager have likely been called upon to mediate their problems with coworkers. These employees need to get along with their coworkers; it's as much a part of their personalities as of their work styles. There's nothing wrong with this, as long as it meets their needs (and doesn't interfere with productivity, theirs or yours).

ESSENTIALS

You can work with people you don't particularly like and still be happy in your job. It's unrealistic to expect you'll like everyone in the group. The more friends and interests you have outside work, the easier it is to work with people you don't consider to be your friends.

Whether employees like each other or not, it's still important for them to be able to work together or to share a project. This can be a challenge (which could be the understatement of the year!). The most effective way for a manager to bring people together in collaboration and cooperation is to stay focused on the job and its tasks—what the job requires and how well the employees do or don't complete those tasks. This helps them—and you—tolerate differences in personality. It also requires outstanding communication skills and the ability to wear several hats all at once.

Cora and Ted worked in the same department in identical jobs, though you'd never know that if you watched them in action. Anyone who saw Cora could describe her in a single word: ambitious. She always had her climbing gear ready, figuratively speaking, to advance to the next rung on the corporate ladder. She wasn't too careful about whom she stepped on along the way, and was extraordinarily gifted at getting others to do the work so she could take the credit. Cora managed to always be present whenever upper management appeared, either talking a good line on the phone or dropping names to her manager, Scott. While Cora's coworkers despised her because she often grandstanded at their expense (even in front of them), Cora's clients adored her and often sent letters complimenting her to the company's CEO. Her personality aside, Cora was actually very good at her job. Her accounts were always current, and she consistently exceeded her sales goals.

Ted, on the other hand, was popular with his coworkers—not because he was kind and generous (although he often was), but instead because he was honest and straightforward. He was known for telling it like it is even if he knew people wouldn't be happy. People always knew where they stood with Ted. Even employees who didn't like Ted's personality or found him abrasive valued his opinions and his intellectual curiosity. Ted wasn't afraid to stick his neck out, even if he knew his position would displease upper management. At times this frustrated Scott, but he respected Ted's processes and knew Ted thoroughly researched a matter before taking a position. Clients either loved Ted or hated him.

Cora and Ted did not get along with each other. When both were in the same meeting, the tension palpably intensified. However, their differences sometimes were the ideal complement on certain projects. When Scott needed them to collaborate, he knew his communication skills had to be in prime working condition. He would start the process by calling them into his office, and praising each for what he or she brought to the project so the other also heard. This established the ground rules for them working together. Then Scott outlined the specific responsibilities he wanted each to handle; he had worked with them long enough to know that if he failed to do this, both of them would shut down and nothing would get done on the project and each would blame the other. Scott finished the meeting by offering Ted and Cora each the opportunity to comment and disagree if they wanted to do so. Then he got a verbal commitment from each of them that they would do the tasks and functions he assigned them.

Scott scheduled regular meetings to monitor progress, always in his office to keep their personalities isolated and free them from the temptation to show each other up in front of other employees. He continued to praise each in front of the other, and to solicit their feedback and comments. If necessary, Scott adjusted assignments to keep the project on track and its workload equitably balanced between the two employees. When the project ended, Scott held a debriefing meeting to discuss how things went and identify any areas for improvement the next time around. Although the process required more involvement from Scott than was ideal, it kept both Ted and Cora contributing from positions of strength. They probably won't ever like each other, but they are learning to work together for the benefit of the department and the company.

ALERT

Attempting to get employees who don't like each other to work harmoniously together doesn't always work despite a manager's best efforts. Putting people on project teams to force them to cooperate can backfire. Don't jeopardize other team relationships and the integrity of the project by trying to engineer the impossible.

Scott's approach was highly innovative. In his work group and with Ted and Cora, it worked. Not all managers can handle such a situation in this way, or care as much about protecting the egos and sheltering the personalities of employees, even top performers. Gloria was such a manager. She viewed such intervention as coddling, and refused to be dragged into what she perceived as personality issues. She believed the strong would prevail, and the company didn't need those who didn't. She simply let her employees loose to see who would rise to the top. Typically this was someone who was adept at corporate politics, though not the most skilled or experienced employee in the department. When Ken announced in a cross-departmental meeting that he was his department's project manager, Gloria said nothing. She let him assume control, even though he wasn't actually a manager.

Gloria's office was in a different building, so she wasn't with her work group most of the time. She checked in occasionally, but otherwise left the department to operate on its own. Ken's bossy demeanor and know-it-all attitude soon alienated the department's employees, who then just ignored him. The department also grew resentful toward Gloria for refusing to step in and put Ken back in his place. Within six months, seven of the department's twelve employees had resigned. Gloria got promoted to director, overseeing numerous departments, and became even more distant.

Employees expect managers to "protect" them, to watch out for their interests and to be involved enough to understand the personalities in the group and put protections in place to assure that equality is maintained. When this doesn't happen, employees grow resentful and frustrated. Morale slides, taking productivity with it. Sometimes the issues that drive employees away seem minor, yet reflect an underlying problem with trust and betrayal. In Kevin's department, window offices were at a premium. They were awarded to project managers whose longevity entitled them to move out of the "stable" of cubicles and into the more spacious and private environment of an office with real walls and a door. The window was the crowning bonus.

Everyone knew and honored the pecking order for window offices. Then Kevin arrived and made no secret of his dissatisfaction at having a cubicle in the center of the large room. He complained, loudly and frequently, that he felt like a mouse in a maze. Just as loudly and frequently, Kevin announced his intention to move into the next available window office. He wasn't going to wait around for all the others to move through their paces; he was going to have his cake and eat it, too. A window office opened up, and even though it was supposed to go to Rhonda who was out of town, Kevin indeed moved in.

When Rhonda returned, she couldn't believe that her manager had simply allowed Kevin to do what he wanted to do. Not wanting to make a big deal out of something that seemed so petty, Rhonda asked her manager, Sondra, why she hadn't intervened. "It's just an office," Sondra said. "And you spend three days a week out of the office anyway. As long as you have a desk and a computer, what difference does it make? Besides, there's nothing in writing that defines who gets what offices. I can't really kick Kevin out so you can move in."

Many managers do not want to involve themselves in issues such as these because they are uncomfortable with feelings and emotions, and don't like conflict. But failing to become involved can cause tension that disrupts teamwork and productivity. Employees feel their managers don't respect them when managers fail to look out for employees' interests (it's that parent hat again). You can be proactive, and avoid conflict, by building in structure that helps employees work together. It's easy enough to head off situations like Kevin and Rhonda's battle over the window office when your department has written policies and procedures that define appropriate actions. Sometimes bureaucracy is a manager's best friend!

Managing Stress

There are a lot of reasons for stress in the workplace, and each individual has unique triggers. In general, workplace stress is the result of fatigue—working long hours—and competing demands, either at work or at home or in combination. Most people feel the greatest amount of stress when they're working hard and feeling that they're not getting anything in return for their efforts and sacrifices. For some people this is money, though more often it is recognition that is lacking. Money loses much of its charm after a while (and to some extent is required by law anyway), but praise for work well done lives in memory for a long, long time. Life beyond the workplace further adds to stress. It seems that what makes the office pressure worse is that our home lives are not always what they should be. Either life at home is great but we can't really enjoy it, or it is not so great so there is no relief from work even when we leave the workplace.

ESSENTIALS

Remember these words of wisdom from entertainer Carol Burnett the next time you're stressed out: "When you get into a tight place and everything goes against you, till it seems as though you could not hang on a minute longer, never give up then, for that is just the place and time that the tide will turn."

Stress is really about balance. A certain level of stress is necessary in life, of course—without it, we don't feel motivated or interested. But when there is too much of it, we don't feel motivated or interested, either. If life is all work, fasten your seatbelt—a crash is inevitable. So what can managers do? In the first place, recognize the symptoms of your own stress. These include:

- Anxiety and worrying about things you can't change
- Sleeplessness
- Fatigue
- Flying off the handle
- Depression
- Feeling sorry for yourself
- Engaging in passive-aggressive behavior

Even if you don't see these symptoms when you look in the mirror or listen to yourself when you're talking with employees, the people in your work group have learned to read your mood. They might not know what to do with their interpretations, but they become less effective because you are less effective. Doug is a manager who wears his heart on his sleeve. When he's happy, which is most of the time, everyone knows it and they feel happy, too. But when he's stressed out, everyone knows it—and they take cover. Employees see the anxiety in Doug's face and hear it in his voice, and they know enough to stay out of the way. When he's stressed, Doug becomes short-tempered and sharp-tongued, quick to deliver barbed comments. He also tends to overlook details, which become just that much more work to add to his stress load. Once the stress lifts and he can see clearly again, Doug finds himself apologizing for his actions and comments.

Avoidance might be a good diversionary tactic, but it doesn't work over the long haul. An environment based on avoidance becomes confusing and frustrating for everyone. Eventually employees lose track of whether this is a stress day or the storm has blown over, and they're not sure how to behave. As the manager, you've already established the "stress protocol" for your department and your employees. If it's not the one you want everyone to follow, change it. Managers need to set examples, and being open—even about stress—is one of them.

- If you're feeling stressed, go into your office, close the door, and take a few slow, deep breaths. If you meditate or do yoga, take ten minutes to indulge these great stress relievers.
- Tell your employees that you're feeling stressed, and offer a brief explanation for why. "I didn't get enough sleep last night, and I have to get this report finished by noon." This often makes you and your employees feel better.
- Try not to say things you'll regret or have to apologize for later. The "count to ten" rule comes in handy in times of stress. Ten seconds is not too long to pause before responding to a question or a comment, and can save all involved considerable embarrassment and frustration.
- Remind yourself that this is a temporary situation, and it too will pass.
- If a few days off would help, take them. Your department and the company will survive without you.

You also need to watch your lifestyle, and encourage your employees to do the same. If you are overwhelmed by your workload, what will make the situation better? Are you taking too much on? Not delegating? What should you do? What can you do? Stress starts with you, so set a positive example (you're already setting an example of some sort; now's your opportunity to shape it into the one you want to set). What do you need to do when you are stressed out? Do you need a vacation or a long rest? Is so, take the time and do it. And encourage your employees to do the same.

Sometimes stress builds up in the department and the manager is not aware. There might be rumors circulating about layoffs and plant closings, causing people to fear for their jobs and their security. Actual layoffs or closures, or bad news about the company's products or stock values, also cause people to become concerned (sometimes overly) about their futures with the company. Sometimes employees become resentful when they perceive that one employee is doing less work than the others. And sometimes personality conflicts are severe enough to cause stress for those involved as well as those who catch the fallout. Signs that the people in your department might be feeling too much stress include:

- Rumors and excessive gossip
- Groups of employees congregating at one employee's workstation, in the break room, or in the restroom—this behavior is often closely related to rumors and gossip
- Discord and disharmony—people just not getting along with each other
- A noticeable and unexplainable drop in productivity or efficiency
- A general bad attitude—people bad-mouthing other employees, managers, upper-level executives, the company, or its products

When you see these signs, it's your responsibility to get to the root of the problem. Talk to people and be a sounding board. Being able to talk about worries and fears is one of the most effective ways to put them in perspective, even when there are grounds for their existence. Things are seldom as bad as people imagine them to be, but the imagination's power knows no boundaries when unleashed. Problems won't disappear by themselves, no matter how desperately you wish they would or how hard you try to ignore them.

Clark was a very laid-back, nonstressed kind of person. As a manager, he preferred to stay on the periphery, letting people and problems work themselves out. While this approach was fine for Clark, it didn't work well for most of the employees in his department. Several people were aggressive, domineering, and territorial. Clark's hands-off attitude gave them free reign and the impression that he approved of their behavior and tactics. Other employees were either less experienced or did not deal well with aggressive people. This created an imbalance of input. Mild-mannered employees with good ideas got squelched by their more belligerent colleagues, who bullied through their ideas and suggestions. There was much in-fighting and just plain bad feelings. It was a stressful environment to work in because either tempers flared or people just walked away and seethed.

Despite Clark's impression of calm and aloofness, in truth the thought of becoming involved in any sort of confrontation or conflict sent him into stress overload. So rather than stepping in he stepped back, hoping that the reasons for the arguments and discord would go away as mysteriously as they had appeared. Of course, there was nothing mysterious about it. People had opposing views and didn't know how to express them without being adversarial. But these kinds of problems seldom fade away. In fact, the stress usually intensifies before it breaks, and the resulting explosion often leaves damage behind.

It's important for managers to get in the middle of things, to find out what's wrong, to talk with people about their concerns and fears. Put on your parent hat and have your coach hat ready—it's your job to set parameters and establish rules. Sure, some people are going to be unhappy. But they're unhappy now. At least when there are rules in place and it's clear that you intend to enforce them, you begin to re-establish a sense of fairness and equity. And yes, if you confront people some of them are likely to push back, just to see if they can and how far you'll bend before you snap. It's a test, just as it's a test when your six-year-old decides bedtime is when he feels like hitting the sheets, not when you tell him goodnight. As a parent it's your duty to establish boundaries for your children that provide them with what they need, whether or not they know or agree that they have such needs. The same holds true in the workplace. You are the manager, and it's your duty to set the limits for behavior and performance.

Creating a More Comfortable Workplace

There's no doubt about it—the workplace's physical and social environments are key factors in whether employees are satisfied and content or dissatisfied and stressed. With so much attention focused on trimming costs to hold down prices, many companies find themselves struggling to define what's essential and what's extravagant. It's a shifting line. Often, creature comforts are dependent on the economy. When times are good, companies lease or build enough space to accommodate niceties such as employee lounges, exercise rooms, recreation areas, and snack counters. When the economy tightens, the employee lounge might become cubicle heaven (or hell, depending on your perspective) so the company can consolidate its employee force and lease space to other businesses. Employees who want to blow off steam might need to head for the sidewalk or the parking lot. When people are happy to just be employed, they don't complain about not having free popcorn or bottled water. As anyone who's been in the job market for very long can tell you, comforts come and go.

FACTS

In a 1999 Gallup poll, 94 percent of working Americans were satisfied with the relationships they had with their coworkers and 82 percent were satisfied with the relationships they had with their bosses or immediate supervisors.

Swings in formality also affect the workplace environment. In the 1980s, most large companies were very formal. They had stringent, almost uniform-like dress codes that even stipulated shoe styles, grooming standards, and whether men could wear facial hair (usually not). People weren't allowed to have personal items displayed in their cubicles or work areas, and couldn't eat or drink at their desks. The philosophy behind this was that such structure kept the employees and the workplace focused on work. Without distractions, management gurus of the time believed, people would be more efficient and productive. Clients and customers could feel that anyone within a company could provide identical service.

Twenty-some years later, "open market" offices are the trend, with large rooms filled with desks or sometimes with three-sided cubicles. Business gurus now believe that people are most efficient and productive when companies encourage individual talents and abilities. In other words, people are not all alike so it makes no sense to act as though they are. Most experts agree that it's important for employees to be able to personalize their offices, to feel comfortable, and to bring some sense of home, or their personalities, into the office. This gives people a sense of control. It is also important to allow some flexibility to allow for differences in personal style as well as scheduling start and end times, lunch breaks, and other activities. Unless there are practical reasons for everyone to follow the same time structure, the work environment needs to offer some flexibility, some sense of individual expression, and some sense of control. When people have too many rules, they either look for ways to break them or they leave.

Psychological comfort is important as well. Managers need to be willing to look at the emotional and the psychological dynamics in their departments. They need to acknowledge that people have feelings, and they have to be able to talk about feelings. They also have to be able to both support and confront so they can maintain an environment where people can be productive and grow. Although "therapist" is not a hat managers should wear, they do need to look for symptoms of discord and dysfunction so they can take steps to minimize the impact before it gets out of hand.

This often means encouraging employees to get enough rest, and to take breaks and vacations to recharge and reinvigorate their bodies and their spirits. Most companies should be able to permit employees to occasionally take an afternoon off, or come in late after working late the night before. Although how employees use benefits such as vacation time is really up to them, managers should encourage every employee to take some extended time off. This is good for the employee, and it's good for the company. Even machines don't run without occasional down time.

Psychological comfort is also about taking an interest in each employee's life beyond work. Take the time to understand each employee as a unique individual and develop a way to appreciate each person for who and what they really are. Share your interests with employees, so they can see that you, too, have a human side. You need to be a resource for your employees when they need to express concerns and receive guidance; this happens only when employees perceive you as a person who cares about them and their needs. In the end, it's this human touch that creates an environment where the real tasks—getting the work done—can be carried out.

CHAPTER 12

Guiding Your Own Career

When you're involved in guiding the careers of others, it's easy to overlook the need to monitor and direct the course of your own career. This can be a costly oversight—for you as well as for your company. You made it to the head of your work team, and now you're caught up in the day-to-day functions of managing.

Keeping Your Skills Sharp

As a manager, you don't just manage people and their workloads. While you are probably not an expert in every function or task that the employees in your department perform, you should have considerable expertise in key jobs—manufacturing processes, art direction and account management, lab techniques, whatever functions are your department's responsibilities. After all, you make decisions that affect productivity. If you're not keeping up with all of this and are instead delegating everything, at some point you won't be able to make the important decisions you need to make. You won't have the information you need, and instead will be relying on others to provide it. This puts your whole team at risk. The leader has forgotten how to program in C++? Then how is he going to guide the team on what it should do when there is a quality control problem, customers are complaining, and the group needs to decide where to go next?

It can be fun to sit in your offices and manage. But you have to remember how to get your hands dirty, because that's what got you this far and that's what is going to keep you valuable to the company. In today's dynamic and sometimes volatile job market, knowing how to do the work is the only form of job security you have. Your department might grow, and your career along with it. Your department's functions might get rolled into another department's administrative structure, squeezing you out of a job. If you need to change departments or companies, you'll need to establish yourself as both a manager and a subject matter expert. Interview questions will address your management skills, to be sure, but will also target the processes you will be managing. If you don't have the answers, you're not likely to get the job, either. If you're a manager whose primary strength is your people skills, you're the manager most likely to get left behind when downsizing or a power struggle hits. When you let your primary job skills erode, you leave yourself few options.

Sean and Christine were both managers at Artful Advertising. Sean had worked his way through the ranks from delivery clerk to customer service manager. On his way, he'd held jobs in just about every department in the company, and knew the workings of the company better than most people understood the details of their jobs. Sean also had the rare ability to get along with almost everybody, which is how he ended up getting promoted to manager of the customer service department. Even irate customers calmed down when Sean took their calls or came to the front counter to listen to their complaints. Sean had been in his position for five years, and had allowed himself to become comfortable. Processes and procedures changed, but he didn't do much to find out how. As long as he knew enough to oversee the efforts of his employees to address customer service issues and handle the difficult situations himself, Sean didn't feel a need to keep up on the details of every aspect of the company's functions. After all, he was a manager and his job was to manage.

FACTS

The U.S. Bureau of Labor Statistics projects a 15- to 20-percent increase in the number of management positions by 2008 for which candidates will need at least a four-year degree as well as work experience.

Christine was the production manager. She had started as a film assistant in the printing department seven years ago, and worked in various positions including copy writer and account representative. Her strongest asset as a manager was her ability to delegate. One reason Christine was so effective was that she knew everyone's jobs well enough that she could do them herself, so she knew who to assign to which projects. Under Christine's direction, the production department operated smoothly and efficiently. She was also a familiar presence in concept meetings. Christine could brainstorm about creative direction, discuss the latest trends in advertising and marketing, and analyze the competition. Christine could look at an ad and offer suggestions for its direction, then turn around and edit a press release. The employees in her department respected Christine as a manager they could come to for anything.

Then Artful Advertising's CEO retired, and there was an intense internal struggle for power. One of the two vice presidents vying for the vacated top spot favored consolidating departments to streamline operations, while the other advocated acquiring a smaller competitor to expand the company's market presence. In the end the consolidator won out. The realignment trimmed six management positions, and the managers who wanted to stay with the company had to apply for the jobs they wanted. The new executive management regime wanted managers with diverse capabilities. Although Sean had once known the company inside and out, he let his knowledge and his skills slip. His interview went poorly, and he chose to resign before the final decisions came down. Christine was promoted to director of what became the production division, responsible for overseeing the art, copywriting, design, and printing departments.

There are many ways to keep your core skills sharp. If you are a working manager, you have daily exposure to the changes taking place in your profession. Pay attention to these changes, even if it seems they don't affect you directly. Many companies will pay, or reimburse, you for costs related to keeping your skills current or learning new skills that are relevant to your job. Even if you're not technically a working manager, it's a good idea to keep yourself involved in the functions of the jobs within your department or work group. At a minimum, you should:

- Enroll in any workshops or classes your company offers. Large companies often have training departments that develop and deliver classes to teach customer service skills, quality improvement methodologies, computer and technology skills, and other subjects relevant to the needs of the company's employees.
- Maintain active membership in relevant professional organizations. Don't just sign up and pay your dues; go to the meetings, conferences, and workshops. Network. Build relationships with people who work for other companies.
- Maintain any licensure or certification essential to work in your core skill area. If you are a licensed professional working in an area that doesn't count toward the hours your state requires to maintain licensure or certification, work some evenings and weekends in a job that will give you countable hours (sometimes volunteer hours count).

- Take continuing education courses. Some professions require continuing education, while in others it's optional. It's always to your advantage to stay abreast of current developments in your career field.
- Continue your formal (college) education. If you have a two-year associate degree, go back for a four-year bachelor's degree. If you already have an undergraduate education, consider a graduate program. Many degree programs have options targeted at working adults, including evening and weekend classes, Internet classes, and correspondence classes.

Of course, it is possible for a manager's core skills to be in management. Some people excel in directing and mentoring, and might not have core skills in the areas they supervise, though this is becoming increasingly uncommon as companies continue looking for ways to get the most from (or for) the least—known in corporatese as efficiency in resource management. Management generalists tend to know a little bit about a lot of things and often have specialized education in management theories, principles, and practices. If you are such a manager, it's all the more important that you remain ahead of the curve when it comes to changes in trends and approaches. And it's still a good idea for you to develop some skill strengths in areas that will continue to be important across the board in business. Learn the basics about the key tasks employees who report to you perform, so you understand their contributions and how each piece fits into the whole. This also helps you to delegate more effectively, and to monitor progress as well as outcomes using measures that are relevant and appropriate.

FACTS

A 2000 Gallup poll reports that 78 percent of Americans believe recent changes in technology that have changed the landscape of American business have been good for the country. The poll also reports that 89 percent of Americans use e-mail, 60 percent use e-mail in place of making telephone calls, and 95 percent use the Internet to find information.

Technology Rules

Ours is a technology-driven society. From doctors to hairdressers, we use computers to schedule appointments, order supplies, and communicate with employees and customers. In just one decade (the 1990s), America leaped from room-size to desktop computers. The transformation revolutionized not only the way we work but also the way we live. Computers have replaced typewriters and calculators, graph paper and record books. Cellular telephones and wireless modems make it possible to work from literally any location. Facsimile machines, e-mail, and the Internet have greatly reduced the need for surface mail and courier deliveries. Software programs make it easy for people with modest skills to perform sophisticated tasks, from word processing applications that allow you to integrate text and images into formatted documents to financial applications that let you track and report any accounting functions.

ESSENTIALS   As a manager, you need to know how to use technology to improve your staff's productivity and efficiency—and when technology is not the answer. A manager who is a technology leader really has an edge in today's workplace!

Managers have to make decisions about technology. They need to know the technology related to their fields. Even in companies that have information technology (IT) departments, it's department managers who will need to know what software is most appropriate for their needs. Which financial software should the company purchase for the accounting department? The manager of accounting will get that question first. Is he or she keeping up in technology? What direct marketing database software should the marketing department use? The marketing manager needs to know, and also must be able to justify the department's need to computerize these kinds of functions. What image should the company's Web site strive to present? Should it be humorous, sophisticated, use the latest whiz-bang animated graphics and streaming video? Should the company produce materials in formats that can work on the Web as well as in print? If you're a manufacturing manager, you better know about

CAD/CAM and ERP and just-in-time and all of the other buzzwords, and be able to talk about what software products might be best used within that environment.

And then there is worker productivity. Do you need to think about a networked system? Does it need to serve just within the department or among all departments? Do the sales representatives need handheld organizers or can they get by with laptops? What productivity software should you consider for the sales reps? Do they need to have promotional literature with them or should they be able to do PowerPoint presentations from their laptops?

A manager who can use technology to his or her advantage can be the department's star. Employees love to be on the leading edge, and they generally recognize the value of technology in keeping their own careers up to date (not to mention in making their daily tasks achievable). It's fun, and it can add a new challenge and excitement to work when simply updating your knowledge is not the whole picture. (These days, it's less important to have a head full of facts than it is to know how to use the Internet to get those facts quickly). When you, the manager, are a well-informed advocate for the technology that makes the work lives of your employees easier, you encourage loyalty among employees. They feel that you have their best interests at heart, and are willing to take action. The increased productivity that results from the right technology makes the company feel more loyal toward you.

ESSENTIALS

Some managers believe they are up on technology, yet it is their administrative assistants who do all the work. If you don't really understand the technologies that are part of your daily work life, enroll in classes to bring yourself up to speed. It'll be an investment that could save your career.

The knowledge this requires means not only understanding the technology but also how to cost-justify it. Read professional journals within your field and join professional associations and organizations to keep yourself abreast of relevant technology. This will serve you well in your current job, and could be the key to other jobs. Most job interviews will include questions about technology. Even if the interviewer doesn't know the full scoop, he or she will know the latest buzzwords. You will need to be able to talk intelligently, and with real-world knowledge.

Does technology frighten you? Don't be ashamed to admit that it does, and don't feel that you're alone. Technology is frightening. It's scary to walk into work one day and find out that everything familiar has become obsolete. You have budgets to balance and productivity to maintain; it doesn't seem fair that on top of everything else, you also have to keep track of the moving line between the past and the future—and walk it. It's scary for you and it's scary for your employees. But knowledge empowers. When you're reading the journals and even all those annoying advertisements that come every day in the mail about this upgrade and that improvement, you're building a knowledge base. Draw from it! You won't know everything, but then no one does. What matters most is your ability to know when you need to consider technology upgrades, and what technology makes sense for your department or work group.

There are plenty of ways you can update your knowledge level, easily and fairly effortlessly. You can:

- Make a friend in your company's IT department and learn what criteria the "experts" use to assess new equipment and software.
- Ask questions when sales representatives come calling. Find out why a change is really an improvement—or if it's not. And sometimes what's touted as an upgrade is nothing more than the current version in new clothes, with a lot of flash that turns out to be nothing but fizzle when it comes to functionality.
- Ask experienced users what they like and don't like about the computer equipment and programs they use. Get a variety of opinions to see what patterns emerge. Although anecdotal, this kind of information helps you weigh marketing hype against real-world experience.

Technology is relentless, whether you dread it or embrace it. Professions and the world of work constantly change and much of this is driven by technology. Those who don't keep up get left behind—companies as well as people. The Ride Smooth Trucking Company computerized its route scheduling in 1992, a move that put it at the leading edge of its industry. When Ride Smooth Trucking's senior truck drivers no longer wanted to, or couldn't, drive, the company offered them office positions at the company's headquarters. It sent them through a two-week training program to learn how to use the computers and software. After completing the training, they scheduled the pick-up and delivery routes for the other drivers. Time passed but the company's technology remained unchanged; the drivers-turned-desk-jockeys were comfortable using the equipment and procedures.

The trucking industry hit a slump by the late 1990s, as technology (surprise!) made it less necessary for businesses to ship materials by highway. MegaTransit Corporation bought out Ride Smooth Trucking, and offered office personnel the opportunity to apply for similar jobs in its administrative offices located in the same city. The schedulers felt confident that they would slip seamlessly into MegaTransit's system—after all, they'd been using computers to handle shipping and driver's schedules for years. The hands-on test MegaTransit gave them was a rude awakening. Ride Smooth Trucking had not upgraded its systems since installing them. The pre-Pentium computers so familiar to the schedulers still ran DOS and DOS-based applications. The current generation of PCs that functioned in gigahertz rather than megahertz on Windows operating systems was as foreign to the schedulers as if they'd never seen computers before. Not one of them was able to qualify for a job with MegaTransit.

Your job may not require a handheld organizer—yet—but chances are your company (or the company you want to work for some day) might decide to go this route. You need to be able to adapt, if not be one of the leaders in adopting current technology. You can only sit back for so long, maybe long enough to take a breath. The technology you laugh at today might crunch out your pink slip next week. Managers who really excel in their organizations often do so by introducing or supporting new technology. This contributes to others—the employees who report to them as well as their superiors—perceiving them as innovators and leaders.

Reading Between the Lines

Every day, companies lay off employees and managers. Could you read the writing on the wall telling you that your job was in jeopardy? Harold, like many managers, missed the signals. Over a period of two or three months his superiors shifted his responsibilities to other managers, gradually isolating him. He was not assigned to any projects that would last more than a few weeks. Instead of updating his resume and renewing contacts, Harold joked about his "good" fortune. Although he had seen upper management ease other managers out using these same tactics, it never occurred to him that the same thing now might be happening to him. Those other managers had all been incompetent fools, not respected by their employees or upper management. Harold's employees, on the other hand, considered him one of the guys and often invited him out for drinks after work. Sometimes Harold's boss even joined them.

Sure, production had been down a bit the past two quarters or so. But every company in the industry was going through a slow time. These cycles were normal, and sales would climb again in due time. The problem was, upper management wasn't interested in due time. It wanted improvements now; stockholders were getting anxious. Harold's boss, a company vice president, had taken Harold to lunch several times in recent weeks to probe for explanations and solutions. Harold interpreted the meetings as camaraderie and commiserated with his boss's concerns rather than offering proposals for immediate improvement. He failed to sense the seriousness of the situation, and misread the tone and intent of his boss's indirect questioning. When Harold received a layoff notice, he was the only one who was surprised.

Being in middle management might insulate you from the pressures at the top and the struggles at the bottom of the corporate ladder, but don't let it isolate you from reality. You are only as good as your last success, and only for as long as others remember it (which is never as long as you do). If your company begins laying off staff, don't let yourself get lulled into a sense of false security because you're a manager. Managers are not inherently immune to staff reductions. In many situations, in fact, managers might find themselves among the first to go.

ALERT

As a manager, you are judged not only by your own performance, but also by the performance of your employees. If your department's productivity is down, it looks like your problem—regardless of the real reasons (which might have little to do with you personally).

If you suspect that your job is on the line or a layoff is imminent, is there anything you can do to save yourself? Usually not, unless the issue is purely performance (and this should never be a surprise to you, just as it should never be a surprise to your employees when it comes time for their performance evaluations). Ask your direct superior; sometimes he or she will be able to give you a straight answer. Recognize, however, that often upper management cannot give you advance notice that you are about to be laid off or your job is about to be eliminated. Sometimes a sympathetic manager might give you a heads-up, but this could be at great personal risk. Most companies have policies and procedures they must follow to avoid discrimination and wrongful termination claims. It's always a good idea to be prepared to find yourself on the seeking end of the job hunt. If your company is downsizing or reorganizing, it's critical. Here are some ways you can stay ready for whatever changes might come your way:

- **Keep your resume current.** Every time you attend a training program or workshop, take on new responsibilities in your job, complete a major project, or achieve a key success, update your resume. At the very least, pull out your resume every six months to review it.
- **Network.** Collect business cards from people you meet at professional gatherings and even social events. Once a week, make it a point to call, have coffee with, or go to lunch with someone you know who works for another company that has people who do what you do.
- **Determine how your skills and experience could translate into positions in fields other than the one you're currently working in.** Could you teach, work in health care instead of the computer industry, be a customer service manager in an auto dealer's service department rather than in a retail setting?

- **Consider volunteering in positions different from your job.**
  In addition to fulfilling needs within your community, this will help you
  to expand your skills and extend the network of people you know.
- **Try to set aside enough financial resources to carry you through
  three to six months of unemployment.** This is a challenge for most
  people, who tend to live from paycheck to paycheck. Just setting
  aside a small amount from each check—as small as 2 to 5 percent—
  can quickly add up to a tidy emergency fund.

According to a 2001 Gallup poll, more than half of working
Americans would be unable to make it longer than a month
without significant financial difficulties if they lost their jobs today.
One in six could last only a week. And only one in ten has the
resources to last a year.

Change Is the Only Certainty

The only thing that's certain in today's business environment is that
nothing is certain. Although change has always been inevitable, it hasn't
always happened at the speed of light as it seems to now. Take the
dot-com world. In the last two years of the 1990s and into the first
quarter of 2000, anyone who could connect these two words could get
a big money job. By the first quarter of 2001, most of these people were
working in very different jobs in very different situations. Within less than
three years, the dot-com cycle zoomed from zero to infinity and down to
near zero again. For those who can remember the late 1970s, a similar
cycle swept through the computer industry; first there were dozens, then
there were just a few.

The days of moving into a nice middle management job in a "safe"
industry like insurance or banking or manufacturing, calmly serving out
your days in a predictable empire casually, or even ferociously, protecting
your turf are gone. Even people in supposedly safe, monolithic companies
are subject to sudden change. Tides rise and fall—within industries,
companies, and professions. Being in management doesn't protect you

from those rises and falls. Rather, it offers opportunity and vulnerability in equal doses. You can't have one without the other.

Mergers and Acquisitions

Anyone with a job in the 1980s, or maybe not working yet but at least watching TV or reading the newspaper, learned of a new trend in business: mergers and acquisitions. A company that is doing well buys out a competitor that is not doing so well. Sometimes the buyer is bigger than the company it acquires; sometimes it's a small company that has a big appetite. Before this time, companies simply went out of business when they could no longer compete. Other companies picked up their customer bases, but the dying company faded into history.

The mergers and acquisitions trend has not gone away, however. In fact, in the 1990s the trend expanded when companies were created with the sole goal of being acquired. The idea was to create a small company based on an idea or a technology that could be eventually swallowed by a larger company who needed it. People were expendable. Companies treated them well while they were there, providing almost unimaginable creature comforts and stock options that turned the lucky into millionaires. But when the need for their contributions evaporated, so did their positions. Employees were resources to be used and discarded.

Companies often do very little to get their employees ready for these mergers and acquisitions. Beyond rumors, employees hear little and know even less. A company's stock price is vulnerable to rumors, and quite frankly that becomes more important than the feelings and concerns of employees. Managers do sometimes get advance warning that a merger or acquisition is pending. They might even have a voice in determining who will stay and who will be let go in their departments. If you find yourself in this situation, you'll quickly discover that it's a mixed blessing. On the one hand, the manager can help assure that decisions are based more on merit rather than being utterly random. On the other, you must be fair and objective. You must also recognize and accept that you truly are in the middle. It is your role to carry out upper management's intentions and plans, even though you might feel your first loyalty is to the employees who report to you. As much as you would like to sneak in a few hints or even make a few midnight phone calls to certain employees to give them a heads-up, you can't.

No, it's not fair. But it is the only way to be equitable. No one enters into a job with the promise of perpetual employment (and few people really expect this to be the case). Companies exist for purposes beyond providing paychecks and benefits to employees, and in the end their objectives win out. Employees with the right skills and experience will stay; others will go. This is one of those times when it's nice to have performance evaluations and job descriptions handy; these erstwhile bureaucratic annoyances become quite useful when it comes time to make objective decisions.

FACTS

Slipping information to employees about pending changes within the company can do more than just jeopardize your career. Having information get out before the company is ready to announce it could jeopardize the company's competitive position. Information that influences decisions to buy or sell stock could violate federal securities regulations, putting you on the wrong side of a criminal investigation. If you know about coming changes, keep the knowledge to yourself unless it is your role to announce it to your department.

Joseph, the managing editor at *Read Me!* magazine, came into work on Wednesday morning eager to see the layout for the issue about to go to press. Instead, a contingent from the publisher's office was waiting to see him. Before Joseph had his morning coffee, his world turned upside-down. MegaMedia Corporation had acquired *Read Me!* and would be absorbing the magazine's editorial and administrative functions into other corporate divisions. Joseph could accept one of several editing jobs (none of which were management positions) with MegaMedia, but there were jobs for only two of the seven people on his staff. The publisher and the new management wanted Joseph to summarize the experience and qualifications for each employee, to help decide who would receive job offers. Everyone else would receive a severance package including four weeks' pay and three sessions with a relocation counselor.

Joseph was a rather casual manager who encouraged creativity and scorned bureaucratic interference. He knew each employee's strengths and weaknesses, but didn't do formal performance evaluations because he felt holding people accountable to arbitrary standards stifled the free expression necessary to make the magazine succeed. MegaMedia wasn't interested in free expression or Joseph's views. It purchased *Read Me!* because the magazine's demographics were strong in areas where other MegaMedia publications were weak. All that the corporation wanted was to keep sales and circulation figures high and costs low.

Because Joseph could not provide evaluations or other formal documentation to support his perspectives of employee performance, MegaMedia's HR department required each employee to apply and interview for a position with MegaMedia—forcing them to compete with one another, and know that they were, to stay employed. MegaMedia cut Joseph completely out of the selection process since he really had nothing to contribute, and ultimately offered him a severance package instead of a job. Joseph was a talented editor and a good manager, except for his resistance to conforming to company policies that he felt had no useful purpose. This cost him the chance to help make decisions that could benefit his employees as well as his job.

Mergers and acquisitions can be as difficult for the employees who stay as it is for those who are let go—managers as well as employees. If you are a manager who stays to become part of the new structure, you have your work cut out for you. Your cheerleader hat is going to get a lot of wear.

- Always break the news to each employee individually, whether the person is staying or leaving. Although a group meeting might be easier for you, it could be very difficult for people who react emotionally to the news. There's nothing easy about hearing that the world you've become accustomed to has suddenly changed through no fault of yours—and there's nothing you can do to change things now.
- Allow people who are losing their jobs to gather their belongings and leave with dignity. Some employees might want to say good-bye to their coworkers, but most people aren't very good with good-byes and

prefer to leave without a lot of attention. People who are friends will arrange to meet if that's what they want to do.

- Meet with the surviving employees as soon as possible, to explain what has happened and why. Hold this meeting in a location where it is safe for people to vent about their feelings. They might feel angry that friends are now out of jobs and guilty that they still have regular paychecks.

- If your department is gaining new employees as a result of a merger, before they arrive explain to the other employees why they are getting jobs when other people were let go. Sometimes all you can say is "that's just the way it is," but it's important for you to say even this to acknowledge that employees need to hear a reason.

- When new employees arrive, welcome them and do your best to make them feel comfortable, even if you must set aside personal feelings to do so. It's not their fault that they're in this situation any more than it's your fault.

Mergers and acquisitions often mean that new people and potentially a new corporate culture have to be integrated. When Grapevine Applications and SophistiWare merged, it was a match made in heaven for stockholders but a clash of cultures for employees. Grapevine was a small company located just outside San Francisco. Its hundred or so employees were California-casual, wearing cut-offs and sandals to work. SophistiWare was a larger company based in Chicago. Its several hundred employees dressed to the nines—men and women alike wore trendy suits to work every day. Though Grapevine purchased SophistiWare, SophistiWare's president was tapped to run the new company.

Grapevine's employees were unhappy about this. Grapevine's president was a hands-on leader who knew each employee by name. SophistiWare's president, by contrast, was as formal as his attire. He didn't want to know names; he only wanted to see results. Doug, the HR manager, tried to ease the transition for his employees. He met with them as a group to point out some of the strengths of the merger. "We're in a very competitive environment, and quite frankly our opportunities are shrinking," he told them. "We need them, and they need us. It's about the bottom line and about survival, pure and simple."

Doug let his employees express their concerns, but he held a firm line. People had no choice but to conform if they wanted to keep working at the company, and that was just the way things were. They needed to work together to make the adjustment to the new company's structure, procedures, and place in the market. Doug made sure everyone always knew what was happening and why, and how the changes affected jobs and responsibilities. To let people know he understood their concerns, he made jokes about finding a shirt and tie to match his cut-offs. This helped everyone to maintain some sense of commitment to a company that all knew would never be the same again. Doug sent California employees to Chicago in small teams, to get to know their counterparts and better understand SophistiWare's processes. He also had small teams of Chicago employees come to the San Francisco office for the same reasons. When Chicago employees were visiting, Doug tapped into the department's petty cash fund to pay for a barbecue to let people socialize and get to know each other.

Although Grapevine's employees weren't happy about all the changes, they felt loyal to Doug and even to the new company because Doug rallied them into a support group for each other. They still had some bad feelings about the merger and the new company as a whole, but they formed positive feelings about the individuals they met. Although the road was sometimes bumpy, they continued to function as a very productive department.

You might feel fairly insignificant when others come in to restructure your department and the ways your employees work. But you're the only one, really, who can make it all work. Even if you feel you won't want to remain with the new company that results from an acquisition or a merger, it's in your best interests to do all you can to make the transition a success. It's always better to leave on a high note, with people at various levels of the organization singing your praises. You'll feel better about yourself, and you might open doors you didn't know existed. People notice your actions and their consequences; it's up to you to shape them to present the perspective you want others to see and remember.

Restructuring and Downsizing

Companies restructure or downsize to conserve resources and cut expenses, generally because the marketplace has become viciously competitive and there's no longer any way to stay profitable without significant changes. Sometimes these are desperation measures attempting to pull the company back from the brink of bankruptcy or closure. While an acquisition or a merger generally has benefits for both companies (even if some people lose their jobs), a restructure or downsize almost always means you're just losing employees unless your department is merging with another department.

Restructuring and downsizing have become more the rule than the exception in today's business world. Industries change rapidly, technology changes rapidly, and companies across industries have learned that survival means being nimble. The companies that survive and thrive are those that can make quick changes within the organization to mobilize to meet the next challenge. Big companies like IBM and AT&T constantly redesign themselves, creating new departments and divisions as well as developing new products and services. Networking, Internet services, wireless communication—unknown terms just a few years ago—have become the buzzwords of the current business environment.

Companies must be able to meet opportunities and demands, and employees must be ready to be shaken up along the way. Even stodgy industries like insurance are changing seemingly overnight. New consumer trends (including lack of interest) mean new expectations for products such as life insurance. Companies have to redesign their products and services to meet these challenges, which often results in a completely new appearance. Sometimes this means the functions of departments that once specialized in certain services become resources distributed throughout the company.

ESSENTIALS

As a manager, you have to be ready to meet the demands of restructuring and downsizing in two ways. First, you need to prepare your employees and support the company by making the changes work. Second, you have to protect your own career.

Although it's difficult to be the bearer of bad news, it's to your advantage to at least have this opportunity. Often, managers know about pending changes but can't tell anyone. Rosalyn heard in September that her company would reduce its workforce by 30 percent in February. She attended countless meetings in which managers struggled to figure out how to meet increased expectations with fewer resources. In these meetings, the managers reviewed and assessed the skills and strengths of each employee to make decisions about who would stay and who would be let go.

The people in Rosalyn's department suspected there were changes in the offing, and several with whom she had close relationships came to her to ask what was up. But she couldn't tell them the truth, so she had to tell them nothing was going on as far as she knew. This didn't make sense to the employees, but because they trusted Rosalyn, they accepted her response. Even when Rosalyn started cutting back the long-term commitments for the three who would lose their jobs, she couldn't warn them to start looking for other jobs. She had to just gradually isolate them, let them finish their current projects but not assign them to new ones. Upper management worried that if employees knew their jobs were about to end, they would either lose interest in their work or leave before the company was ready for them to go. The company needed them to complete their current projects, even though that meant withholding the truth from them. Rosalyn held out hope that things would change and she wouldn't have to lay off anyone; that hope was what made it possible for her to pretend nothing was wrong.

When the day finally arrived for Rosalyn to issue pink slips, the employees who had come to talk to her earlier about the possibility of staff reductions were very angry—even the ones who didn't lose their jobs. Rosalyn talked individually with each employee being laid off, explaining that it was purely economics and had nothing to do with performance. But word quickly got out that Rosalyn had known for several months that this was coming and had not only failed to warn people but had also lied to them when they asked her about it. Employees, both surviving and laid off, felt Rosalyn had betrayed them and told her so. There was little Rosalyn could say; they were right.

After the laid-off employees left, Rosalyn called a meeting with the survivors. She explained that she understood and accepted their perceptions of the situation, but wanted the opportunity to explain her actions. She told each remaining employee that she was very sorry to see each laid-off employee leave, but there had been no choice about cutbacks if the company itself was going to survive. Then she pulled out some charts and reports and started talking about the company's economic status. She showed employees what the company had to produce in terms of billable days just to cover operating costs and make a minimal profit. Everyone was surprised at what it took to keep the company running. The meeting gave them a greater understanding of the challenges the company faced and also an appreciation for the careful way in which the company had approached the downsizing.

Another dimension of the downsizing was restructuring. Several other departments that had also laid off employees were consolidating, which meant Rosalyn's department was gaining employees and functions from other parts of the company. Rosalyn discussed how these employees would fit into the department, and allowed her employees to decide how to reorganize the department to accommodate them. Rosalyn concluded the meeting by thanking the employees for the good work they'd done, and expressing her confidence that their strong performance would continue.

Communication is critical in times of challenge. As much as possible (and only when the company is making the information available to employees), managers should try to let people know what actions the company is considering and how these actions might affect individuals. As a downsized or restructured department moves forward, it's important for the manager to be sensitive to workflow, personality conflicts, confusion over who does what, and potential problems. The restructured group might perceive its manager as somewhat of a stepparent, with partiality toward his or her original employees. If you are this manager, you might feel damned if you do, damned if you don't. Employees are likely to accuse you (or the company) of overworking them to increase profits. Sometimes there is a grain of truth in this perception; the company wouldn't have downsized in the first place if it could support all of its resources. Doing more with less, whether equipment or people, is always a challenge.

This will undoubtedly lead you to reconsider your own career. Although you must be cheerleader, mediator, parent, and coach for your employees, you might not believe in the company's new direction. And sometimes when departments are restructured, managers are among the first to go in an effort to shave costs while retaining the people who actually do the work. You need to be ready to move within the company or to another company. This is the reality of the marketplace. Companies want loyalty, but at the same they expect us to accept change and be ready to move. They are not there to provide us security for life. As we said earlier in this chapter, you need to keep your professional or non-management skills current. Stay abreast of current thinking and technology in your field and in general. These are the factors that will help you make a move when you need to. There is nothing sadder than a person with twenty years in at Bank Big Money who basically knows nothing more than how to survive at Bank Big Money.

Keep Looking Forward

No doubt being a manager represents achieving a key career goal for you. This is a good thing, of course, and an accomplishment of which you should feel proud. But don't rest on your laurels. The world around you is changing, even if your little environment seems stable. Keep your eyes and ears open for new opportunities. It doesn't hurt to interview for a job or two each year, just to keep your interviewing skills honed. While your history forms the foundation for your future, what used to be won't necessarily prevail in the years to come—witness Beta Vision videotapes and eight-track tape players, slide rules and typewriters. Keep your career in your hands, not at the mercy of factors you can't control.

APPENDIX A

Glossary

Acquisition—When one company buys another.

Age Discrimination in Employment Act of 1967—Federal legislation that made it illegal for companies with fifteen or more employees to discriminate in hiring, pay, promotion, and firing practices against people who are age forty or older.

Americans with Disabilities Act of 1990—Federal legislation that established requirements for employers with fifteen or more employees to provide reasonable accommodations for individuals with disabilities.

Body language—The unspoken messages a person's posture and gestures convey.

Cliques—Groups, usually small, that form around specific interests and then exclude those who do not share those interests.

Contingent jobs—Temporary jobs that are expected to last nine months or less. See also **Temporary employee.**

Corporate culture—The pattern of beliefs and behaviors that exists within an organization; a company's code of conduct.

Desk rage—Manifestation of workplace violence consisting of threatening or abusive language and behavior.

Dot-coms—Companies that sell their wares (products or services) via the Internet; term derives from the electronic, or Web, addresses which have ".com" as the last element.

Downsizing—Reductions in workforce and sometimes production, usually to accommodate a downturn in the economy.

Downturn—Situation within the economy when sales and earnings drop, causing companies to tighten the budget belt. Often marked by consolidations and restructuring.

EAP (Employee Assistance Program)—Collection of services, usually for counseling and related needs, available as an employer-paid benefit.

EEOC (Equal Employment Opportunity Commission)—Federal agency that oversees compliance with federal laws and regulations to support fairness and prevent discrimination in the workplace.

Equal Pay Act of 1963—Clarifies equal pay for equal work to specifically prohibit employers from paying women less than men for performing the same jobs.

Exemption—When an employee is not protected under federal law from practices otherwise regulated by the FLSA, such as work hours, paid overtime, and equal pay for equal work.

Fair Labor Standards Act (FLSA)—Federal legislation originally passed in 1938 and modified through the years; defines many aspects of employment compensation, including the standard of a forty-hour workweek, minimum wage, child labor limitations, equal pay for equal work, and compensatory time calculations.

Family Medical Leave Act of 1993 (FMLA)—Federal legislation enacted to require employers to provide unpaid time off from work for an employee to care for a new child (newborn or adopted), a seriously ill family member, or because of their own medical conditions, without losing their jobs. The FMLA generally applies to companies that employ twenty or more people.

FTE (Full Time Equivalent)—Way to address staffing based on full-time employment of forty hours per week. Two people sharing a full-time position are each .5 FTE; someone working thirty-two hours a week is .75 FTE.

Internet—Worldwide network of computers that serves as the infrastructure for electronic information and commerce.

Job sharing—When two people share a single position, including its tasks and responsibilities, salary, workspace, and other elements. Usually the division is equal, though sometimes one person might have a larger share than the other.

MBWA (Management By Walking Around)—Refers to the management style of mingling with employees on a regular basis to understand their day-to-day activities, accomplishments, and frustrations.

Mediation—The process of finding common ground, of seeking win-win solutions to differences and disagreements that will be acceptable to both parties.

Mentor—An accomplished professional who takes a novice under wing to guide him or her in making appropriate career choices.

Merger—When two or more companies combine staff and functions to create a single company.

NIOSH (National Institute for Occupational Safety and Health)—An agency of the U.S. government that monitors and reports on workplace health and safety issues. Unlike OSHA, NIOSH does not conduct inspections or enforcement activities; as a division of the Centers for Disease Control, NIOSH's primary functions are data collection and reporting.

OSHA (Occupational Health and Safety Administration)—A federal agency responsible for enforcing federal workplace safety laws, rules, and regulations.

Paradigm—A clear and unmistakable pattern of behavior that is widespread in its acceptance.

Policies—Written guidelines an employer creates that establish procedures for complying with laws and regulations, operational functions, and behavior expectations.

Productivity—Ratio between effort and costs expended and results.

Restructure—When a company reorganizes its operations to function more competitively.

Shadowing—Allowing employees to observe actions and behaviors without participating in them, as a learning experience.

Surf—To explore the offerings of the World Wide Web.

Telework—Working from home or another location different than the regular workplace; also called telecommuting or distance working.

Temporary employee—Person whose job is expected to last nine months or less; sometimes called a contingency worker or more casually, a temp. Temporary employees often fill in for regular employees who are out for an extended time (such as for maternity or sick leave), or to bolster staffing during peak seasons.

Title VII, Civil Rights Act of 1964—The component of this federal legislation that makes it illegal for companies with fifteen or more employees to discriminate on the basis of race, color, religion, gender, or national origin in hiring, pay, promotion, and firing.

WIIFM (What's in It for Me)—Refers to the interest people have in knowing how they benefit from situations and decisions.

Workaholic—Person who works excessively, to the extent that work activities interfere with or prevent a life beyond the job.

Work style—Combination of skills, knowledge, and personality that determines how an individual approaches job functions.

World Wide Web—Also known as www; the prefix for most electronic addresses. The interfaces and structures that make it possible to post and locate information on the Internet.

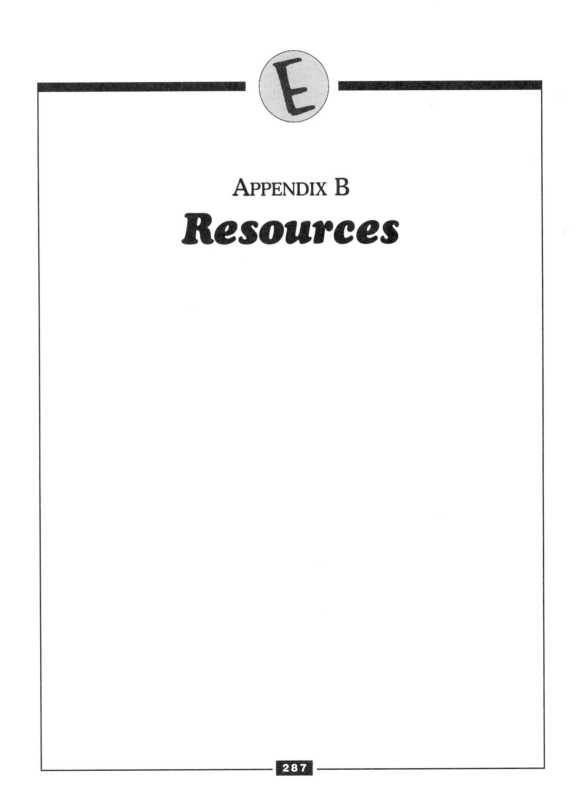

Appendix B
Resources

The "business and career" section of any major bookstore contains thousands of titles. Some cover the staples of business and management— the things that remain pretty much the same through the years. Others address topics of current interest. The best way for you to stay informed about what's going on in the business world, in your industry, and in your career field is to read, read, read. Subscribe to (or go to the library to read) magazines and journals relevant to your profession, and also to those that cover related information such as technology or industrial psychology.

The Internet is also an abundant source of information. Nearly every professional organization has a Web site on which it posts information of general interest to those in the field. Some sites require membership to access most (and sometimes all) content. Others provide certain content for free and require a subscription (or membership in the sponsoring organization) for access to the most pertinent and detailed information. And some Web sites provide content that is available to anyone who visits the site. General Web sites such as those sponsored by government agencies (such as the U.S. Department of Labor, OSHA, and EEOC) provide a wealth of information at no cost, including interpretations of employment law and regulations.

The resources listed here are general and likely to be enduring. The best way for you to stay informed as a manager and as a professional is to maintain a balance among books, periodicals (journals and magazines), and Web sources. Doing so keeps you grounded in the standards as well as on the cutting edge of new developments and practices.

Books

Ken Blanchard and Sheldon Bowles, *Gung Ho! Turn on the People in Any Organization,* William Morrow & Co. (NY), 1997.

Kenneth Blanchard, Ph.D., and Spencer Johnson, M.D., *The One-Minute Manager,* Berkeley Publishing Group (CA), 1993.

Marcus Buckingham and Curt Coffman, *First, Break All the Rules: What the World's Greatest Managers Do Differently,* Simon & Schuster (NY), 1999.

William C. Byham, Ph.D., with Jeff Cox, *Zapp! The Lightning of Empowerment: How to Improve Quality, Productivity, and Employee Satisfaction*, Fawcett Books (NY), 1998.

Stephen R. Covey, *The 7 Habits of Highly Effective People*, Simon & Schuster (NY), 1989.

Albert Ellis, Ph.D., and Arthur Lange, Ed.D., *How to Keep People from Pushing Your Buttons*, Birch Lane Press (NY), 1994.

Keith Harary, Ph.D., and Eileen Donahue, Ph.D., *Who Do You Think You Are? The Berkeley Personality Profile*, HarperCollins Publishers (SF), 1994.

Spencer Johnson, M.D., and Kenneth Blanchard, Ph.D., *Who Moved My Cheese? An Amazing Way to Deal with Change in Your Work and in Your Life*, Putnam (NY), 1998.

Jon Katzenbach and Douglas Smith, *The Wisdom of Teams*, Harper Business (NY), 1994.

Stephen C. Lundin, Ph.D., Harry Paul, and John Christensen, *Fish! A Remarkable Way to Boost Morale and Improve Results*, Hyperion (NY), 2000.

Marlane Miller, *Brainstyles: Change Your Life Without Changing Who You Are*, Simon & Schuster (NY), 1997.

Julie Morgenstern, *Time Management from the Inside Out*, Henry Holt & Company (NY), 2000.

Bob Nelson, *1001 Ways to Reward Employees*, Workman Publishing Company (NY), 1994.

Roger von Oech, Ph.D., *A Whack on the Side of the Head: How to Unlock Your Mind for Innovation*, Warner Books (NY), 1983.

Deborah Tannen, Ph.D., *Talking from 9 to 5: How Women's and Men's Conversational Styles Affect Who Gets Heard, Who Gets Credit, and What Gets Done at Work*, William Morrow and Company, Inc. (NY), 1994.

Paul D. Tieger and Barbara Barron-Tieger, *The Art of Speed-Reading People: Harness the Power of Personality Type and Create What You Want in Business and in Life*, Little, Brown and Company (NY), 1998.

Periodicals

Red Herring Magazine

This monthly magazine, established in 1993, covers the business of technology. The online version is available at *www.redherring.com*. Subscribe online or call (800) 627-4931.

Industry Standard

This publication covers the Internet economy including news, analysis, and new products and services. Industry Standard's online version is available at *www.thestandard.com* and a print edition is available by subscription (forty-eight issues a year). Subscribe online or call (800) 395-1977.

Fast Company

The online version of this publication (*www.fastcompany.com*) features limited free content and extended subscriber content. A print version, twelve issues per year, is available by subscription. Subscribe online or call (800) 542-6029.

Web Resources

Center for Research in Electronic Commerce
www.cism.bus.utexas.edu
Provides information, reports, and advice for Internet-based commerce. Numerous private and public organizations cosponsor the CREC.

CNN Financial News
www.cnnfn.cnn.com
An electronic news site reporting on current business and industry trends.

The Gallup Organization
www.gallup.com
Reports Gallup poll findings. This site also has a section about management, with articles and information as well as poll analyses.

MaturityWorks
www.maturityworks.org
Sponsored by the National Council on Aging (NCOA), this site provides information for and about older workers.

Monster.com
www.monster.com
This commercial job placement Web site provides articles and information about business and career topics for both managers and employees.

Nolo Self-Help Law
www.nolo.com
This site features legal information, books, software, and forms for both personal and business matters.

U.S. Bureau of Labor Statistics
www.stats.bls.gov
Extensive data and analysis of employment trends in the United States.

U.S. Department of Labor
www.dol.gov
Extensive information about employment laws and issues, as well as links to numerous federal Web sites for more detailed materials.

U.S. Equal Employment Opportunity Commission
www.eeoc.gov
This site provides information about fair labor practices, anti-discrimination laws and regulations, and filing discrimination complaints, as well as about pending or completed discrimination actions and lawsuits.

U.S. Occupational Health and Safety Administration
www.osha.gov
This site provides information about workplace safety and health, including injury prevention suggestions, OSHA requirements and inspections, and compliance.

U.S. Small Business Administration

www.sbaonline.sba.gov

Much useful information for small and family businesses.

Workplace Doctors

www.west2k.com/wego.htm

The Web site of communication consultants Dan West and William Gorden, this site features questions and answers about matters involving the workplace.

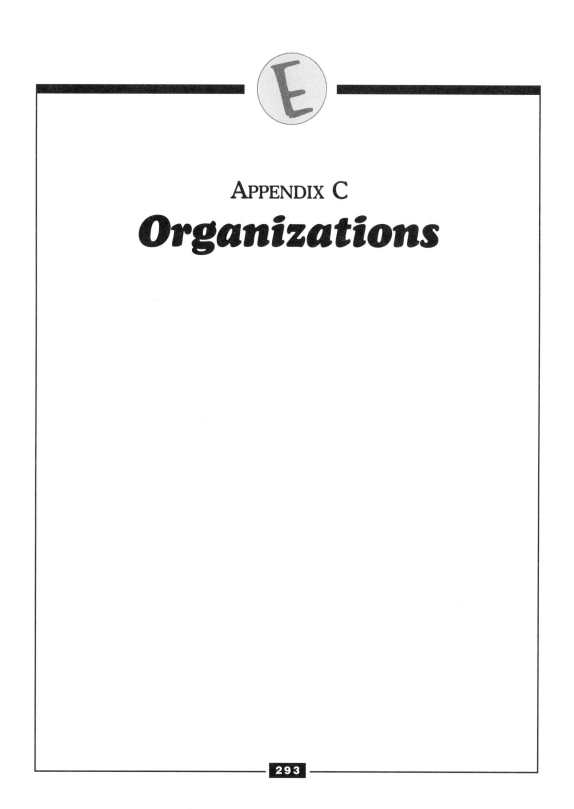

APPENDIX C
Organizations

There are professional organizations for many career fields, from accounting to industrial engineering to technology. There are also organizations specifically for people in management. It is to your advantage to belong to at least one professional organization. This helps you stay abreast of changes in your field, keeps you in touch with others in your profession, and often provides a source for continuing education opportunities. There are hundreds, if not thousands, of such organizations; most you can learn about through your company or by talking with others in your field. Here, we'll list a few of the major organizations of interest to managers in general.

American Management Association

This membership-based management development and training organization provides seminars, conferences, and special events for the more than 700,000 managers and executives who are members worldwide. Contact the American Management Association online at *www.amanet.org* or at:

American Management Association
P.O. Box 169
Saranac Lake, NY 12983
Phone: (800) 313-8650
Fax: (518) 891-0368

American Marketing Association

The American Marketing Association is the professional organization for marketing practitioners, managers, and executives. Founded in 1937, the Association today has 45,000 members in 100 countries. The Web site (*www.ama.org*) provides free information and also features extensive resources for members only, including a reference library and job posting center. For more information, visit the Web site or contact:

The American Marketing Association
311 S. Wacker Drive, Suite 5800
Chicago, IL 60606
Phone: (800) AMA-1150 or (312) 542-9000
Fax: (312) 542-9001

American Society for Training and Development

The American Society for Training and Development (ASTD) is a membership association representing professionals in workplace learning and performance fields. ASTD conducts and reports on research, provides education and seminars, and serves as an information clearinghouse for its members. Learn more by visiting ASTD's Web site at *www.astd.org* or call ASTD at (800) 628-2783.

Toastmasters International

Toastmasters International has clubs in cities throughout the United States (and the world). Look in your local phone book to find one near you, or contact your local Chamber of Commerce. The goal of Toastmasters is to help people build their communication and leadership skills through public speaking and by organizing and conducting meetings. Visit the Toastmasters International Web site at *www.toastmasters.org* for more information.

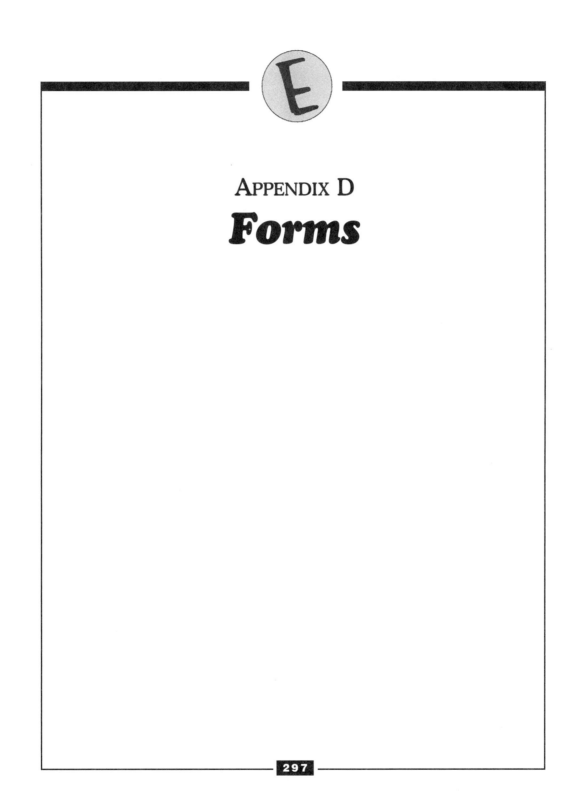

APPENDIX D
Forms

Companies wouldn't survive without forms and documentation. However, most companies use paperwork specific to their needs. Generic forms and documents often don't provide the level of detail necessary to be useful. Several Web sites provide information and sample forms that can provide a foundation for the forms and documents you need for your company. In addition, many professional organizations have developed materials relevant to the profession or industry they serve that are available to members.

Nolo Self-Help Law
www.nolo.com
This Web site contains extensive information about legal issues involving the workplace as well as downloadable forms.

U.S. Small Business Administration
www.sbaonline.sba.gov
This Web site provides comprehensive information for small business owners, including guidelines for managing employees and sample forms.

Society for Human Resource Professionals
www.shrm.org

HRTools.com
www.hrtools.com
This online resource offers extensive information about all aspects of human resources, including staffing, legal compliance, training and development, benefits and compensation, and workplace safety. The site offers a wide variety of standard forms (downloadable).

HR.com
www.hr.com
This Web-based company offers services and information for human resource management, training, and jobs. It features extensive free content as well as downloadable forms and reports. Visit the site to learn more, or contact the company the old-fashioned way:
HR.com
220 Julia Avenue
Mill Valley, CA 94941
Phone: (877) 472-6648

Index

THE EVERYTHING SERIES!

BUSINESS & PERSONAL FINANCE

Everything® Budgeting Book
Everything® Business Planning Book
Everything® Coaching and Mentoring Book
Everything® Fundraising Book
Everything® Get Out of Debt Book
Everything® Grant Writing Book
Everything® Homebuying Book, 2nd Ed.
Everything® Homeselling Book
Everything® Home-Based Business Book
Everything® Investing Book
Everything® Landlording Book
Everything® Leadership Book
Everything® Managing People Book
Everything® Negotiating Book
Everything® Online Business Book
Everything® Personal Finance Book
Everything® Personal Finance in Your
　　20s & 30s Book
Everything® Project Management Book
Everything® Real Estate Investing Book
Everything® Robert's Rules Book, $7.95
Everything® Selling Book
Everything® Start Your Own Business Book
Everything® Time Management Book
Everything® Wills & Estate Planning Book

COOKING

Everything® Barbecue Cookbook
Everything® Bartender's Book, $9.95
Everything® Chinese Cookbook
Everything® Chocolate Cookbook
Everything® College Cookbook
Everything® Cookbook
Everything® Dessert Cookbook
Everything® Diabetes Cookbook
Everything® Easy Gourmet Cookbook
Everything® Fondue Cookbook
Everything® Grilling Cookbook

Everything® Healthy Meals in Minutes
　　Cookbook
Everything® Holiday Cookbook
Everything® Indian Cookbook
Everything® Low-Carb Cookbook
Everything® Low-Fat High-Flavor Cookbook
Everything® Low-Salt Cookbook
Everything® Meals for a Month Cookbook
Everything® Mediterranean Cookbook
Everything® Mexican Cookbook
Everything® One-Pot Cookbook
Everything® Pasta Cookbook
Everything® Quick Meals Cookbook
Everything® Slow Cooker Cookbook
Everything® Soup Cookbook
Everything® Thai Cookbook
Everything® Vegetarian Cookbook
Everything® Wine Book

HEALTH

Everything® Alzheimer's Book
Everything® Anti-Aging Book
Everything® Diabetes Book
Everything® Hypnosis Book
Everything® Low Cholesterol Book
Everything® Massage Book
Everything® Menopause Book
Everything® Nutrition Book
Everything® Reflexology Book
Everything® Stress Management Book

HISTORY

Everything® American Government Book
Everything® American History Book
Everything® Civil War Book
Everything® Irish History & Heritage Book
Everything® Middle East Book

HOBBIES & GAMES

Everything® Blackjack Strategy Book
Everything® Brain Strain Book, $9.95
Everything® Bridge Book
Everything® Candlemaking Book
Everything® Card Games Book
Everything® Cartooning Book
Everything® Casino Gambling Book, 2nd Ed.
Everything® Chess Basics Book
Everything® Crossword and Puzzle Book
Everything® Crossword Challenge Book
Everything® Cryptograms Book, $9.95
Everything® Digital Photography Book
Everything® Drawing Book
Everything® Easy Crosswords Book
Everything® Family Tree Book
Everything® Games Book, 2nd Ed.
Everything® Knitting Book
Everything® Knots Book
Everything® Motorcycle Book
Everything® Online Genealogy Book
Everything® Photography Book
Everything® Poker Strategy Book
Everything® Pool & Billiards Book
Everything® Quilting Book
Everything® Scrapbooking Book
Everything® Sewing Book
Everything® Woodworking Book
Everything® Word Games Challenge Book

HOME IMPROVEMENT

Everything® Feng Shui Book
Everything® Feng Shui Decluttering Book, $9.95
Everything® Fix-It Book
Everything® Homebuilding Book
Everything® Landscaping Book
Everything® Lawn Care Book
Everything® Organize Your Home Book

All Everything® books are priced at $12.95 or $14.95, unless otherwise stated. Prices subject to change without notice.

EVERYTHING® KIDS' BOOKS

All titles are $6.95

Everything® Kids' Animal Puzzle & Activity Book
Everything® Kids' Baseball Book, 3rd Ed.
Everything® Kids' Bible Trivia Book
Everything® Kids' Bugs Book
Everything® Kids' Christmas Puzzle & Activity Book
Everything® Kids' Cookbook
Everything® Kids' Halloween Puzzle & Activity Book
Everything® Kids' Hidden Pictures Book
Everything® Kids' Joke Book
Everything® Kids' Knock Knock Book
Everything® Kids' Math Puzzles Book
Everything® Kids' Mazes Book
Everything® Kids' Money Book
Everything® Kids' Monsters Book
Everything® Kids' Nature Book
Everything® Kids' Puzzle Book
Everything® Kids' Riddles & Brain Teasers Book
Everything® Kids' Science Experiments Book
Everything® Kids' Sharks Book
Everything® Kids' Soccer Book
Everything® Kids' Travel Activity Book

KIDS' STORY BOOKS

Everything® Bedtime Story Book
Everything® Bible Stories Book
Everything® Fairy Tales Book

LANGUAGE

Everything® Conversational Japanese Book (with CD), $19.95
Everything® French Phrase Book, $9.95
Everything® French Verb Book, $9.95
Everything® Inglés Book
Everything® Learning French Book
Everything® Learning German Book
Everything® Learning Italian Book
Everything® Learning Latin Book
Everything® Learning Spanish Book
Everything® Sign Language Book
Everything® Spanish Grammar Book
Everything® Spanish Phrase Book, $9.95
Everything® Spanish Verb Book, $9.95

MUSIC

Everything® Drums Book (with CD), $19.95
Everything® Guitar Book
Everything® Home Recording Book
Everything® Playing Piano and Keyboards Book
Everything® Reading Music Book (with CD), $19.95
Everything® Rock & Blues Guitar Book (with CD), $19.95
Everything® Songwriting Book

NEW AGE

Everything® Astrology Book
Everything® Dreams Book, 2nd Ed.
Everything® Ghost Book
Everything® Love Signs Book, $9.95
Everything® Meditation Book
Everything® Numerology Book
Everything® Paganism Book
Everything® Palmistry Book
Everything® Psychic Book
Everything® Reiki Book
Everything® Spells & Charms Book
Everything® Tarot Book
Everything® Wicca and Witchcraft Book

PARENTING

Everything® Baby Names Book
Everything® Baby Shower Book
Everything® Baby's First Food Book
Everything® Baby's First Year Book
Everything® Birthing Book
Everything® Breastfeeding Book
Everything® Father-to-Be Book
Everything® Father's First Year Book
Everything® Get Ready for Baby Book
Everything® Getting Pregnant Book
Everything® Homeschooling Book
Everything® Parent's Guide to Children with ADD/ADHD
Everything® Parent's Guide to Children with Asperger's Syndrome
Everything® Parent's Guide to Children with Autism
Everything® Parent's Guide to Children with Dyslexia
Everything® Parent's Guide to Positive Discipline

Everything® Parent's Guide to Raising a Successful Child
Everything® Parent's Guide to Tantrums
Everything® Parent's Guide to the Overweight Child
Everything® Parenting a Teenager Book
Everything® Potty Training Book, $9.95
Everything® Pregnancy Book, 2nd Ed.
Everything® Pregnancy Fitness Book
Everything® Pregnancy Nutrition Book
Everything® Pregnancy Organizer, $15.00
Everything® Toddler Book
Everything® Tween Book
Everything® Twins, Triplets, and More Book

PETS

Everything® Cat Book
Everything® Dachshund Book, $12.95
Everything® Dog Book
Everything® Dog Health Book
Everything® Dog Training and Tricks Book
Everything® Golden Retriever Book, $12.95
Everything® Horse Book
Everything® Labrador Retriever Book, $12.95
Everything® Poodle Book, $12.95
Everything® Pug Book, $12.95
Everything® Puppy Book
Everything® Rottweiler Book, $12.95
Everything® Tropical Fish Book

REFERENCE

Everything® Car Care Book
Everything® Classical Mythology Book
Everything® Computer Book
Everything® Divorce Book
Everything® Einstein Book
Everything® Etiquette Book
Everything® Great Thinkers Book
Everything® Mafia Book
Everything® Philosophy Book
Everything® Psychology Book
Everything® Shakespeare Book

RELIGION

Everything® Angels Book
Everything® Bible Book
Everything® Buddhism Book
Everything® Catholicism Book

All Everything® books are priced at $12.95 or $14.95, unless otherwise stated. Prices subject to change without notice.

Everything® Christianity Book
Everything® Jewish History & Heritage Book
Everything® Judaism Book
Everything® Koran Book
Everything® Prayer Book
Everything® Saints Book
Everything® Torah Book
Everything® Understanding Islam Book
Everything® World's Religions Book
Everything® Zen Book

SCHOOL & CAREERS

Everything® After College Book
Everything® Alternative Careers Book
Everything® College Survival Book, 2nd Ed.
Everything® Cover Letter Book, 2nd Ed.
Everything® Get-a-Job Book
Everything® Job Interview Book
Everything® New Teacher Book
Everything® Online Job Search Book
Everything® Paying for College Book
Everything® Practice Interview Book
Everything® Resume Book, 2nd Ed.
Everything® Study Book

SELF-HELP

Everything® Dating Book
Everything® Great Sex Book
Everything® Kama Sutra Book
Everything® Self-Esteem Book

SPORTS & FITNESS

Everything® Fishing Book
Everything® Fly-Fishing Book
Everything® Golf Instruction Book
Everything® Pilates Book
Everything® Running Book
Everything® Total Fitness Book
Everything® Weight Training Book
Everything® Yoga Book

TRAVEL

Everything® Family Guide to Hawaii
Everything® Family Guide to New York City,
 2nd Ed.
Everything® Family Guide to RV Travel &
 Campgrounds
Everything® Family Guide to the Walt Disney
 World Resort®, Universal Studios®,
 and Greater Orlando, 4th Ed.
Everything® Family Guide to Washington
 D.C., 2nd Ed.
Everything® Guide to Las Vegas
Everything® Guide to New England
Everything® Travel Guide to the Disneyland
 Resort®, California Adventure®,
 Universal Studios®, and the
 Anaheim Area

WEDDINGS

Everything® Bachelorette Party Book, $9.95
Everything® Bridesmaid Book, $9.95
Everything® Creative Wedding Ideas Book
Everything® Elopement Book, $9.95
Everything® Father of the Bride Book, $9.95
Everything® Groom Book, $9.95
Everything® Mother of the Bride Book, $9.95
Everything® Wedding Book, 3rd Ed.
Everything® Wedding Checklist, $9.95
Everything® Wedding Etiquette Book, $7.95
Everything® Wedding Organizer, $15.00
Everything® Wedding Shower Book, $7.95
Everything® Wedding Vows Book, $9.95
Everything® Weddings on a Budget Book, $9.95

WRITING

Everything® Creative Writing Book
Everything® Get Published Book
Everything® Grammar and Style Book
Everything® Guide to Writing a Book Proposal
Everything® Guide to Writing a Novel
Everything® Guide to Writing Children's Books
Everything® Screenwriting Book
Everything® Writing Poetry Book
Everything® Writing Well Book

. . . .

We have Everything® for the beginning crafter!
All titles are $14.95.

Everything® Crafts—Baby Scrapbooking
1-59337-225-6

Everything® Crafts—Bead Your Own Jewelry
1-59337-142-X

Everything® Crafts—Create Your Own Greeting Cards
1-59337-226-4

Everything® Crafts—Easy Projects
1-59337-298-1

Everything® Crafts—Making Cards with Rubber Stamps
1-59337-299-X

Everything® Crafts—Polymer Clay for Beginners
1-59337-230-2

Everything® Crafts—Rubber Stamping Made Easy
1-59337-229-9

Everything® Crafts—Wedding Decorations and Keepsakes
1-59337-227-2

Available wherever books are sold!
To order, call 800-872-5627, or visit us at *www.everything.com*.
Everything® and everything.com® are registered trademarks of F+W Publications, Inc.